Say It with Music

Say It with Music

The Life and Legacy of
Jane Froman

by
Barbara Seuling

Boxing Day Books
Princeton, Illinois

Editor: Paula Morrow
Book Designer: Ron McCutchan
Printed in the United States of America

Library of Congress Control Number: 2007934930

ISBN-13: 978-0-9798332-0-5
ISBN-10: 0-9798332-0-5

The excerpt from "I Believe" on page 232 is used by permission; words and
music by Ervin Drake, Irvin Graham, Jimmy Shirl and Al Stillman.
Copyright © 1952 (Renewed) 1953 (Renewed) Hampshire House, New York.

Review by Ralph Lewando on page 93, published 1/7/1935, is used by
permission of the Pittsburgh Post-Gazette.

This book is for Jane

and all that she inspired

CONTENTS

PART III

PREFACE

I FIRST LEARNED about the remarkable Jane Froman when I was a child growing up in the forties. My parents had mentioned her in passing; something about a terrible accident that happened in the middle of her career. I heard her sing on the radio and admired her velvety voice. I watched her on early TV variety shows with Milton Berle, and saw a beautiful woman who sang, laughed a hearty laugh, and who radiated elegance and warmth.

It was not until 1952, when I saw the movie of her life, *With a Song in My Heart,* that I learned the full story of this brave, accomplished singer who, on her way to entertain troops for the USO in World War II, was seriously injured in a plane crash. During her long struggle to walk and sing again, she not only married the co-pilot who had held her afloat until rescue came, but became a national symbol of faith and courage. My adolescent heart thumped wildly at the drama and romance of it all.

I followed Jane Froman's career devotedly, and was fortunate enough to meet the woman as a teenage fan and to enjoy a long friendship with her. It became clear as I got to know her that she had more of a story to tell than had appeared in the movie. Once, during dinner at her home in Columbia, Missouri, Jane talked about her family and showed me a soup tureen that had been painted by her grandmother, a pioneer woman who had raised a huge family while pursuing a career in china painting. I think it was at that moment that I knew some day I would write the rest of Jane's story.

Research for this book confirmed what I had believed all along: Jane's courage and tenacity had not come to her in one inspired leap after the crash; it had been there from the start, in the roots of her strong and determined forebears who settled in Missouri two generations before her.

Jane knew what she wanted early in life. She wanted to sing, and to be able to do it as expertly as possible. When she shifted her focus from classical music to popular, she demanded no less of herself than to give each song everything she had learned from her vast musical training. Singing was her reason for being, and even when her health and her marriage crumbled around her, singing kept her to her course. Not even the terrible crash that nearly cost her her life, and which left her with crippling injuries, stood in the way of her singing. Jane Froman would sing until she couldn't anymore.

The movie was fine, but the full story of this remarkable woman, who sang her heart out for anyone who would listen, deserves to be known. I only hope I did justice to it.

Barbara Seuling
Landgrove, Vermont

ACKNOWLEDGMENTS

IT TOOK A great many years to complete this book and there are a lot of people to thank. I am indebted to every one of them, starting with Jane Froman Smith herself, who gave me the encouragement to dare, and Rowland Haw Smith, who supported my forging ahead with the book after Jane's death.

A huge debt of gratitude goes to Barbara Buoncristiano, who during the last few years has been by my side, at my call, doing every kind of difficult bidding or research that I threw her way. She is as tenacious a researcher as I have ever known. She has traveled with me on several research trips at her own expense, helped me interview people, found files and photographs I didn't know existed and has tracked down people who were missing; she even came up with the title for this book. I don't know how I could have done the book without her. She is a true and devoted friend and she makes me laugh. How could I possibly ever thank her enough?

Talking to people who knew and worked with Jane was vital to my capturing the woman as well as the performer. My debt to those who were willing to be interviewed is huge.

John Curtis Burn was most generous and candid with his recollections of Jane. I am grateful for his willingness to discuss with me personal matters of some delicacy, and for his trust in me to handle them with propriety.

Joyce Lasky Liskin shared with me many experiences as Jane's secretary, personal assistant, and friend. Her stories were moving, enlightening, and often amusing, yet always respectful of the woman who was not only her employer but her good and trusted friend as well. I found her insights invaluable in showing Jane as a real person behind the public image. I am proud to have her as my friend.

Ervin Drake loved talking about working with Jane and writing her television show and even played some of his songs for me, a treat I will never forget.

There are three people who will never know how grateful I am for their contributions to my book, and for this I am truly sorry. They are the late Milton Berle, who spoke to me from his table at the Friars' Club, remembering Jane affectionately; Ruth Barnard, Jane's former therapist from Menninger's, who, at the age of 92, still had that great sense of humor that had endeared her to Jane; and Sid Feller, whose musicianship Jane so admired. Along with his wife, Gert, and daughter, Debbie, Sid welcomed me into his home and treated me like family. Listening to him describe working with a master musician like Jane was a highlight of my research.

I want to express my appreciation to the scores of people who offered advice, encouragement, and help as I gathered information for this book and then assembled it. These include, alphabetically, Audrey Baird, Edward Beddoe, Don Bolognese, Max Cole, Richard Copenhaver, Bill Crawford, Jane Canedy Crow, Diane Dagley, Sheldon Duchin, Robert Easton, Bo Edwards, Ellen Friedman, David Froman, Michelle Froman, Mark Fuller, Shirley Gilroy, Joann Grandi, Len Guitar, Rosa Roux Guitar, Richard Harcourt, Joan Hecht, Jimmy Hourigan, Mark Hudson, Carol Kennedy,

Liz Kennedy, John Konzal, Karen Ledderer, Valerie Lemon, Thomas Lisanti, Jim Lowe, Barbara Manzo, Deena Meiner, Greg Olson, Robert Paulson, Carol Peck, Evelyn Peck, Robert Quackenbush, Dick Rademacher, John Randolph, Randy Roberts, Dodie and Pete Seagle, Dr. Hugh Stephenson, Carol Stess, Bill Stolz, Jack Taylor and Henny Youngman.

My utmost appreciation to the extraordinary staff of the Western Historic Manuscript Collection, under the directorship of David Moore, for their endless patience and thorough attention to detail during every one of my visits to the collection. I also want to thank Bonnie Brouder, Special Projects Coordinator, President's Office, Columbia College, who has been most patient and helpful during my visits and who has made materials on Jane easily accessible. Sincere thanks also to Deborah Thompson of the Boone County Historical Society for her assistance in making historic materials available to me in my research, and for the annual celebration honoring Jane's life and career at the Walters-Boone County Historical Museum. I am also in the debt of Ned Comstock, curator of the Twentieth Century–Fox Archive at the Doheny Library of the University of Southern California and to Haden Guest, curator of the Warner Brothers Archive (special collection), at USC WB Archives, School of Cinema-Television, University of Southern California.

I thank Robert Beck for making the best quality recordings available to me whenever I needed them. Preserving Jane's voice with the most up to date technical means has been his mission, and all Froman fans can now benefit from his devotion to that task. Preserving Jane's musical spirit is equally important, and thanks to Nollie Moore and his great work with the Jane Froman Singers for doing just that.

Special thanks to Susan, Dennis, Elizabeth and Pamela Seuling, who have been cheering me on from the beginning. Their constant interest and enthusiasm has been a light in my life all the way through.

Thanks, too, to my incomparable writers' group, always there for me and guiding me upward and onward: Bonnie Bryant, Miriam Cohen, Sandra Jordan, Peter Lerangis, Ellen Levine, Fran Manushkin, Norma Fox Mazer, Harry Mazer and Marvin Terban. And to my students who have heard bits of the story and have been eagerly urging me on to the finish line.

Heartfelt thanks to Ron McCutchan for his sharp artist's eye that made this book beautiful to look at and hold, and to Paula Morrow, my wise and patient editor, whose devotion to making this book at one with my vision is deeply appreciated. Working with them, sometimes into the long hours, has made this a true joy of teamsmanship as well as a labor of love.

My partner, Winnette Glasgow, has been there from the first glimmer of the idea and has been my advisor, first reader, pillar of support and most caring and constructive critic. She is the best friend a writer could have.

The plane had gone down; that much she knew. She had awakened in the icy waters somewhere outside the city of Lisbon and had been rescued by Portuguese fishermen. Now she lay on a hospital bed, her pain numbed, but sickeningly aware that something was terribly wrong. She knew her left leg was barely attached below the knee—but it was the other leg doctors pointed to, shaking their heads. She did not have to speak their language to know they were saying that the right leg had to come off.

Waiting her turn for the operating room, she heard the unmistakable sounds of suffering around her. Where was the girl with whom she had switched seats on the plane? What about the young co-pilot who had held her afloat in the water? He had been badly injured himself. In the dim light of this foreign hospital, not knowing the answers to these questions, or whether she would still have her leg when she came out of surgery, she did know one thing for sure: she had to hold on.

The women in her family were not the complaining kind. They had been through more than she ever would, and had never quit in tough times. Neither would she.

PART I

1

THE BLOOD OF ADVENTURERS
1848—1907

ASKED ONCE IF she had ever wanted to be anything but a singer, Jane Froman replied, "My earliest ambitions were to be a circus rider and jump through hoops. That seemed to me the most glamorous possible career."

Great drama, whether in grand opera, the Broadway stage, or the circus, left a strong impression on the singer from the very beginning. Being born into a family of colorful and adventuresome people could have had something to do with it.

Jane Froman's grandmother, Ellender Weston, was born in Pope County, Arkansas, on December 1, 1848, the same year that gold was discovered in California. Ellender's father, like so many others, quickly fell victim to gold rush fever. He loaded his wife and four young children into a covered wagon and set off for California when baby Ellender was just a year old. Weston "had the blood of adventurers in his veins," the records say. Among Weston's colorful forebears were the trailblazing pioneer Daniel Boone and an aide-de-camp to George Washington. Even Jean de la Fontaine, author of the world-renowned fables, had a place in Jane's family tree.

When the Weston family set out, lands west of Missouri were still wild and undeveloped. Railroads went as far as Kansas. The only feasible way to make the journey, carrying goods and family, was to cross the plains and mountains by covered wagon. The Westons joined a wagon train with forty other families.

Halfway into their journey, where Denver, Colorado now stands, the train halted to dry a supply of buffalo meat. While they were stopped, cholera broke out among the caravan, severely reducing their numbers. A few weeks later they continued westward with fewer than one man for each wagon, leaving behind a small graveyard on the site of their encampment.

The journey took eight months and three weeks before they crossed the California boundary. Weston and his group landed in Red Bluffs. Weston did better than a lot of others. In the next year and a half, he struck gold often and secured their fortune. Now was a good time for the family to return East to educate the children. At Salt Lake City, however, their plans changed when their wagon teams were stolen.

Weston went to General Patrick E. Connor, who had arrived in town with troops under his command. They were on their way to establish a settlement at Fort Douglas, Utah. Weston claimed protection as a United States citizen and was allowed, with his family, to join them. The family lived at Fort Douglas for several years, with Weston helping in the work of building the settlement. Ellender grew up at the Fort, where life and death were never far apart.

On the night of January 29, 1863, fourteen-year-old Ellender attended a dance at the fort. It was to be a night that made history. She later recalled:

> I was there that night. We were dancing, a large crowd of young people, when the call to saddle and boots was sounded. Thirty-two of the young men who hurried from the dance floor were found dead the next day.

In retaliation for several raids on their settlement by neighboring Indians, General Patrick Connor and his troops had made a surprise attack on a Shoshone village of about 400 people, killing approximately 272 men, women and children, including their Chief, Bear Hunter. The Bear River Massacre, as it came to be known, was one of the most ravaging massacres of Indians in American history.

Weston took his family north the following year to live in Fort Bridger, Wyoming. Ellender, now fifteen, was often at her father's side as he chatted and gossiped with the founder of the fort, Jim Bridger. Young Ellender found in Bridger a colorful man. He was the famous trapper and fur trader who had been the first white man to discover the Great Salt Lake in Utah. Generally seen with a female Indian companion or two, Bridger knew the mountains better than almost anyone. Speaking English, French and Spanish, plus six Indian languages as well, he became a legendary guide. He and his partner, Louis Vasques, had built Fort Bridger in 1843 as a trading post along the Oregon Trail to serve the heavy wagon train traffic as western migration increased.*

At Fort Bridger, young Ellender Weston met Thaddeus Barcafer, a young soldier from Clark County, Ohio. Barcafer's duties included the quelling of Indian riots and later, helping to build the Union Pacific railway. Life at the military post had toughened Ellender for constant hardship and danger. With the same grit and determination that drove her father, she met her challenges without complaint, satisfied

---

* One of the wagon trains that used Fort Bridger was the ill-fated Donner Party, which became trapped in the Sierra Nevada mountains during the winter of 1846-47. Nearly half of the Donner party died, and some resorted to eating their dead in an effort to survive, making it the most famous tragedy in the history of the westward migration.

that she was one of the few young people to have experienced firsthand the development of the west. She was ready for the next adventure. Ellender and Thaddeus were married at the Fort, and their first child, Pearl Garnett Barcafer, was born a year later. Ellender was barely seventeen.

The young Barcafers left the west after Thaddeus suffered a gunshot wound in the right shoulder and was awarded a veteran's pension. They traveled to Idaho Territory, which had been recently organized and signed into law by President Lincoln, then on to Ohio, and finally Missouri, where they settled in 1873 to raise their growing family. They purchased a huge house on East Jefferson Street in the town of Clinton, Henry County, which was to be their home for many years. By the covered porch of the house, Ellender planted a pink rambling rose bush that had traveled with her on the wagon train.

The first of the Barcafer children born at the Clinton home, on January 15, 1874, was Anna Tillman Barcafer, who was to become Jane's mother.

It was a musical family, with everyone singing or playing an instrument. Anna's great-great-uncle, William Woodin,* was a composer. Still, Anna's musical talent was a true gift, and it was recognized at an early age. She began playing the piano at five years old, and before graduating from Franklin High School in Clinton, she was earning money as an organist in a country church.

At sixteen, the young prodigy was sent to the Chicago Musical College, where she studied piano for two years. Piano competitions were held every year, and students with

---

* Woodin later became Secretary of the Treasury under President Franklin Delano Roosevelt.

The forceful Barcafer women: Jane's mother, Anna Tillman (upper left), her sisters and mother (center). Aunt Pearl is at top, center.

the highest grades were chosen to enter. Anna, with grades from 98 to 100 percent in her exams, competed with hundreds of students for the prize, a diamond-studded medal, and won both years.

A serious student, Anna nevertheless had her share of beaus at school. One was Florenz Ziegfeld, the son of the president of the College, who would one day become the producer of the famed Ziegfeld Follies.

Anna received her teacher's certificate from the college in 1892 at the age of eighteen. At her commencement, she played piano in a concert with the Chicago Symphony Orchestra.

She continued to sing and play the piano in concerts and afternoon musicales in Clinton and nearby St. Joseph, sometimes with her sister Maude playing violin. When musicians of renown, like the great Paderewski, gave recitals in Chicago, Anna went to hear them.

It was at this time, singing in the matinee entertainments of polite society, that Anna met a young man, Elmer Ellsworth Froman, from St. Joseph. Froman was a well-known young businessman who held a responsible position buying lingerie with the Hundley-Frazier Dry Goods Company. Although little is known about Elmer, genealogical records tell us that he was born June 29, 1868, to William Gist Froman and Mary Sherard Froman. William's father, Lorenzo James Froman, came from Hardin County, Kentucky, and moved to Clinton County, Missouri, where he became a judge. His wife was a descendant of the Gist family of Maryland, who settled in Baltimore County in the late 18th century and who helped lay out the city of Baltimore. One member is said to have been a surveyor with George Washington.

Elmer had a beautiful tenor voice and sang in local music programs. Anna and Elmer often appeared in the same recital, occasionally singing a duet. The two young singers were ideally suited for the lead roles in an amateur production of *Giroffe Giroffa* at the Tootle Opera House in St. Joseph, performed on October 27, 1894. Reviewers liked Anna as "Paquita," remarking on her sweet voice and lovely face, and added that she was not a bad actress, either. Elmer's "Pedro" was "well-acted and sung, in a voice sweet and dear." He was praised as "one of the best tenors in St. Joseph."

The couple continued to pursue their musical interests; Anna seemed more inclined to make a career of hers. In

1897, at the age of twenty-three, she moved to St. Joseph to teach piano while she continued to sing and give solo piano concerts in the area.

After a long and musical courtship, Anna Tillman Barcafer and Elmer Ellsworth Froman were married on March 7, 1898, in the Barcafer home. The *Clinton Eye* reported:

> She is possessed of a more than ordinary musical talent and is highly cultured both in vocal and instrumental music. . . . She has made the lives and hearts of Clinton people brighter, happier and better by her songs. Willingly singing for concerts, churches, social occasions and making the burden lighter when hearts were saddest, she has been the "sweet singer in Israel," loved by everybody.

The young couple left on the afternoon train for St. Joseph. The St. Joseph *Gazette* spoke highly of both Elmer's and Anna's accomplishments and congratulated the city of St. Joseph that the young couple had decided to make their home there. Their future looked exceedingly bright.

Elmer remained in the dry goods business. Anna continued to give piano lessons, and her pupils performed in student concerts. After nearly four years of marriage, Anna decided to go to Europe to continue her piano studies.

The talented Anna was welcomed in the greatest French and German conservatories of the day, winning awards and honors in both. She studied with Fidele Koenig in Paris and was invited to sing at the American Church in Dresden, appearing in many programs there. She studied the pipe organ while she was in that city.

At the end of two years of studies abroad, Anna returned home. She and Elmer moved to University Heights, a burgeoning community just outside of St. Louis, with new houses, a race track, an amusement park, roadhouses and taverns and even a street car that brought people from St. Louis to the amusement park and back again. Anna established a private studio for teaching.

It was an especially exciting time, because St. Louis was then commanding the nation's attention as the site of the 1904 Louisiana Purchase Universal Exposition, or World's Fair. The city represented America's youthful outlook as gateway to the expanding nation and the new century. Anna Froman was asked to be a featured vocalist at the dedication of the Kentucky, Maryland, New Jersey and Illinois Buildings and at receptions in the Missouri Building. She sang in a number of Missouri Day programs as well as special concerts for distinguished visitors.

It would appear that Anna's career was on the rise, but that was about to change. After nine years of marriage, at the age of thirty-three, Anna gave birth to a daughter. Anna and Elmer sent out eggshell-colored cards, with small pink bows woven into them, announcing the arrival of Ellen Jane Froman on November 10, 1907. One can imagine the joy brought by those announcements.

Elmer continued to work in dry goods, advancing in position and singing on the side. Anna kept up with her musical activities in the community but, always one to do her best at any undertaking, she threw herself into motherhood with everything she had. In a carefully kept baby book she recorded Ellen Jane's every event, as though such things had never happened before to anyone: "first ride on street car Feb. 13, 1908"; "first tooth was discovered—August 22, 1908"; "first knew she had hands Jan. 28, 1908"; "walked alone on

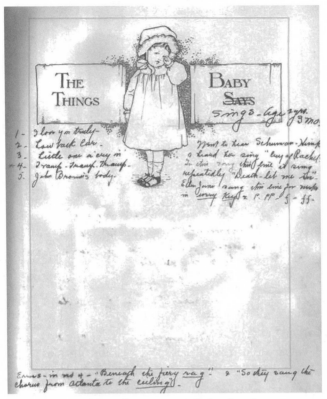

A page from Jane's baby book

her first birthday Nov. 10, 1908 Forest Park." A lock of blond baby hair was kept in its pages, as well as Ellen Jane's first bib and her first attempt at sewing. On a page labeled "The Things Baby Says" the word "Says" is crossed out and "Sings" is handwritten over it in ink. A list of songs includes "I Love You Truly," "Tramp, Tramp, Tramp" and "John Brown's Body." No precious moment was overlooked.

At being a mother Anna Froman excelled, but it was a far cry from the concert stage.

2

A MUSICAL FAMILY
1908–1918

ELLEN JANE WAS only a toddler when she began to show signs of the musicality that ran through both parents' families. Her mother wrote, many years later:

> We were living in St. Louis at the time. . . . Jane was three years old; and she, at that early age, showed signs of musical talent. One day when I was giving a lesson, she sat apart—very quiet and listening intently, and if I looked around to her, she would give me a sweet smile of approval as if to say, "Mother I understand."
>
> This particular pupil was having a difficult time producing for me the light Italian "ah"—which is the basis of good singing. After I had finished the lesson and let the pupil out the door, I returned to the piano to straighten up the music. I felt a tug on the back of my skirt. Looking, there stood Jane, who said, "Mother, I can sing light 'talian ah," she said, and she proceeded to do just that! Then and there I gave her her first music lesson—at the age of three.

Unlike most children her age, Ellen Jane never minded bedtime. That was when Mama, her music lessons and activities behind her, could spend time alone with her, and they always sang. Jane's mother remembered those precious times in later years.

I would rock her to sleep in a semi-darkened room, and we would sing together. She could sing and hum songs—and even arias—before she could talk. As she grew sleepier, the hum would grow softer and softer, and finally it would stop altogether with a sleepy gasp. Then I would put her in her little bed. I soon began to teach her the child's prayer, and to my surprise, she put an "en" on every line—so it went like this:

> Now I lay me down to sleepen,
> I pray the Lord my soul to keepen;
> If I should die before I waken,
> I pray the Lord my soul to taken.
> Amenen.

Anna Froman took three-year-old Ellen Jane to see the great singer Madame Ernestine Schumann-Heink performing in *The Cry of Rachel*. She wrote:

Jane sat entranced, but I didn't realize the profound impression it made on her until the next day. In the morning, I suddenly heard my daughter ranting and screaming in her bedroom. There she was clubbing one of her dolls against the wall and repeating the tragic line from the opera, "Death let me in." Her little voice raged in imitation of the great singer.

Jane, age two

Was Anna simply reading her own musical interests into the little girl's behavior? Was it wishful thinking that her daughter, the offspring of two musical parents, would also have great talent? One can only speculate, but Mama's reports of Ellen Jane's early signs of musical talent are convincing.

When Ellen Jane was five years old, Anna gave birth to another child, a daughter, but this birth brought only sadness. Margaret Ann was born with spina bifida, a deformity of the spinal column. She lived only four and a half months.

The only reference to this event—that there was another child born to Anna and Elmer Froman—is a tiny squib in the back of Jane's baby book that Margaret Ann "entered into rest Tuesday, March 4." A typewritten poem, with no author's name, was glued to the back of the book about a child being taken away by angels to join the children in heaven.

It is likely that Jane did not know about Margaret Ann until she came into possession of the baby book many years later. No one can recall Jane ever mentioning a sister. John Curtis Burn, Jane's second husband, felt that he would have heard about it if Jane knew, as they shared so many details of their lives.

Around this time, Ellen Jane was sent to her grandparents' home in Clinton, to recuperate from a throat infection. At least, that was the explanation given. It was common to shield young children from unsettling experiences, even more so than now. Sending Ellen Jane off to stay with relatives was typical of how a young child might be removed from a troubling situation in the early part of the twentieth century. In this way, her parents could visit Margaret Ann in the hospital and deal with her death and burial and their own grief without having Ellen Jane be aware of the trouble.

When Anna Froman arrived in Clinton to join Ellen

Jane after Margaret Ann's death, she arrived alone. Elmer was not with her. No explanation was given, and Jane was left to wonder what had happened. Did she think, as most children do when parents separate, that it had something to do with her? Mama was the only one who knew what had happened and she would not talk about it. She had locked Elmer Ellsworth Froman out of both their lives. Jane never saw her father again, nor did her mother ever speak of him again.

In all the scrapbooks, clippings and photographs Anna saved over her career and Jane's, there is not a single portrait of Elmer. There is one torn candid photo of a young man in a playful pose who looks like he had a good sense of fun. If this is Elmer, the picture is a clue to the couple's differences. The dour, more sophisticated Anna was many things, but playful was not one of them.

The tragedy of losing a child certainly could have rocked an unsteady marriage, but there is no evidence that there was discord before this. Although Elmer's job involved travel, and he must have been away from home frequently, that alone does not suggest problems. Ellen Jane adored her father. Except for Anna's refusal to talk about it, and the notable lack of proof of Elmer's existence in an otherwise well-documented family, there is no evidence of a rift in the marriage. Mystery surrounds his disappearance to this day.

Friends and relatives have tried to put the pieces together about Elmer's disappearance. They knew he was a salesman and that his territory was the south, where he traveled with trunks loaded with women's dresses and ball gowns. A cousin reported that Elmer had been in Atlanta and that he had left his hotel one morning, without a hat, and never returned. No official records, census or otherwise, could confirm his disappearance or death. Meanwhile, the brokenhearted little girl had to figure things out for herself. Jane wrote, many years later:

> As time went on, I began to realize that something I did not understand and which worried me was very much amiss between those people I loved so dearly. I had been very close to my father, and missed him terribly.... What had occurred, why they parted, what caused the pain that separated these gifted young people, remained locked in Mama's heart and she never revealed to the wondering daughter who loved him why Papa had gone another way.

It is no wonder a terrible stutter erupted around this time that was to plague Jane all her life. While there is no single explanation for stuttering, many psychologists believe that it comes from repressed anger. Certainly the sudden shock of losing her father and being sent away could provide that, but whatever the cause, the stutter was here to stay. Anna Froman, hoping that proper vocalizing would counteract her child's speech difficulties, taught Jane careful breathing and perfect enunciation. Perhaps Mama's training helped, as Jane was able, throughout her life, to sing or deliver certain rhythmic lines without a sign of the stutter. Other stutterers have also found the rhythmic delivery successful; it is a phenomenon that puzzles even the experts.

Mama and Ellen Jane now lived in the family home on East Jefferson Street in Clinton. The house was big and busy. Jane described the Barcafer family as "forceful, forthright people, of high integrity and principle, all musical to their talented fingertips."

> There were 13 brothers and sisters presided over by my Grandfather and Grandmother Barcafer. . . . They all sang

and played and performed in the family orchestra in their home. They were all proficient in music, both classical and current, and sang from kindergarten on, as did I. . . .

I remember Grandma—she sang, of course—in all her imposing stature and ceaseless activities . . . she was never too busy to listen to rehearsals . . . or to correct any careless passage. . . .

Jane remembered her grandmother vividly.

Grandma was up at 4 A.M. and kept going all day long. I never remember her wearing glasses. She was not only beautiful, but she had the most gorgeous pair of eyes I've ever seen. They were large and true violet. And this before makeup and eye shadow and all the rest of it. With all their beauty, those deep big eyes never missed a trick. . . .

Grandma sang as she tended to her many activities—mending their clothes, churning the butter, tending the garden which supplied the family vegetables and fruits which she canned and preserved. An amazing and energetic woman, born into a tough pioneer family, she was an artist, too. On the top floor of the old house, she taught painting and did her own delicate china painting.

She made exquisite lace. Those strong fingers were never idle. She was nothing if not ingenious. Her last two children, Aunt Ellen and Aunt Thad (Thaddea in the family Bible) came very close together. They were tiny toddlers at the same time. Trying to keep up with them in their very early days, Grandma couldn't keep up with her orders for her china painting, which kept coming in from all parts of the world. One fine day she picked her two babies up in her arms and planted them down on a blanket in her studio on the top floor. Each of the four tiny hands she covered with molasses, and then placed in each a feather. Well, she got on with her china painting and they were kept busy!

Although most of Ellen Jane's aunts and uncles eventually moved on to lives of their own, they never abandoned their musical heritage. They spread their talents in communities across the country, wherever they settled.

Ellen Jane's favorite aunt was the eldest of the Barcafer children, Aunt Pearl, who later moved to York, Nebraska, with her own family. Aunt Pearl had clearly inherited the strong traits of the Barcafer women.

What a remarkable character she was! She weighed 250 pounds and taught swimming at the Y.W.C.A. for 50 years. She sang regularly in the choir for 45 years until asked to desist. . . . She was active in everything that was going on in town in all the years she lived there, from making huge tubs of cole slaw for the annual church social to keeping up the morale of delinquent women in the York jail. But she did it in her own way, you may be sure.

One of Aunt Pearl's good friends in town was the matron of the York prison. Called away on urgent personal matters, this matron asked my Aunt Pearl to hold the job until she returned. Nothing daunted, Aunt Pearl went to the prison, took charge, and began counseling the women, some 20 of them, two of whom were murderers. And she had them all singing, too. . . .

In the course of her duties at the prison, Aunt Pearl learned that the gals in her charge had a hankering to go to the movies. She could see nothing against it and wrested permission from the prison authorities to take the group to the local movie palace. She saw nothing amiss in marshaling these jailbirds through the streets of York, Nebraska. Had she not extracted from every last one of them a solemn word of honor (among thieves and murderers, to boot!) that they would not betray her trust? Had she not counseled them on behavior and deportment and shown them how to improve their complexions, to care for their hair, to sew and mend, and to behave like responsible, respected human beings? Doubt never entered her mind that she would have any trouble whatsoever on her hands, and of course she didn't. As a reward for their good behavior, after the movies Aunt Pearl marched her companions into the ice cream parlor, sat them down at little tables, and treated each of them to a plate of ice cream of their choice before delivering them back to their prison quarters at the appointed hour.

Ellen Jane's dear Aunt Pearl was known and admired far and wide. The great orator William Jennings Bryan was a good friend of Aunt Pearl's lawyer husband, Frederick Gilbert, and a frequent visitor to their home, where the table was always heavily laden with Pearl's good cooking. Aunt Pearl knew white radishes were a great favorite of Bryan's and never failed to put a large bowl filled with them, grown specially for him, at his place at the table. "Everyone else had to be content with red ones," wrote Jane, clearly amused.

It was Aunt Pearl who taught Ellen Jane to keep her little hands busy with needlework. Ellen Jane loved the attention Aunt Pearl would pay her, teaching her to knit, crochet, tat, and sew. It seemed Aunt Pearl always had time for the lonely little girl. Those lessons enabled Jane, later, to make her own clothes when she couldn't afford to buy them, and to regain the use of her right arm and hand when they were badly damaged.

Mama had to earn a living for both of them now and she did it, of course, through music, singing in the choir, teaching music in Clinton's public schools and giving piano lessons wherever she could at fifty cents a lesson.

Shortly before Ellen Jane's sixth birthday, Mama enrolled her as a day student in the Holy Rosary Convent in Clinton, where she was to receive her early education. Even though the family was not Roman Catholic, the Sisters of St. Joseph looked after the shy little girl and let her board there when her mother had a job in another town.

Although she was the youngest child at the convent, Ellen Jane's talent was already evident. The nuns were enchanted by her lovely voice and fussed over her. Little girls with any accomplishments were expected, on request, to display them, but the attention only increased Ellen Jane's anxiety.

How I hated to have Mama leave me! It was terrible for me to see her go. I recall in those early years singing for some convent visitors "La Marseillaise" in French as I had learned it in school, with tears streaming down my cheeks. Mama had just left. From the end of the convent garden where it passed I could hear the chugging of the train growing fainter and fainter, leaving me a very lonely and frightened little girl. It was my darkest hour.

With no other children her own age at the convent school, Ellen Jane had a difficult time. Although Mama gave Ellen Jane vocal direction, and she was awarded every honor in music the school had to offer, her musical talents were not enough to protect her from the cruel taunts of her classmates. She was the nuns' pet. She didn't have a father and her mother worked. Worst of all was her stuttering. The children laughed when she was called on to recite and the words wouldn't come out. The nuns finally stopped calling on her.

It was a lonely childhood, in which she developed an unusually strong bond with her mother. Ellen Jane took refuge in singing, where, like magic, the stuttering never interfered. She lapped up the vocal training her mother gave her. As long as she could sing, she would be all right. It was a lesson that stayed with her all through her life.

Ellen Jane Froman was soloist at all the school's concerts. She played Snow White in the school play. Sometimes she sang in local choirs or at occasional socials and parties in town. At eight years old, she made her first musical appearance singing solo in Gaul's oratorio, "The Holy City" at the Christmas service of the Clinton Baptist Church.

Because she had a musical ear and a natural aptitude for the piano, Ellen Jane could play everything she heard. When the carnival came to town, the merry-go-round played "Oh, You Beautiful Lady," and she picked it out on the piano. She played "The Butterfly" by Merkel by ear. At the convent, however, she was made to practice, and she resented it. Her piano teacher would play a piece and then give it to her. Ellen Jane would play it perfectly—in the wrong key. Once, impatient with the long practice hour, when she knew she could play anything anyway,

Age seven, in costume

Ellen Jane bit the piano savagely from one end of the music stand to the other, leaving big tooth marks in the finish. Mother Superior sent for Mama, who saw to it that all the dents in the piano were professionally removed, paying for the repairs out of her meager teacher's salary.

When Jane told this story many years later, it was with an ironic addendum to the story. Many years later, she was to sing a song seated atop a piano and was seating herself just so when she felt a sharp pain. Darned if the piano hadn't bitten her back, after all those years!

Mama watched with some consternation as her daughter's rebellious nature continued to reveal itself. In her loneliness at the convent, Ellen Jane turned to devious methods for amusement. She watched through the transom as the nuns shaved their heads. She showed what she thought of the horrible food served at the convent by slipping down to the dining room at night and pouring cereal all over the floor. She developed a fascination for people who were considered "bad," going home to play with a girl whose mother was considered "loose," for which she got her first switching.

As adolescence approached, she watched, intrigued, as the older girls lowered baskets from convent windows at night to be filled with candy and fruit by their beaus. Ellen Jane had beaus too—a boy by the name of Buena Vista Ashenhurst who gave her candy valentines, and Clifford, who rode to school on a white horse.

Ellen Jane looked forward to those occasions at the Barcafer home when Mama was in town and they could be with other family members, some of them now married and returning for a visit. Those were the best times.

Always, when the lively Barcafer family got together,

it ended in an evening of good music. The orchestra might consist of Mama playing the piano, Grandpa Thaddeus playing his flute, Maude on the violin, and other family members joining in with their voices and instruments.

On one festive occasion, there were sparklers. Ellen Jane got too close, and her organdy dress caught a spark and burst into flame. Mama, thinking fast, rolled her in a rug to put out the fire. Ellen Jane was badly burned, but Mama's good reflexes saved her from serious harm.

Between visits, Ellen Jane wrote to Aunt Pearl. Even at age seven, she realized letter writing was a way of communicating without having to stumble over spoken words.

March 6, 1915

Dear aunt Pearl I am going to thank you for all your nice petticoats you made me

I tell God to bless you every night and I ask God to bless Fred to be shure you come here soon to Clinton mo and bring fread with you because I want him to sing to me when I was a baby they tickled me so.

I hope you will come soon when spring comes will you come ar be fare that because mother and I are going to St. Louis next month say have you got any more of those black and dark red cherries on the cherrie tree well I think it is time fare me to stope because the 10 o clock whistle has jest blown, so

I will haft to stop here is a kiss for both of you.

I send my love to you. grandma sends her love too.

Dear aunt Pearl and uncle Fred with love
Ellen Jane

and again just before her eleventh birthday:

Dear Aunt Pearl,

    I write to tell you how glad I was to recieve that coat.

    I think it is lovely of you to sen it to me. this is only a note of thanks because we have company, Aunt Thad is her and little Jack, he is the cutiest thing I ever saw, well I must close.

yours sincerely

your loving niece,

Ellen Jane Froman

XXXX

love love love

P. S. give my love to Uncle Fred

        Mother sends her love to both

It is not surprising that Ellen Jane's favorite picture at the time, saved in a scrapbook, was of a little girl and a mailbox, so cherished that her mother saved it along with childhood valentines and letters.

Ellen Jane finished grade school at the Holy Rosary Convent at age twelve. She was a good student in the arts, but not exemplary in math and other dogmatic subjects.

Thaddeus—Grandpa Barcafer—died in 1915. Grandma Barcafer remained for a while in the home her family had occupied for more than half a century. When she moved to Fort Worth to live with her daughter Ellen, now Mrs. H. G. Lindsay, it was time for Mama and Ellen Jane to move on. Mama got a position teaching in the little college town of Columbia. This time, Ellen Jane went with her.

3

A CAMPUS GIRLHOOD
1919—1927

M AMA HAD HER heart set on getting a good education for Jane, and when Mama wanted something, she usually got it. Christian College, in Columbia, Missouri, was the best girls' school in the area, with a fine scholastic record and an impressive course of study.

Christian College was "more than a finishing school"; it had been founded as a women's college on a par with most men's colleges, in a day when college attendance for women was unusual. The girls were not directed toward the usual subjects for women relating to household duties and the decorative arts such as "ornamental wax-working" or "hair wreath embroidery"; at Christian they would get a full college education.

In "The Circular of the Christian Female College," the purpose of Christian College was stated clearly:

> It is desirable that no young lady will seek admission into this school, who is not determined to devote her whole energy and attention to her moral and mental improvement. Those who cannot, for the time being, abstract their minds from the fascinations of society, or who aspire merely to a superficial or fashionable Education, are earnestly advised to seek elsewhere....

John Augustus Williams, the first president of the college, was concerned that women had so few options; they could marry, work as domestics, or teach. Although he did not remove "Domestic Science" from the curriculum, students—young women—were encouraged to pursue "a thorough and extensive course in the Mathematics, in Natural Science, in Belles-lettres, in Natural History, in Language, and in Philosophy."

Williams soon established the school's reputation for excellence in music. Christian College's first budget included "the engagement of four pianos."

Mama joined the faculty and struck a deal with the respected school, arranging to give singing lessons to the girls enrolled at the college in return for twelve-year-old Ellen Jane's education: four years of high school and two years of college.

At last, Mama and Jane had a place of their own, a tiny apartment on the college campus. To Jane, Columbia meant more than school and a place to live. She had found a community in which she felt totally at home, and she was to carry its character in her heart forever. Jane wrote:

> Our roots during the next six years at Christian became planted irrevocably in the charming hospitable town of Columbia, Missouri . . . in which the University of Missouri played so important a part. . . .

Columbia was in a part of the state known as "Little Dixie," named for those earlier migrants who not only brought the desire for higher education to the state but brought a good bit of the Old South to the area. It surfaced in their love of heated politics, their respect for tradition and culture, and their abiding faith in religion.

Mama seemed happy in her new life. When she finished with her duties as the head of the Voice Department, she gave Ellen Jane voice lessons. Mama saw to it that her daughter was taught in the classic tradition, beginning with properly supported breathing, unbroken phrasing, pure vowels, and flawless diction. Ellen Jane was to have a sound vocal foundation, with no tricks or shortcuts.

Besides teaching at the college, and her private training of Ellen Jane, Mama sang in many church choirs of different faiths. It was inevitable that her daughter and star pupil would follow that path. Mama recalled:

> A choir leader called me on a Sunday morning to say that one of the sopranos was ill, and asked if I could bring along someone to fill in temporarily. I took Jane. It was the first time she had sung in public, and she was uneasy and anxious to do well. After the services, she watched as the choirmaster approached us. He practically ignored her as he spoke to me, but what he said was, "Mrs. Froman, I intend to let the other soprano go and use your daughter permanently." I didn't like the idea of Jane's getting the work because of the other woman's misfortune, and I told him so. "Someone else will get Jane if I don't," he insisted. "You can't hide your daughter's voice."

At school, Ellen Jane took part in all the activities that she possibly could. She loved anything to do with the theater or music and took part in school plays and musical revues. Often, her voice won her featured roles. She studied ballet, doing toe dances to popular melodies. It was in high school that Jane developed a lifelong love for the theater.

She loved sports and excelled in basketball and swimming. Christian College's brand new swimming pool was considered the largest and most beautiful of any institution

Dancing with other girls at school

in the Middle West. The white tile floor, the pool with blue tile lane markers, and the shower walls of gray imported marble were exquisite. The pool was lighted by twenty-three frosted windows and an overhead skylight.

Jane, an excellent swimmer, knew the pool well. One day, probably with that feeling of invincibility most teenagers possess, she climbed up to the rafters and jumped into the pool.

Years later, when Sue Meyers Gerard was hired as swimming instructor, a myth had grown around their famous alumna. Her jump had turned into a dive. Even a jump seemed dangerous. Gerard worried that teenage girls in her charge might try to emulate the singer they admired so much.

Gerard climbed the ladder to the rafters. "Never could she have survived a dive," Gerard exclaimed. "The pool was 25 feet wide at the 'deep end.' It was only 7' 2" deep at the drain! The diving board extended out over the drain! Pool drains are, of course, in the very deepest part in order to receive every last drop of water when draining or cleaning. . . ."

Gerard jumped, feet first. It confirmed her suspicions.

"I made it clear to my students," Gerard added, "that to DIVE (head first) would be suicide! I had that ladder removed from the pool deck promptly."

At Christian College, the very same talent that had set Jane apart at the convent now brought her into contact with people. Her status had changed, with Mama's position on the faculty giving them the respectability and sense of belonging that had eluded them before. At last Jane felt accepted, sure of herself and at ease; there was no sign of her aching shyness, and her persistent stutter seemed less obvious. She was popular, a model of geniality and personal charm. She made friends easily, participating in all the activities a college town could offer, and said yes to every chance to have fun. Whenever there was a gathering, she sang. Sometimes in the dorms at St. Clair Hall she kept on past curfew so that the housemother would have to come in and ask her to stop. She sang, and sang, and sang, for the sheer pleasure it gave her and others.

Drawing room musicales were the popular form of entertainment in polite society, and Jane and her mother sang duets at many. Jane wrote:

> I recall an evening during the Christmas holidays at Brentmoor Park with Anna Froman, mezzo-soprano, and Ellen Jane Froman, soprano, in a "musical evening." A line on top of the program for the evening read: "Music is able to change the feelings of and traditions of a nation.—Cicero."

Mama and I opened the evening with a duet, "A Stream Full of Flowers" by Carda Ciola. I sang Rachmaninoff's "The Soldier's Bride," and Mama sang "The Abbess" by D'Earlanger. There were more duets and more songs, with these Yuletide selections: "The Birthday of a King," "The Virgin's Lullaby," with everyone, as I remember, joining in the singing of "Silent Night," the words of which were printed on the program which had accompanied the engraved invitations from our music-loving hostess.

Mama's salary did not allow the luxuries some of the other girls in St. Clair Hall had, like fashionable new clothes.

A high school photo

The college girls didn't just follow fads, but showed a genuine flair for creating original clothing styles. Jane loved what they wore. Evening clothes were smart and sophisticated while daytime sports clothes were, according to Jane, "the most dashing in the world!"

Copying the latest styles from pictures in magazines and catalogs, Jane cleverly fashioned a wardrobe, sewing her own clothes. "A splash of color here, a bunch of cherries there, a startling bit of silk, and I was as stylish as any of them," Jane wrote, looking back on those times. "By careful planning I was able to stretch the two dollars I received for singing in the choir on Sundays to cover my actual needs. It was slim pickin's, but I managed."

Being a town girl, or "Tee Gee," had certain clear disadvantages. Ellen Jane was expected, as the daughter of a faculty member, to set a good example. Rules—if they seemed unfair—had always set her rebellious nature in motion. She was campused once for going to town after hours, and got caught smoking a cigarette—her first—in another girl's room. When Mama found Ellen Jane with a cigarette, she was profoundly shocked. Christian College forbade smoking. Anna Froman remembered the incident vividly.

"You'll have to report yourself to the student council," I told her.

"But mother, I had only two puffs," she said.

We talked further about it, though, and the upshot was that—very unhappily—Ellen Jane reported herself. She was even more upset with their decision.

"It's lucky I didn't take three puffs," she said woefully. "I've been restricted to campus for two months."

Although their funds were always limited, Jane and her mother enjoyed a pleasant life in the most sophisticated circles, where Jane's talents were developed and nurtured. Even during the summers, Ellen Jane studied and sang, when Mama would take her to Oscar Seagle's Summer Colony at Schroon Lake, New York. Seagle, a famous baritone who taught at the Cincinnati Conservatory of Music, had founded a musical camp for students in the heart of the Adirondacks. Its many acres included a lake, a main house called "the Farmhouse," several small rehearsal shacks in the woods, each with a piano for practicing, and plenty of fresh air. The colony was part school, part summer playground. Professional singers who were in musical comedy or opera, like Louise Homer, the great Metropolitan contralto, came to Schroon Lake every year to work with the students and be near Seagle, their mentor. Mama spent five summers as one of Seagle's assistants at the colony and brought Jane along to study with him.

Always, Jane sang—at parties, fraternities, and pep rallies when the Missouri Tigers played. There were jam sessions in the evenings before turning in, and Jane sang for the girls after dinner in the gym. She sang at commencement exercises

Jane (standing third from left) at the Seagle Colony; Mama is seated at right in front row

and starred in the annual revues of the Elks and the Rotarians. *The Savitar,* Missouri U's yearbook of 1922, lists the musical comedy *All Aboard* as the Elks' annual production, with Ellen Jane Froman as one of the leads in a plot involving a double love triangle.

Anna Froman organized Christian College's first vocal sextette, which later expanded into the Double Sextette. This musical group became one of the college's most revered performance groups and is known today as the Jane Froman Singers.

In costume for play at the Elks

Christian College had established its own radio broadcasting program with WOS in Jefferson City, the state capital, so Anna Froman arranged frequent trips for the sextette to sing at the station, with Ellen Jane as the lead singer. Good roads had not yet been built, and the thirty-mile trip was made mostly on dirt or gravel roads in Model-T Fords. When it rained, side curtains were put up to keep mud from splashing in. It was after one of these dusty, bumpy journeys that Ellen Jane Froman sang over the air waves for the first time.

The College Widow, the Christian College annual, noted in her senior year the organizations in which Ellen Jane Froman participated: the Missouri Club, composed of college women who were native Missourians; the As We Like It

Club, designed to promote interest in contemporary literature; the Mary Arden Club, created to foster an interest in
the dramatic arts and the study and presentation of plays.
Her superior vocal ability was noted:

> *She's laughing and singing, and always gay.*
> *We're looking for her in Grand Opera some day.*

On a bright Wednesday morning in June, 1926, Ellen
Jane Froman received her Associate Degree in French and
her Associate in Arts degree to teach in the public schools
of Missouri. Mama, a respected and honored member of the
faculty, loved and admired by everyone, looked on proudly.

Ellen Jane was uncertain about her plans for the future.

Academically, she was only a fair student, but in anything to do with the arts, she excelled. She was not too set
on a career—perhaps she would marry after finishing school,
or earn her living by teaching, as Mama did. She loved to
write. That was one reason why the School of Journalism at
the University of Missouri appealed to her, but it was not the
main reason.

The University of Missouri's School of Journalism was
the unlikely producer of an annual musical revue. The revue
sounded like fun. Jane enrolled in the school and, sure enough,
before the end of her first semester, she had the lead role in
Bagdaddies, a musical comedy written by two J-School
students from Texas, Tom Mahoney and Chesley L. Manly.
Two other students, Fred Ayer and Elmer E. Taylor, Jr., wrote
the lyrics and composed all the music. It was performed on
December 6 and 7, 1926, in Hall Theatre at the University
of Missouri. On the program Ellen Jane Froman is listed as

playing Helen Cooley, daughter of a Kansas City businessman. Her big solo came in Act II, when she sang "Mystic Moon."

The Columbia *Missourian* agreed that the show was a hit:

> . . . Miss Ellen Jane Froman all but ran away with the show. . . . From the time Hurley Kaylor raised his baton until the grand finale was being sung, the many present were witnessing entertainment of a quality seldom presented by amateurs, several of which bordered on the professional in the production last night.

Bagdaddies was an unrivaled success for the School of Journalism, largely because of Jane. Longtime Columbia resident and journalist Jack Taylor remembered it well. "Jane was a new note in leading ladies. For once the journalism show had a girl with poise, stage presence and a swell voice. News of her success got outside the confines of the campus."

A booker for the Skouras Theatres in St. Louis, who attended one of the performances, thought so, too. He hired Jane to do a week at the Grand Central Theater in St. Louis, performing for their annual children's Christmas show. Jane wrote:

> A pretty little girl named Betty Grable shared the dressing room with me. We talked about it many years after when we were in Hollywood. . . . Gene Rodenmick and His Merry Maniacs headed the bill, which also presented Gene's Kiddy Follies with Ellen Jane Froman, the "Blues Singing Co-ed of Missouri U." It was my first contact with show business. I was paid $100 for the week—$75 of which I blew on a fancy beaded dress, high fashion in the roaring '20s.

The expense of the beaded dress was rare. Jane had no trouble spending money if she had it, but she seldom did. Although modest in her personal wardrobe, she felt she had a public image to uphold, and put all her extravagance into that. This concept would carry through the rest of her career.

For her journalism class, Jane worked as an intern at the St. Louis *Globe Democrat,* doing court reporting, general assignments and book reviews. The venerable Dean Walter Williams considered her an outstanding writer and a promising journalist.

Jack Taylor remembered Jane in college days as

> . . . a gay, likable girl, friendly and easy to stare at. She smiled a lot, sang a great deal, and made her way around town as if she was always in a great hurry. If you happened to be near, you could hear Jane humming to herself as she flitted about on the streets or university campus.

She looked and acted like any coed, racing around on a bicycle or attending the home games of the Tigers, wrapped in a raccoon coat—the rage in the twenties—that Mama had managed to buy for her.

It was inevitable that the popular Jane was pledged to Kappa Kappa Gamma, for she had often sung for the girls prior to her enrollment at the University. When it was her turn to join, her initiation involved counting all the windows in the University Hospital. She was in great demand, especially during rushes, when girls came to check out the various sororities and decide which one to join. Many girls were lured to Kappa Kappa Gamma by Jane's singing.

Stella Scott, chaperone at the sorority, remembered that Jane sang for various campus groups and, when asked to sing

Singing for her Kappa Kappa Gamma sisters

at the house, she never refused, although she had to be constantly warned by the chapter president to "cease singing after quiet hours."

Scott also remembered that Jane was shy.

> She always had a smile for everyone she met, but she was really a very quiet girl and invariably allowed others to make the conversation. She was very reserved, almost timid.

Most likely, it was the stuttering that prevented Jane from joining in the conversation. Singing was safe; so was keeping quiet.

There was no serious boyfriend, although Jane never wanted for male company. Young men were drawn to her, in class, at parties, and at dances. They were there when she sang at church or attended the various college activities. They walked across the campus with her just to be in her company. Jane was a pal to them all, rather than a girlfriend to one. Getting close to others was not easy for the shy Jane, and she could avoid intimacy by being everyone's chum.

Rowland Smith, a college friend who was later to become her third husband, knew her then but never had a date with her because there was always a crowd waiting—a fellow had to book a date with Jane months in advance.

The *Kansas City Star* reported:

> Many a college boy has parked his collegiate Ford outside the Conservatory at Christian College and waited until Jane had finished a lesson with her mother. And many an M.U. student caught his only glimpse of the inside of a church when he sat in the back-row pew waiting for the weekly choir practice to end so that he might walk home with Jane.   •

Church was a constant in Jane's life. She was in the choir and sang solos at the First Christian Church, while her mother accompanied her on the organ. The charismatic Reverend Walter Haushalter was not only a brilliant, spellbinding speaker whose sermons were heard weekly on WOS in Jefferson City; he was also tall and handsome, and Jane was sure to be there when he delivered the sermons.

Clearly, Jane was having a ball. She won letters in basketball and tennis and excelled in swimming. She loved to write and was good at it, but her first love was singing. After studying piano and voice with her mother, she was a skilled and talented vocalist not much interested in other studies, so she didn't pay much attention to them. Without regrets or pretension, she confessed that if ever there was a choice between a fraternity dance and a school book, she was at the dance.

It was with utter shock that Mama received the news that Jane had flunked out of school. This gifted daughter, in whom she had invested so much, and who had Barcafer blood in her veins, had done the unimaginable: she had failed at her responsibilities. With few words, and practically overnight, Mama called on her connections, and Ellen Jane Froman was dispatched to the Cincinnati Conservatory of Music.

4

AWAY FROM HOME
1928—1932

THE SWIFT MOVE from Columbia to the Conservatory in the fall of 1928 brought Jane to her senses. Mama, through her strength and determination, had earned them a place in the Columbia community. Now, for her pains, she had been publicly disgraced. Once again, Mama would be giving up things she needed for herself so she could pay Jane's tuition at the conservatory. Jane made up her mind to take her studies more seriously and restore her mother's faith in her.

She would build upon the excellent musical and vocal training she had already received from her mother to further develop her performing artistry. She studied in earnest voice, harmony, and theory, and worked diligently on the classical repertoire.

One day, while walking down the hall, Jane discovered auditions in progress. She inquired and learned they were for the Corinne Moore-Lawson Scholarship, open only to seniors. Although it was Jane's first year at the conservatory, she begged to be heard and was so insistent that the judges consented to hear her. She sang her first song. There was silence. They asked her to sing again, and she did—four songs in all. She won the scholarship, which was for $300, enough to pay her tuition. She was ecstatic.

When word of Jane's scholarship reached Columbia, Mama received one telephone call after another congratulating her on Jane's good fortune. Most were from friends but there was one from the Mayor of Columbia, William Hetzler.

"I want to tell you that this city is very proud of your daughter," he said.

She thanked him for calling and forgot about it, but he didn't. The next day the mayor sent flowers for Jane—and for Mama. There were more phone calls. Soon it became clear that the mayor's real interest was in Anna Froman, not Jane.

Jane put everything she had into her studies. The conservatory hired for their faculty only the best musicians in their respective fields. Jane worked with Oscar Seagle, her instructor from Schroon Lake days and Mama's old mentor. She studied singing with renowned tenor Dan Beddoe, who taught her a method for practicing the vowel sounds, which she used throughout her career. The pattern of the exercise was a simple scale using one breath for each step of the scale, singing *hung, yee, oo, oh, ah.* Then, after taking another breath, the sounds were repeated on the next step up the scale, going through the singer's entire range. From this exercise, Jane learned the power and value of resonance. Jane wrote to her mother:

> My lesson with Beddoe yesterday was wonderful! They always are, for he is fond of me, as everybody says. I vocalized up to a high C—just as easily as could be. He just beamed and turned to the accompanist and said, "Isn't that a glorious voice?" He always keeps me an hour—and makes John Brigham wait (he comes right after me).

I'm learning "By the Sea," "Siesta" by Besly, "The Unforeseen"—Cyril Scott. The last is something I've always loved since I heard it at Seagle's. My tone is getting so large—and I'm so happy.

As Beddoe's pupil, Jane performed in a conservatory recital, singing an aria from *Le Reine de Saba*, by Gounod. Anna Froman pasted a clipping about the event in the scrapbook she kept on her daughter's career. She added a handwritten note: *One of my happy days.*

There were times when Jane admitted frustration with the math and technical side of music, particularly in conquering harmony. It was the only subject she didn't like, and she had to get help to muddle through it, but she did.

By now, her voice had become a rich, well-focused mezzo-soprano. At this time she sang with the idea that she would eventually sing opera. She even had an offer from the Chicago Civic Opera Company. "Just barely an offer," Jane commented. "Thirty-five a week and a chance to sing in some small soprano roles. The old-timers warned me against it. 'If you go into an American opera company like that, you'll never get anywhere,' they said. 'You either have to come in as somebody important or you're never important.'"

One day, the Dean called Jane into her office and informed her that her mother had married the mayor of Columbia, William J. Hetzler. Jane was as surprised as anybody.

"Mother eloped on me!" she told her friends.

Mama and the Mayor moved into a new and sprawling home at 1 West Broadway in Columbia. Anna Froman Hetzler retired from teaching, ready to take on the busy life of the first lady of Columbia. One can only imagine the shock of this news, as Jane and her mother were so close. Once again, Mama had orchestrated an event that was to mean a major change in Jane's life for which she had had no warning or preparation. Jane very quickly came to terms with the situation. She could not let her feelings set her back. All that mattered now was getting on with her life.

I realized all too clearly that Mama no longer belonged to me alone, and

Mama's favorite picture of Jane

since she had another life to lead I could not continue to be her responsibility. Something had to be done about it. . . .

The scholarship had paid for her tuition, and Jane sang in churches and did choir solos for five dollars every Sunday, with a little more for funerals, to earn a bit of spending money. For a time, she actually lived on that, but to be sure Mama wouldn't have to worry about sending her money for clothes and other items, Jane went to Miss Bertha Bauer, the president of the college, and told her she needed work for pay. After this declaration of her independence, Jane would never again let anyone pay her way.

Miss Bauer got bookings for Jane at parties, teas, and soirees. Full of spirit and vitality, and with a beautiful voice as well, Jane was a natural to entertain at these. She made herself a gown for these occasions, but when the one and only evening gown was not sufficient for all her bookings, Miss Bauer gave Jane two more.

It didn't take long for Jane to be in great demand at these private parties. She sang the traditional fare of operatic arias and art songs as well as "pops," all in the same evening, and played her own piano accompaniments to them all.

There was a new popular music that was taking the country by storm. Until now, popular songs had come from the European tradition, "parlor songs" or songs from operettas. Young American songwriters like Vincent Youmans, Jerome Kern and George Gershwin were changing all that, digging deep into the multiethnic roots of American culture for their rhythms and melodies. Jane was drawn to this music— and stubbornly followed her own instincts in spite of her mother's desire to see her classical training put to good use.

At one of the musical parties Jane met Powel Crosley, Jr., owner of the largest independent radio station in the country, WLW in Cincinnati. At 500,000 watts, the station could be heard anywhere in the world. Crosley, an industrialist, inventor, and businessman who owned everything from the local baseball team to the radio station, had ventured into the broadcasting business to sell more of the radios his company manufactured.

Jane accompanied herself at the piano as she sang her rendition of "St. Louis Blues," a hot number called "There'll Be Some Changes Made," and other songs. When Crosley heard her, he came up to her.

"How would you like to be on the air?" he said.

Jane said she thought it might be fun.

"Come out and do an audition," Crosley said.

She did just that, arriving at WLW the next morning to audition with the station's musical director, Grace Raine, who would later be instrumental in shaping the voices of Doris Day, Rosemary Clooney and others to sing on the radio. Jane was put under contract immediately and that same night, at age twenty-three, began her radio career singing a jingle for "Tom's Toasted Peanuts." It paid her ten dollars and was her transition from talented student to professional singer.

At first, Jane's voice did not adapt well to the air waves. In her first broadcast, her unfamiliarity with the microphone betrayed her. Frightened, she sang louder—to be sure listeners far away could hear her!

Before radio, Jane didn't have to develop a microphone technique. She sang naturally, able to project to a large audience without the help of amplifiers, but radio was different. The microphone and the studio held onto and magnified sounds. Jane became aware that she had to change her style. Standing close to the mike, she sang into it from the left, putting her hand to her ear occasionally to ascertain the true tone of her voice, or resting her arms on the pedestal nearby. This felt comfortable and resulted in the best effects.

Mama, in her exalted position back in Columbia, politely accepted the compliments that came her way from people in town who told her they had heard Jane singing popular music on the radio, but she winced a little at the idea of her daughter wasting her God-given talents.

No such thought entered Jane's head. Each night she sang for a different sponsor: one night she sang for Heatrola, and another for King Paste. Her original pay was ten dollars per program, but soon she was offered $85 a week and a position as a staff artist, which meant that she was on call at any time. Sometimes her day went from 5:30 A.M. when the farmers got up to 2 A.M. the following morning.

Despite her strictly classical training, Jane made lively show tunes and ballads a part of her repertoire. Radio was the perfect medium for this new music. Although many listeners enjoyed hearing Jane sing refined songs like "Sea of Rapture," and "Do Not Go, My Love," many more wanted to hear the popular tunes of the day, like Harold Arlen's "Get Happy," Irving Berlin's "Blue Skies," Vincent Youmans's "Tea for Two," and Jerome Kern's "Can't Help Lovin' Dat Man." She found she enjoyed them enormously. When sung by Jane, they sounded a cut above the conventional. She sang a mixture of jazz, ballads, opera, and torch songs, and her popularity grew.

It takes one's breath away to think that as Jane was starting her singing career, entertaining at parties, songs now taken for granted as part of the Great American Songbook were then the "new" music.

It's curious to see this development in Jane's career taking place shortly after the shock of Mama's marriage to Mayor Hetzler. Could she have been, perhaps, all too ready to give Mama a similar jolt? Jane's anger came out in her own creative ways over the years. Forging ahead into a world of popular music, after all those years of Mama's devotion to the classics, must have ruffled her mother's feathers. Nevertheless, Anna Hetzler, stoic Barcafer woman that she was, never said a word.

In spite of paying jobs on the radio, Jane continued her musical education as a serious voice student. She sang in concerts with the Cincinnati Symphony and was chosen principal soloist in the Christmas concert of the Cincinnati

Conservatory of Music—a production of Debussy's *The Blessed Damozel* under the direction of the great Fritz Reiner, with a chorus of three hundred voices. Jane sang the aria from *Le Reine de Saba* at commencement exercises—the only student outside the graduating class invited to sing—and Mama journeyed to Cincinnati to hear her. That same night, Jane was over at WLW singing the latest ballads on the air.

WLW was called "the Nation's Station," for good reason. Its network programming reached from coast to coast and provided entertainment all through the day and evening, all week long. Many performers got their start at Powel Crosley Jr.'s station, people like Rosemary Clooney, Red Skelton, Doris Day, the Mills Brothers and Fats Waller. Soap operas also got their start on WLW, when Crosley let Proctor & Gamble Company sponsor some daytime dramas. For one of them, *Honey Adams,* Jane supplied the vocals for actress Virginia Payne, who would soon be known to soap opera fans as Ma Perkins.

It was at WLW that Jane met Don Ross, a staff singer for the station. One half of a song-and-dance team called Brooks & Ross, Don had been on the vaudeville circuit for years, and his show business experience was vast—Jack Brooks, tenor, and Don Ross, baritone, had been all over the country and in Europe. Jane's only knowledge of the business was garnered during her stints in college in *Bagdaddies* and at the Grand Central Theater in St. Louis. Don had gone from vaudeville to night clubs to radio and worked with many sponsors. The more Don talked and revealed how much about the show business world he knew, the more Jane was fascinated.

Jane found Don brash and somewhat conceited, but was in thrall to his show business expertise. Don, meanwhile, felt that Jane was spoiled. She didn't think much of his phrasing when he sang; he thought she could use some lessons in microphone techniques. After a quarrelsome beginning, during which they were required to sing romantic songs to each other, they became the darlings of the air and soon became inseparable, one with a hunger to learn, the other slipping into the role of instructor smoothly and easily.

As the son of a Presbyterian minister, Don found himself at odds with his father, who disapproved of his son's love of the theater and ambition to be a part of it. In spite of this, Don took any job that kept him close to the smell of greasepaint—ushering, selling tickets, prompting. At times he was penniless, and even broke a leg once hopping a train. But he was persistent. He had achieved moderate success in vaudeville as a partner in Brooks & Ross, but his real skills came into play behind the scenes, in writing, producing, and managing.

Don, charming, handsome and knowledgeable about all sorts of stage business, saw in the lovely and talented Jane the makings of a star. She was smart, but just a small town girl when it came to stage presence. He made himself indispensable to her by teaching her how to present herself in this newer "pop" style—how to hold her hands when she sang, how to smile, walk and turn. Jane lapped it up and let Don, with his incredible experience and knowledge, lead her.

The two young people were seen as WLW's bright young couple, admired for their fresh, eager looks, their youthful appeal, and their promise. They sang together at Cincinnati's Hotel Sinton. Local papers and radio fan magazines saw them as a team and ran feature after feature on them.

Back in Columbia, Anna Hetzler tuned in to hear Jane sing. It must have been a difficult time for her. What had happened to her daughter's classical training and repertoire, so carefully nurtured? Jane reflected on this in later years, as she imagined Mama hearing, over the air waves,

> . . . the voice she had loved and trained in all the enduring beauty of the classics, singing the blues, torch songs and ballads in such vivid contrast to the strains of Mama's own musical heritage.
>
> But gallant, loyal gal that she was, she evidently took it in her stride though she never really approved, I'm sure, of the songs she heard me singing on the air.

The hectic pace that Jane set for herself finally took its toll. In the fall of 1930, she contracted double pneumonia, but continued to sing and study until she was forced to take a break to recuperate. She visited her namesake, Aunt Ellen, now in Mineral Wells, Texas, where she relaxed and soaked up the dry southwestern sun before she returned to the conservatory.

Bandleader Paul Whiteman, one of the most popular bandleaders in America, must have heard Jane sing, because he sent a wire asking her to audition for him. Alas, her tonsils were giving her trouble and had to be removed. She couldn't audition—she was told not to sing for six months. Jane could not wait that long and returned to her radio singing in two months. Her voice was noticeably improved, but having missed the opportunity with Whiteman was a disappointment.

When, some time later, WLW offered to send Jane out of town to a mountain resort for a well-deserved rest, she naively thought they were being kind. Little did she know they had heard Paul Whiteman was coming to town. When Jane learned that another opportunity had been missed, she was stunned. It was a hard lesson.

Jane relied on Don more and more as he taught her, helped her with business decisions, and became her companion. Convinced of Jane's talents and appeal, Don set up carefully chosen auditions and negotiated better and better contracts for her. Jane's reputation was growing rapidly, and she was in demand. It was inevitable that Jane let Don make career decisions for her, and he did so eagerly. She wrote:

> Don Ross had show business in the very marrow of his bones, and he had stardust in his eyes. He was convinced I had the making of a star, and felt I had been in Cincinnati long enough—the time had come to move to greater fields. I had been in Cincinnati two years.

Don arranged for auditions for Brooks & Ross and for Jane at WBBM, the Chicago outlet for CBS, the Columbia Broadcasting System. Brooks & Ross were hired in a minute, but Jane overheard Walter Preston, the musical director, say, "I wouldn't give that girl $25 a week." Although it crushed Jane, it infuriated Don, who knew instinctively that Jane could be a big star, if they would only buy his pitch.

He was aggressive in his pursuit of Jane's career, often irritating people with his arrogant manner. There is no doubt that Ross genuinely believed in Jane's talents as a performer, nor that his methods paid off. Jane's looks and talent made up for his shortcomings.

When CBS turned Jane down, Ross went to NBC—the National Broadcasting Company—the other big radio station in Chicago. He made an appointment for Jane to audition for a commercial, the term used in early radio days for any program with a sponsor. This was an important chance, because the station's musical director, Paul Whiteman, would be there. He still had not made contact with Jane.

In the excitement of getting to her audition on time, Jane caught her heel, fell down a flight of stairs and broke her ankle. Determined not to miss her chance this time, she got up, brushed herself off, and made it to the audition, asking to be carried in and placed before a table with a microphone on it. She sang one song after another—four numbers in all. Important people—potential sponsors—listened to her over a loud speaker in another room. At the end of the session, learning she had a job, she promptly fainted from the pain in her ankle. Just before blacking out, she heard Paul Whiteman's voice saying, "I've been trying to get hold of you for a long time."

NBC accepted Jane with great enthusiasm. Whiteman signed her to a three-year contract to appear over the NBC-WJZ network in Chicago, under his personal direction. Her pay was $350 a week. Whiteman introduced her on a new program, with his protégé, Matt Melnek, a twenty-four-year-old violinist and composer, as her bandleader. Success was instantaneous. Jane states in her memoir:

> "Pops," as everyone called Paul Whiteman, gave me my own orchestra . . . and a 15-minute show across the board, every day in the week at 6:15, immediately after Amos 'n' Andy, top comedy team on the air. To follow them meant that I was beamed into every sitting room in the country—at least for a few minutes.

High on the success she found all around her, Jane believed she could do it all and continued her studies at the conservatory in Cincinnati, living at the dorm there and commuting over 260 miles to sing with Paul Whiteman's band in Chicago. The prestigious Three Arts Club in Chicago, composed of all the best musicians in town, invited Jane to join. She did, enabling her as a member to move into living quarters at the club.

"I'm afraid the more and better jobs I got, the less I went to the conservatory," she confessed, "but I did complete two and a half years of study."

Jane sang with Whiteman at one o'clock on Sunday, and Don, now a continuity writer and radio announcer with the station, came on with his program at five. At seven o'clock Jane was back on the air with still another program, for Iodent toothpaste. Listeners dubbed her "the Iodent girl."

Anything with a dangerous element still fascinated her, and she now drove a car. Always in a hurry, she was driving a little too fast when a tire blew out and the car turned over, pinning her underneath. She got away with a broken arm, a fractured leg and other minor injuries. For two weeks, she had to be carried into the studio.

Whiteman liked Jane's deep rich sound and wanted her to sing regularly with his band. Most singers would have leaped at the chance to work with a band as popular as Paul Whiteman's, but singing with a band, even one as popular as his, was too restrictive for Jane. She declined the offer.

Jane was still shy, in spite of her public success. Her stutter followed her in all social situations; it could even be greatly amusing. Once, when a Chicago music publisher came to see her and he stuttered, they almost could not start a conversation, and it broke them up in laughter.

On the radio she was able to develop an intimacy with her audience without the anxiety of having to struggle through conversation. In front of the microphone, she felt comfortable, relaxed, and rarely had trouble. Her speaking lines were limited, with someone else introducing her, or with a very short script requiring her to speak as the lead-in to a song.

Study at the conservatory had given Jane a free and relaxed manner as she sang; she had learned the importance of being at ease in order to emit good sound.

In an article that appeared in *Radio Stars* magazine, an observer of a radio broadcast wrote that as Jane sang "Harlem Lullaby," her eyes looked out over the audience's heads, and seemed to "fasten on some vision high behind the limits of this puny ceiling as though she visualizes the countless listeners within the beating reach of the sound waves that carry her voice, and to that vision she sings."

Those who knew Jane before her radio days missed the old Jane and the more classical style of her naturally projected and trained operatic voice, but the younger crowd responded well to her more modern adaptation, preferring the sounds and rhythms of Broadway and the new songwriters.

Dubbed "Radio's Melody Queen," "Radio's Loveliest Songbird," "Radio's Sweetest Songbird" and other affectionate titles, Jane led a more public life now. She had new publicity photos made at the prestigious Maurice Seymour Studios in Chicago. Radio fan magazines did one interview after another with her. Many featured her on their covers. She made public appearances for her sponsors, a job that came with her popularity. In her memoir, Jane wrote about this exciting new time:

> Radio sets had sprung up like mushrooms all over the country.... Radio was the new industry, vital and burgeoning, seeking new ideas, new talent, new songs and styles of singing

them, new ways of promoting them. It was the beginning of a new era. Paul Whiteman, who had introduced me to it, was its king, the King of Jazz. I had become Jane Froman, a recognized singer in this new and exciting world of music.

Clearly, there were greater career opportunities in radio than there were in the concert halls. Don had been right. You had to move on to build a career, and that, apparently, is what she was doing. It took a savvy person like Don to know what to do and when to do it. Jane coasted along this way for a long time, leaning on him to guide her career.

Jane seemed ideally suited to radio. Heard regularly over the air, broadcasting from NBC's Chicago studios, she was developing her style of singing a song, bringing to it her vast musical knowledge that had begun with singing in the choir back in Clinton, Missouri. If there was such a thing as a perfect radio voice, hers was it.

Crooners were coming into their heyday. They were described as successors to the Savoyards, troubadours of old, singing of love and throbbing hearts and disappointments. These minstrels of the air sang people off their feet and into the clouds. They sang blues and torch songs. They were Bing Crosby, whose relaxed way with a song made him famous; Russ Columbo, the Romeo of song; and Rudy Vallee, who crooned his Maine "Stein Song" to his heart's content and everyone's delight. And new faces and voices kept appearing everywhere. I crooned too! And I sang the blues!

There were times when home and family—Missouri—seemed very far away. A visit from Jane's Uncle Mark and Aunt Ollie, who had moved to Chicago in 1929, and their son, Temple, helped Jane over those lonely periods and

*Jane was never more comfortable
than as a radio singer*

provided a chance to relax and talk about Mama and Aunt Thad and the Barcafer clan back in Clinton.

Mama was never far from her thoughts. She wrote Mama long and chatty letters, filled with lively reports of her exciting life at the conservatory, carefully placing her forays into popular music in secondary position.

Darling—

. . . How we wished for you the other night! Honie came up for a cocktail—and some other people who are musical also came in—and did we have a real musical feast! Honie had just come from a lesson with Seagle and had her music— she sang and sang—and beautifully too. I sang and Don sang and Paul played, and we all wished for you. The other night we also took Frank Luther out for dinner and we spent the whole evening talking about what a grand person you were. Did your ears burn? . . . .

I am "guesting" on Show Boat this Thursday night—and opening at the Earle Theatre in Washington a week from Friday.

Had the sweetest card from Auntie Gert for Easter— will drop her a line soon. . . .

Much love to you all—

Janey

After six months at NBC, Whiteman asked Jane again to go on tour with his band. Jane was on her way now, and didn't want to settle for singing the chorus of a band number. Singers had been mere accompanists to dance bands until recently, when radio audiences seemed to favor them. Some vocalists were lucky enough to be featured prominently, as Frank Sinatra was with Tommy Dorsey's orchestra, but most had to break away from the bands to find their own careers. Martha Raye, Dick Haymes, Jo Stafford and Mildred Bailey had done it, and Jane wanted to strike out on her own, too. This time, her refusal resulted in some hard feelings with Whiteman, who considered Jane one of his greatest "finds."

Finally, Jane offered to buy her contract from Pops and he agreed to release her. She and Whiteman parted ways. He turned her over to NBC and they placed her under a management contract.

In brief spells from radio work, Jane played theaters around town, including Chicago's hottest one, the Oriental. The offer started at $250 a week for four performances a day but, after weeks of negotiations under Don's management, a contract was signed for $1,000 for a week's engagement plus star billing. On the same bill with her were the extraordinary Mills Brothers, who were a smash hit. Jane, too, was a hit, doing a routine of popular songs of the day, according to *Variety,* the show business weekly, and was held over for another week.

Feeling sure of herself and her ability to please an audience, Jane planned a new routine for the second week, composed of the classics. It was a complete flop. It was a lesson Jane never forgot.

You could hear the waves of boredom thundering down the aisles. I barely got to the wings. What a lesson! It was the same theater, the same singer, the gown was right, the singing was right, but the songs were wrong, dead wrong. They weren't the songs the people in this Oriental audience were in the mood to hear. They wanted to hear music of their own day, not the music of the past. I learned my lesson. I learned that an audience won't be forced.

I got to work and changed all the numbers and gave them the "pops" they loved. We all had a wonderful time. I was again a smash. I brought down the house with "It's Only a Shanty in Old Shantytown." They loved it.

In spite of her busy schedule, Jane kept fit by walking three or four miles around Lincoln Park every morning, and by playing golf. There were no late nights, no parties, no drinking. Other than an occasional baseball game when she got to see the Cubs play, she lived quietly in a tiny one-room apartment close to the studio. She guarded her voice and time almost fanatically. It was a harsh life, being a radio singer, but to Jane, earning the princely sum of $125 a week at NBC, plus the occasional outside booking, it was rich and full.

Wrapped up in her career, singing morning, noon and night, Jane always managed to be there when her home town needed her. She was there at a rally preceding a Missouri-Northwestern game, bringing Don and his partner along to entertain as well, in their old Brooks & Ross vaudeville act.

From time to time, Jane and Don took the Twentieth Century Limited to New York City, where Jane would make guest appearances on various radio shows. It was around this time that Jane met Ireene Wicker, another radio singer who had a program for children on which she was known as "The Singing Lady." Running into each other time and again, they became "radio buddies," a relationship that developed into a lifelong friendship.

Don's influence showed in Jane's confidence on stage. Although she had always deferred to Don on matters of performance and career, she discovered she could now assert herself when it came to music.

During a guest appearance with Rudy Vallee, one of radio's leading crooners, Vallee wanted Jane to sing "St. Louis Blues" in rat-a-tat-tat fast time. Jane had sung the song many times, but in her own bluesy rhythm. She tried to persuade him to let her do it in her style. He insisted on the fast version. When they went on the air and she was introduced, Jane took the stage, then tapped her foot insistently in blues time. After a few bars, the band got the message and played it her way.

That wasn't the only discovery she made in New York.

My most pleasant moment in the big town was the discovery of all those little buttons at my bedside in the St. Regis hotel. When I needed something, a gown pressed in a hurry, service in my room, the papers, I merely pressed a button. I didn't have to force myself to talk into a telephone.

The stuttering never went away; it just seemed unimportant, as long as it could be held at bay. Reporters loved to focus on it, to her dismay. She answered their questions quickly and directly, then diverted the conversation to something more pleasant.

After two years of successful radio work centered in Chicago, and some scouting around, Don felt the moment had come to take the next big step and make the move to New York, the mecca of show business. This time they boarded the Twentieth Century Limited with one-way tickets.

5

NUMBER ONE GIRL SINGER
1933—1934

IT WAS A cold crisp day in January, 1933, when Jane arrived in New York. She had no job and exactly $100 in her pocket. Don's brash confidence was enough to carry both of them.

The Great Depression had left the country demoralized. Life was grim for many, with banks closing, foreclosures on farms, lifestyles changing from middle class respectability to living on the street or as hoboes. A quarter of the nation's work force was unemployed, and people went to great lengths to find any kind of job, hopping on freight trains to get from one place to another. "Hoovervilles," communities of homeless people living in cardboard boxes, had sprouted everywhere. Everyone looked to the new president, Franklin Delano Roosevelt, to lift the country out of its gloom.

Hollywood did its part by making "feel good" movies with curly-haired darling Shirley Temple smiling and showing her dimples on the big screen, Mae West making risqué comedies with W.C. Fields, and Fred Astaire whirling Ginger Rogers lightly into people's hearts. Movies painted a hopeful picture of life being amusing and people being forever young and beautiful and in love—and millions went to see them, forgetting their struggles and hard times.

Newspapers supplied details of the amusing antics of sophisticated society—a life as remote to most readers as a trip to the moon. Glamor was definitely "in," and New York was the capital of it all. People who could not afford to participate found vicarious pleasure in reading about the fascinating lives of the privileged in the columns.

At the Casino in Central Park, Eddie Duchin enchanted patrons with his smooth, romantic piano style. Broadway boasted Jerome Kern's new musical, *Roberta,* about real and phony royalty in Parisian circles. Couples lingered over dinner at Sardi's and took carriage rides through the park. Evening clothes were mandatory at the Persian Room at the Plaza, where members of café society filled the tables.

Jane's looks and style fit the scene. New York was the end of the rainbow. What you did in Cincinnati or Cleveland or Chicago wasn't enough to gain entry to the big time. Your reputation had to precede you, and even then, you still had to prove yourself. Had anyone even heard of Jane Froman here? Would anyone notice her? Would they give her a chance?

They had, and they would, and they did.

The Chesterfield Hour on CBS, a coast-to-coast musical variety show featuring popular singers and bands of the day, had just dropped the Boswell Sisters, a singing trio, leaving one of their three segments vacant. Bing Crosby, the nation's top crooner, had a spot and Ruth Etting, a torch singer and a favorite of Jane's, filled another. Within a week of her arrival in New York, Jane had the third spot.

Don had explored the possibilities on an earlier visit to New York, where he had discovered the impending changes in the Chesterfield program's lineup. He set up an audition for Jane. She sang and a contract was offered, but Jane was afraid to accept it. Even her agent, Charlie Morrison, was against it. A failure now, with a top radio spot in New York, could result in the ruin of the career that had been so carefully and beautifully built to this point. It was too big a gamble. Don wouldn't listen. Sure of himself, and of Jane, he signed a contract for Jane without her permission. It was only one of many major disagreements that arose between Jane and Don on the handling of her career.

Jane was given a two-week trial. *The Chesterfield Hour* aired twice a week, Tuesdays and Fridays at nine o'clock, from a CBS studio at 53rd Street and Broadway. The CBS house band was led by Lennie Hayton. The announcer was Norman Brokenshire. Jane quickly earned the nickname "The Chesterfield Lark" and was signed on permanently after her trial period. Don's big gamble paid off.

Success could be dangerous. Ruth Etting, in one of the other Chesterfield slots, was known for heartrending songs of broken hearts and dashed dreams. Jane's repertoire was wider, as she could sing anything. She was more elegant and sophisticated than Etting, so the the two singers did not clash artistically. Still, Jane came under the scrutiny of the mob, to be sure she was not trying to oust Etting—whose husband and manager was Chicago mobster Moe Snyder. When Snyder decided Jane was no threat, the mob backed off.

Friends later told Jane they would never forget the look on Mama's face when the voice of the "Chesterfield Lark" first wafted into her sitting room at 1 West Broadway in Columbia. Jane wrote of this later.

> Mama, who as Anna Barcafer had been the guest artist with the Chicago Symphony Orchestra and devoted her life to the great classical composers, really looked down her nose at what was going on in the music of the day, which she

never really liked or understood. Sometimes I think it even made her shudder. But she kept that upper lip mighty stiff, a habit she had anyway as I had learned early in my young life.

I, on the contrary, had a great and genuine feeling for those ballads and blues and torch songs then coming into vogue. I very deliberately tried to bring to those "pops" not only

The Chesterfield Lark

the feeling and heart of the songs but the musical taste and knowledge of phrasing and diction I had acquired through the years.

It was my pride and joy as time went on to be able to bring my own interpretations to the unforgettable songs of Gershwin, Cole Porter, Dick Rodgers, Irving Berlin, Hoagy Carmichael and o, so many who have been contributing to the great resurgence of American music. . . .

The Chesterfield Hour catapulted Jane into the big time. Her career zoomed. Audiences responded to the feelings Jane inspired as she revealed the heart of the songs. Her salary went up and up . . . and so did her responsibilities. Radio had become a huge industry, in which millions of dollars were being invested. Jane described it:

It was no longer just pure fun for the fun of singing. You disciplined yourself for every waking hour. You didn't drink, you didn't stay up late at night—I never had anyway— but you guarded almost fanatically your voice, your time, and every bit of your resources, physical and vocal. You were there in that vast studio whenever they wanted you, and they wanted you all the time—morning, noon and night. I was no longer alone in a heavily draped room with a tiny mike, but in the huge new studios with their large and critical audiences, among the most sophisticated in this town of sophisticates. By now that innocent looking little mike had become master. It certainly had become mine.

Jane had always felt the importance of having a real home and worked to make one for herself and Don. They found a charming apartment in Garden City, Long Island, which Jane fixed up to be a cozy haven, away from the pressures of their work. Decorated in bright colors, with plants on the window-sills in colorful pots, the room radiated sunshine. The dining room had an Old Dutch motif with blue and white enamel and tile. Easy chairs covered in velvet, with plenty of books and magazines and ash trays handy, made a warm and inviting living room. Indirect lighting provided soft light everywhere.

During an interview with radio's Dwight Fiske, Jane mentioned a home and children. "Kids mean a lot," she told him. "I want two boys and a girl, and a little house with a tree, a fireplace, and some chintz. And as I've never believed that careers and cradles mix, I'm going to give up the career."

If it surprised the audience, who saw her as a rising star, and who generally believed stardom and motherhood did not mix, it didn't seem a contradiction to Jane. She had gone along, letting her talent and fame take her where they would. Perhaps with the idealism of youth, she felt all things were possible, and that a family was simply in the cards, and she would handle it when the time came.

The apartment in Garden City meant a commute to the studio in Manhattan, where Jane always arrived with a bag of yarn, so she could knit when she wasn't singing. If she did happen to steal some time, it would be to get in a few rounds of golf. Reporters who found her on the golf course would have to keep up with her to get their interviews.

The Chesterfield Hour secured Jane's reputation. She received more offers than she could possibly accept, including some from the big new "picture houses."

Vaudeville, the entertainment that had pleased audiences for an entire generation of performers, had seen its last glory days at the Palace. Movies now reigned and theaters—movie palaces—were built to house them, like the Capitol and the Paramount in New York. The big new "picture houses," as some called them, offered first run movies and, following the movie, a live show on stage featuring dancers, singers, comedians, and all kinds of performers. While full, live orchestras were used for more important films, specially built pipe organs were the main provider of music in all picture palaces.

The theaters built to house these shows were indeed majestic, as extravagant in their decor as the Palace had been for vaudeville. Customers were made to feel like royalty as they walked on plush carpets past mirrored walls, crystal chandeliers, and under gold ceilings. Behind the scenes, elaborate technical equipment and facilities insured lavish productions that would dazzle the audiences.

The Roxy was considered the grandest of all the movie palaces. Its creator and namesake, Samuel "Roxy" Rothafel, called it "The Cathedral of the Motion Picture." Designed by architect W.W. Ahlschlager of Chicago and erected in 1927, it was indeed the showplace of New York City, with its 5,920 seats and multi-tiered balconies.

As luxurious as these movie palaces were, the grandest was yet to come. John D. Rockefeller, Jr., in a commercial liaison with media giant RCA, had built a complex of buildings called "Radio City," which people saw as a sign of resiliency during tough times. The complex included a gigantic movie palace, designed by Donald Deskey. In December, 1932, Radio City Music Hall—the largest theater in the country—opened in New York City. It boasted only a few more seats than the Roxy—5,960—but the seats were widely spaced.

The elegance of architecture and design in a time of depression made Radio City Music Hall a symbol of optimism and hope. It was so spectacular that critics reported, "It has been said of the new Music Hall that it needs no performers."

The Great Stage was the most perfectly equipped in the world, with several hydraulic-powered elevators making it possible to achieve dynamic effects in staging. One elevator alone raised and lowered the entire orchestra. Its enormous gold curtain

Radio City's famous facade

was the largest in the world. The Wurlitzer pipe organ, built especially for the theatre, needed eleven separate rooms to house its pipes.

Radio City Music Hall wanted Jane and made an offer, but Jane declined. She felt it was just too big; all the picture houses were. Eventually, however, she was won over by an offer from one, not as intimidating—the Paramount.

That spring, while Jane was playing at the Paramount, Don heard that auditions were being held for the new Ziegfeld Follies of 1934. Flo Ziegfeld, the Broadway impresario who had brought the American musical revue to astonishing heights with his Ziegfeld Follies from 1907 to 1931, had died, but Billie Burke, Ziegfeld's widow, was eager to pay off his debts and sold the rights to showman Lee Shubert to produce another Follies. Don planned on trying out for a part in the Follies, and asked Jane to come along.

Jane was engaged at the Paramount and had her radio work, but went along with Don to the audition. The producer heard Don's rich baritone voice and signed him right away. He seemed less interested in Jane but at Don's insistence, he agreed to listen to her. She was signed up immediately. The show was to go into rehearsal in June.

Meanwhile, Jane returned to the Paramount again and again. Eventually, Radio City Music Hall lured her, too, and she opened there on Thursday, March 23, 1933.

A production called *Big City Blues* featured musical numbers "On the Ferry," "In a Limousine," and "The Rendezvous," featuring dancers, singers, musicians and comedians as well as the entire company in a spectacular finale. Jane had no lines to speak; she just sang. Also on the program with the live show was a feature movie, *Sweepings,* with Lionel

Barrymore, plus "The Last Mail," a short Aesop fable, and an organist playing the Radio City Music Hall's "Mighty Wurlitzer." It was grand, indeed.

Once *Follies* rehearsals were underway, Jane's schedule was busier than ever as she kept up with her radio work and the picture houses and explored an interesting new avenue—movies.

Warner Brothers had asked Jane to do a short film for them at their studios in Brooklyn. Jane took it on. Yes, the stutter would be a challenge, but movies—with *sound!*—were too important to her career for her to dismiss them. It was probably singing they wanted her for, and not speaking. She signed on, but the script they handed her had hundreds of speaking lines. She panicked.

When it was time to appear at the studio, Jane didn't show up. She didn't answer her phone, either. Warners sent scouts to her apartment, but, scared to death, she feigned illness or pretended she wasn't home. Scouts tried to track her down but she managed to evade them.

Finally, a no-nonsense telegram arrived from the studio. Miss Froman had better appear at the studio by ten o'clock the next morning or face legal action. Under threat of being sued by Warner Brothers, she showed up.

Kissing Time, a two-reel Warner Brothers-Vitaphone "filmshort" directed by Roy Mack, was labeled an operetta. It was a twenty-three minute film with a big musical production number involving the full cast, lots of costumes, and plenty of stereotypes. Jane played a young woman on holiday in a small Mexican village who falls for handsome leading man George Metaxa, but agrees to give him up to save his life and help him escape revolutionary forces led by the powerful and jealous El Toro. Her one song in the film was

"Love, What Have You Done to Me," a bluesy love song. The film was released a month before Jane opened on Broadway in the Ziegfeld Follies.

"We made the picture in four days and I never stuttered once," Jane recalled, surprised at the results. Nevertheless, she observed another problem.

Jane at the time of the Ziegfield Follies

"I had always been taught to sing from way down here—the diaphragm," she said, "—also to open the mouth and give the voice a chance to come out. Well, the Froman mouth was all over the screen.... you have to be refined and dainty when you're singing for the screen." It was a valuable lesson. One can only guess how Mama felt about another popular influence pulling Jane away from her classical training.

Working for the Ziegfeld Follies, Jane met people of the stage and screen whom she had admired all her life. One was Fred Allen, the great wit of radio, who had written the book for the show. Others Jane met in the Follies were dancers Vilma and Buddy Ebsen and actor Brice Hutchins, who was later to change his name to Bob Cummings. A young unknown, Eve Arden, was also in the show; but the person who ran away with the show—and Jane's heart—was Fanny Brice.

When Lee Shubert took over the Ziegfeld Follies, no one knew what to expect. To meet the challenge of living up to its reputation, Shubert had hired Fanny Brice, whose name had become synonymous with the Follies, as she had appeared in every one. No Follies would ever seem complete without her.

Actress, singer and comedienne Fanny Brice was one of the most popular stage performers in the country. Her skill at creating comedy out of her Jewish roots with songs, skits and physical antics, complete with Yiddish accent and lithe comedic movements and facial expressions, left audiences rolling in the aisles. For years, Brice had been trying to find a place in the popular medium of radio to reach an even larger audience, but her particular kind of visual burlesque had not proved effective in that field. On the stage, however, her performances were almost always sold out. Flo Ziegfeld, the impresario, had known a good thing when he saw one, and had hired Fanny back in 1907 when he first produced his Follies in the renamed New York Theater, the "Jardin de Paris."

From the first day in the Follies, Fanny, as everyone called her, took pity on Jane, who looked awkward and terrified as the grand scale of the production seemed to overwhelm her. Someone in the costume department had handed Jane a flat pancake of a hat to wear in the show's finale. Jane, so green that she had no idea that the horsehair creation had to be shaped to suit the contours of the face, walked on stage with the hat flopping. As the curtain went down, Jane heard someone holler, "Hey, kid!" It was Fanny. She looked Jane squarely in the eye and barked, "That's the God-damnedest hat I ever saw."

Taking Jane into her dressing room, she took out a needle and thread, did some bending and blocking, and whipped the limp form into shape. Fanny handed Jane the hat, no longer the ridiculous pancake that had flopped on her head during the show, but now transformed into a thing of beauty. As she worked in her dressing room, they talked. Fanny leveled with Jane.

"Kid, you have a great set of pipes, but you can't walk or talk." Fanny took Jane under her wing, giving her "show biz" lessons—and Jane, ever on the alert for more knowledge about how to present herself as a performer, ate it up. Fanny talked to her about clothes. She paid attention to the smallest details of show business, of how a performer could make her work more meaningful. Under Fanny's tutelage, any awkward mannerisms on stage were forged expertly and deftly into graceful, natural movements, taking Jane's earlier lessons from Don to new heights. That was the beginning of

Fanny Brice

a long and lasting friendship. Jane, who could not tolerate anyone who put on airs, found Fanny's earthy manner refreshing and honest.

With Fanny's help, Jane learned the art of walking across a stage, how to carry herself with head erect and body straight; she learned timing, and what to do with her hands. Fanny watched Jane, corrected her, and made her practice over and over again, passing on to this eager newcomer her own great fund of priceless experience and techniques. Jane was thrilled to learn from a pro like Fanny.

In September, 1933, just before the Follies went on the road to preview in Boston, Jane and Don were married. Mama and her husband, Mr. and Mrs. William Hetzler; Don's father, the Reverend F. E. Ross; and Aunt Pearl were in attendance. There was no fanfare. The pair had been together a long time and everyone saw them as a couple. Life in show business went on as usual, with a new show always in preparation, and new arrangements to learn, and maybe a little golf on the side when they had the time. Don continued to coach Jane and Jane was an eager student who learned well the moves and mannerisms for good stage presence. She, in turn, felt Don had a fine baritone voice and tried to coach him in his singing, using the vocal training she had received from her mother, but he did not take to being taught.

When she and Don finally announced their marriage over the air, Jane added, matter-of-factly, "We've been married for weeks and weeks." The couple's romance delighted audiences. Pictures of them appeared in fan magazines, Jane's on the cover of *Billboard* magazine in August and Don's a few months later. They sang duets on the radio. Bright and breezy, the newly married couple represented a good life, happy times.

The Ziegfeld Follies of 1934 opened for previews at the Shubert Theater in Boston on November 7, 1933. Fanny Brice was brilliant as "Soul Saving Sadie of Avenue A," and "Countess Dubinsky," a Russian socialite whose genteel poverty had led her to a career as a fan dancer. She introduced Baby Snooks, a character who would later become a huge hit in a network radio series. Jane, too, was a great success, introducing the beautiful Vernon Duke songs "Suddenly," with lyrics by E. Y. "Yip" Harburg, and "What Is There to Say?" in a duet with Everett Marshall.

Don, as lead male singer, was also given a song that became a hit: "Headin' for the Last Roundup," written by Billy Hill.

Before each show, in the dressing room, Jane put on her makeup, accentuating her widow's peak with dark pencil to shorten her too-long face, and practiced her speaking lines by thinking of what she was going to say, then saying it over and over, slowly and with care.

There were backstage jealousies, unfamiliar to Jane, as one performer tried to sabotage another. This was not merely upstaging. It could be a pinch or a stab of pain with a fingernail during a song, the trampling of a gown, or the maneuvering of someone to the back of the stage instead of toward the audience. Had it not been for Fanny, the glamorous experience of working in the theater might have given way to a minor battlefield for which Jane was not prepared. Unable to speak up for herself, Jane kept quiet, but Fanny taught her tricks to counteract the shenanigans of other performers who tried to ruin her song and steal the spotlight for themselves. She was learning. One day, she would put this knowledge to good use.

Jane wrote about the production, which had to compete with the Ziegfeld imprint of past years.

> Neither the fascinating beauty of the Ben Ali Haggin tableaux was there, of course, nor the spectacular splendor of Joseph Urban's scenery, but the beauty of the American girl was still glorified in all her fresh, young loveliness.

The show needed polish, but *Variety* and *The New York Times* wrote that with Fanny Brice in the production, the show would be a success. Extensive changes in production and cast, and engagements in Philadelphia, Washington, Pittsburgh and Newark before the scheduled opening in New York, helped to put the finishing touches on it. At last, the show came to the Winter Garden Theater in New York, opening Christmas week, January 4, 1934, just a year after Jane had arrived in New York.

One of Jane's numbers, "Green Eyes," had her come onstage wearing a skintight green sequined dress—so tight she wore nothing underneath. She was a stunning beauty in the spotlight, but as she took a deep breath and hit a high note, she felt the dress give—all the way down the back, from her neck to her knees. Jane recalled:

> It was the most embarrassing thing that ever happened to me. I couldn't leave the stage. . . . I had to stand there and keep on singing as if nothing had happened. So I simply put

one hand in back and held on to the dress for dear life. When I slunk off stage, careful to keep my back from the audience, I certainly must have looked peculiar. . . . but it was nothing to the way I felt!

Jane's appearance in the Follies led almost immediately to cover after cover on the fan magazines of the day and more offers than she could possibly accept.

Jane and Don—now Mr. and Mrs. Ross—were learning that being in a show together as man and wife could take its toll. Columnists gave much attention to the fact that Jane's earnings far surpassed those of Don Ross. They claimed that Don Ross was on the bill at Jane's insistence. Ross bitterly complained to Walter Winchell, the columnist, that he was in show business long before Jane and was given the role on his own merits.

Although rehearsals for the Follies took most of her time, Jane had kept up her radio work. She did shows at the CBS Studios in New York for various sponsors—Chesterfield, Linit, Frigidaire, Iodent—working with bandleaders Ted Husing, Erno Rapee, and Nino Martino. The brilliant pianist, Oscar Levant, was her accompanist. Between shows, she managed to fly to Chicago to appear with Vincent Lopez on Sunday evenings. Commercial air travel was just catching on, and the trip was long, but Jane, enthusiastic about flying, didn't seem to mind. She had not had a night off for a solid year.

Her stutter was under control as far as Jane was concerned. It never interfered with her singing, and someone could be called in to speak her non-singing lines. Actress Arlene Francis, whose voice was in the same register as Jane's, was a frequent stand-in for her when operettas, words and music, were presented on the *Palmolive Beauty Box*.

MGM wanted Jane to hop on a plane and fly out to Hollywood to sing three numbers in a new Joan Crawford movie. It was an appealing offer, but even Jane had her limits. The tight Follies rehearsal schedule forced her to stay in New York.

The Ziegfeld Follies of 1934 was a great hit, and Jane played to wonderful reviews. Her salary was $500 a week, a substantial sum of money in 1934, when a dollar could buy nearly fifteen times what it can today. She was meeting the cream of the theater world, and loving it. There were polls everywhere, in newspapers, magazines, and trade papers, and Jane's name would invariably appear at the top.

Jane shared her success with her mother. She brought Mama to New York and bombarded her with good times. They attended concerts and visited museums. They saw the latest plays on Broadway, including Lillian Hellman's play, *The Children's Hour*, the hit of the season. They visited NBC's studios, where Jane had arranged for Mama to sit in on her favorite musical broadcasts. At the Winter Garden, Anna Froman Hetzler sat through three performances of the Follies, while others had to order their tickets to the popular show twelve weeks in advance.

Jane threw a party for her mother. Everyone was invited, from popular radio soprano Jessica Dragonette and radio personality Ilka Chase, to composer and music critic Deems Taylor, New York Times theater critic Brooks Atkinson, band leader Ray Noble, author Alexander Woollcott and sports hero Jack Dempsey. Ethel Barrymore, the famous first lady of the theater, was also there. Her dignity, charm, and magnificent stature as a human being were impressive. The great actress had been generous when Jane was just starting out in New York, making her feel admired, and Jane was grateful. They became friends. Jane recalled the scene with pleasure:

Mama was the star. Her china blue eyes surveyed the whole scene majestically. On the immaculate pastel blue ensemble she had placed regally the pretty diamond brooch I had bought her when I was first in the chips. A gaily flowered blue hat topped her faultless pompadour. I never saw a hair out of place in those undulating waves she achieved so miraculously. She invariably favored pastels, preferably pink and blues with long gloves to match, and flowered hats. She carried herself with perfect poise.

I'll never forget the sight of her at the party, seated with Ethel Barrymore deep in conversation beside a potted plant. Ethel had great admiration for Mama and always made a B-line for her at a gathering.

Ethel's royal bearing by no means topped Mama's, I can assure you. But Ethel's prowess with a martini far outclassed Mama's modest efforts. As their glasses were filled again and again, I caught Mama pouring her drinks cautiously and surreptitiously into the potted palm. She knew in what department she really was outclassed!

Jane loved having her mother around. Mama coached her whenever they had an opportunity and remained Jane's best friend.

Mama revealed a bit of the "ham" in her beautifully articulated and finely-wrought responses to questions. To one interviewer's query about Jane and Don at home, she answered, brightly,

They live comfortably but not ostentatiously, in one of Manhattan's lovely apartments, with a suite reserved for me when I go for a visit. After an engagement at the theater they return to the apartment for a late supper, rather than joining friends at a cocktail party or night club. Both Ellen Jane and Don know the importance of rest, and the physical fitness that their careers require, and they do an excellent job in guarding their health.

The Follies had brought all kinds of attention to Jane, not only for her remarkable singing talent and style, but for her uncommon good looks. Jane appeared taller than her five feet six inches. Her vocal training had given her a courtly posture and bearing. She had been chosen for the Ziegfeld Follies, known for its celebration of female beauty. Jane was featured in ads and articles about beauty care, giving tips on proper skin treatment and nutrition and the merits of exercise and a good night's sleep. Women wanted to know her secrets and bought up fan magazines by the thousands to read about them.

Success was hers, but not without a price. Her marriage to Don was losing ground. The ball of yarn that was their tightly wound relationship of professional work, companionship, and respect was unraveling. Jane's career was soaring; Don's was not. Don was drinking more heavily than usual. When her contract with the Follies was up on June 1, and the show went on the road, Jane did not go with it. She needed time with Don. Marriage was a commitment to be taken seriously, and she had to work on hers.

No longer bound to the rigorous demands of the Follies, Jane took time off while she and Don drove up to New Brunswick. They cruised the Gaspe Peninsula and toured the Thousand Islands. She played golf every day, getting her score down from 116 to 98, once even breaking 90.

During her break, Jane took only one booking, at the Paramount. The biggest experts in the business of booking talent—Boris Morris of Paramount, Martin Beck of RKO, and others—competed for Jane's appearance, resorting to flipping a coin to see who would book her. Morris won. Coming on near the windup of a 48-minute show, Jane's appearance gave a real kick to the bill. *Variety* said she had a "swell pair of pipes and knew what to do about it." She was never in better form. Paramount kept her for one month, the longest time a radio star had appeared in one theater.

Jane returned to the air late in the summer of 1934 for Pontiac on NBC with Frank Black's orchestra. Whatever else she did, Jane always returned to radio. She had grown into a star as the fledgling radio industry made its way into the American culture. Radio was comfortable, secure. Her voice reached many more people over the air waves in one broadcast than it did in a year with the Ziegfeld Follies. Sponsors liked her, and she sang for a host of the top ones—Buick, Coca-Cola, Gulf Oil, Palmolive, Fleischman's Yeast, Pontiac.

Rarely did Jane make enemies, but once, while she was under contract with Pontiac, the William Esty Agency got upset with her. The agency had auditioned her for a Camel show and had received the OK from management to give her a contract, then discovered that her contract with Pontiac prevented her from doing more than a half hour weekly on a network hookup for any other accounts. Camel wanted her for two half-hour programs a week. Jane, still blasé about business affairs, thought Camel had planned to use her for just one half hour.

Trying to lead an entirely normal life to keep the balance in their marriage, Jane and Don played golf every morning and went to see a picture most evenings, as they were both incurable movie fans. It was only in the afternoons that they went over songs, vocalized, rehearsed and smiled at clients.

It took more than a week to get ready for each weekly program. Songs had to be picked for the program, and new ones were coming out all the time. Once the tunes were chosen, there might be a three-hour conference with the arranger to go over openings and closings. Then another session was necessary to work out a rough version of the song. Jane had to vocalize, work on the arrangement, and study the phrasing of a song before rehearsals for the show even started.

Jane's salary had climbed to four figures a week, making her the highest paid woman on the air. After splurging on an ermine coat, she felt guilty and buckled down to save money, using her sewing skills to revamp her entire wardrobe.

As a performer, Jane was to radio what Eddie Duchin was to supper clubs: a healthy dose of style and sophistication wrapped up in a pretty package. She was called "Park Avenue's Favorite Entertainment." Dressed from head to toe in sequined gowns, wearing diamonds and furs, and frequenting posh restaurants, Jane was no longer concerned about money; it was there to enjoy. Worrying about the future just never occurred to her.

In the fall, Jane cut her first solo recordings with the newly formed American Decca company. One of the four sides cut, "I Only Have Eyes for You," became a hit. Jane had made earlier recordings with Henry Thies and His Orchestra: "Sharing," a song by Benny Davis and J. Fred Coots, and later, "June Kisses," composed by Jack Clifford with lyrics by John Roberts. Recordings had only recently evolved from production on wax cylinders to disks.

In November, Jane did a performance of *Hit the Deck*, a Vincent Youmans musical, on radio station KSD in St. Louis. Engagements were lined up for a tour of the picture houses, for the National Press Club in Washington, as the soloist at Lewisohn Stadium in New York, and at ASCAP and Paul Whiteman concerts at Carnegie Hall.

Everywhere, she sang the music of popular American composers. In turn, the composers looked to Jane to sing their ballads, bringing them to the public with her sophisticated style and taste and finely trained voice.

Mama still had to choke down disappointment that her talented daughter, classically educated, seemed to prefer singing blues and torch songs to opera. However, she respected Jane's choices and her right and desire to sing the music that pleased her. Mama did her best to come to terms with Jane's success in the popular field. One interviewer quoted her as saying, with the proverbial stiff upper lip, "I am very happy that Ellen Jane chose to sing over the radio. An operatic career requires much physical endurance. Opera stars don't last very long, it is too exacting a life."

The nation couldn't have been more pleased. In 1934, Jane was voted the Number One girl singer on the air in every poll in the country. A person would be hard put to turn on the radio and not hear the glorious voice of Jane Froman at any hour of the day or night.

6

DREAMS OF STARDOM
1935 — 1939

L IFE IN ALL its exciting variety continued at a fast pace, with one engagement after another lined up for months in advance. In a time when broadcasting was all live, she did two radio broadcasts in one evening, one for Coca-Cola and the other for Bromo Seltzer, "winding up the season with a bang!" she wrote to her mother. In the mayor's house on West Broadway in Columbia, Missouri, Mama's radio was almost always tuned to one show or another to hear her talented child sing.

Money came in sometimes faster than Jane could spend it. She showered her mother with flowers for her birthday and Easter and sent her lavish gifts—a fashionable new dress in one of her favorite pastel colors, or a string of expensive pearls.

In the spring of 1935, Jane and Don closed up their New York apartment, got in their car and headed west. Jane drove most of the time, as fast as possible. They visited Don's family in Columbus, Ohio, and Jane's family in Columbia, Missouri, staying to watch the Missouri Tigers play football. Driving a snappy convertible coupe, touring in the open air, Jane gained ten pounds, drinking three quarts of milk a day for the calcium, and getting plenty of sleep.

They saw the Grand Canyon and other places of interest,

and got in all the golf they could, trying to enjoy some time together away from the pressures of show business, popularity polls, and a working marriage. In California Jane soaked up the sun, beginning a lifelong love affair with warm climates. On the golf course or sunning herself by the swimming pool in Hollywood, she got a glorious tan, improving her already good looks.

Soaking up the California sun

A friend invited them to visit the Warner Brothers studios, where Jane was asked to make a screen test. Secretly she wanted to do it, but knew her stuttering would be a huge roadblock. *Kissing Time* had taught her that she could do a flawless job speaking lines in an emergency, but the stress was too great; she just couldn't chance it, and she said no.

It surprised her when Warner Brothers pursued her. They made an offer. Would she come and make a test? Don, sensing the rules of the game, advised Jane to play it cool. They played a few holes of golf, got beautiful tans, and acted unimpressed.

In truth, trying to forget about the movies proved impossible. Every young performer aspired to become a big movie star. In spite of her anxieties, Jane wasn't ready to give up the dream.

Movies had become, along with radio, a major form of entertainment in the country. Film was no longer the empire of silent clowns like Buster Keaton and Charlie Chaplin, or exotic romantic exploits with desert sheiks, but had grown in stature with the addition of sound and more advanced lighting and camera techniques to reflect a sophisticated blend of drama, art and music.

For an attractive and talented young woman who had achieved coast-to-coast radio celebrity on *The Chesterfield Hour* and who had been on the Broadway stage in the Ziegfeld Follies, movies were the next logical step to total stardom and all that came with it.

Warners's offer went up. Jane and Don played more golf. Jane's excitement grew but Don remained aloof.

The offer went up again. Don's confidence had paid off and it was rubbing off on her. The stutter had not stopped her in radio, or on the stage, or in the movie short, with music and clever scripting to mask her brief speaking lines. So far, it seemed there was nothing Jane could not do, or conquer. She was persuaded to try. With opportunity knocking, Jane had to open the door, so she stubbornly refused to let her recalcitrant stuttering problem stand in her way. They finally agreed to make the test.

It was obvious Warners was pleased with the results, because they drew up a contract and Jane signed it. She knew little about camera technique and film acting but, as always, was eager to learn.

Warner Brothers had been churning out lots of routine musicals with forgettable plots that could absorb the talents of popular radio stars to see if they were worth developing as screen stars. Studios did not seem concerned over the rumored threat of television; perhaps it still seemed a distant possibility. Nevertheless, if the public wanted to see what their favorite radio stars looked like on the screen, Hollywood would show them before television came along to do it. Rudy Vallee, the popular crooner of the 1930s who was known for using a megaphone to project his voice, was one hopeful; Helen Morgan, who sang songs of heartbreak and loneliness and was especially popular in small, smoky clubs, was another. They put these singers in movies with thinly outlined story lines, merely to show off their voices, hoping to win over their devoted radio audiences. Some made it in the movies and went on to stardom and a life of fame and fortune. Bing Crosby and Bob Hope were two of the lucky ones, but Fanny Brice, as talented and popular as she was, was not; although she made a few films, her brand of physical humor never caught on in films as it had in the theater and, later, on the radio, as Baby Snooks.

Jane and her old singing partner from radio, James Melton, also a newcomer to the movies, were signed to do *Stars Over Broadway*. Melton had been born to radio as Jane had, and loved it as she did, so neither of them banked on movies as a substitute for it. Still, they could neither pass up the opportunity nor ignore the possibilities. Jane, by contract, had first female billing. Others in the cast were Pat O'Brien, Jean Muir, and Marie Wilson. On another set, for Warner Brothers–First National, Don was filming *Broadway Hostess*, with two other radio singers, Phil Regan and Wini Shaw.

The plot of *Stars Over Broadway* was based on a short story by Mildred Cram called "Thin Air," which first appeared in a Hearst publication in November, 1934. A down-on-his-luck talent agent sees his big chance when he discovers a hotel porter with a beautiful singing voice and tries to turn him against his classical training to become a popular radio star. The story, a parallel to Jane's own, must have had a ring of familiarity to it.

The music for *Stars Over Broadway* was created by the talented team of Al Dubin and Harry Warren, who wrote much of the music for Warners's musicals. Dance routines and choreography were under the direction of Busby Berkeley and Bobby Connolly.

Jane and Don rented Eddie Cantor's spacious house in Beverly Hills. It had plenty of rooms, having been home to the Cantor family—Eddie and Ida and their five girls. "It was heaven," Jane recalled, years later. They had servants, a swimming pool, tennis courts, a fancy car, and they even began to behave like movie stars, thinking nothing of taking a leave of absence from the studio to fly to New York just for an Italian meal. In those days it took 36 hours and 19 stops to fly from California to New York. They would stay for two or three days, then return to California.

There was plenty of work to do at Warners before Jane could start rehearsing. An army of speech therapists went to work on her speech impediment. One of the techniques they tried was to have her remain absolutely silent for seven days. She communicated by writing notes, or using sign language to indicate she was hungry or needed a break, pointing significantly at her throat. Concerned friends left her alone, believing she had laryngitis.

Therapists also worked at changing the rhythm of Jane's speech with a method called "swing reading." This involved writing a figure 8 in the air with a finger aloft, then speaking with the rhythm of a steady beat. It was slow at first and then was increasingly stepped up until the pace approached normal speech.

Stories in the fan magazines noted Jane's stuttering, to her despair. "Star of Radio Despite Handicap," they read, or "No Handicap Too Great." The final straw came when she read in a column: "Poor Jane Froman, her terrible handicap, her unfortunate drawback, will ruin her career. . . ." It got her so mad she learned her lines by sheer determination, buying volumes of poetry and reciting lines each night for hours, using the swing method.

Along with speech therapy she had to do breathing exercises, rest regularly and do as little entertaining as possible until her "cure" was complete. Only then would they let her go to the studio and start the picture. In order to insure the total relaxation necessary for success, she was not even allowed to have coffee during this period.

Her hard work seemed to be paying off until she went before the cameras. The barrage of activity on the set and pressure to perform on cue proved overwhelming, and her stutter returned. The director was patient, and the crew understanding. Still, at the end of the week, Jane was a nervous wreck.

Jane admitted her fears. "That awful moment of absolute silence after the director says 'action' and the sound track starts moving sent me into the worst panic I have ever known in my life," she confessed, but she didn't mind the hard work. The schedule that others may have found daunting was no problem for her. She had done the Follies—every night and a matinee twice a week, plus a weekly radio broadcast. Her natural drive to do well was a factor, too. She wanted to learn—camera techniques, film acting, anything she could to enlarge her cache of show business know-how—and she wasted no time learning it and doing it well. She looked forward to the weeks ahead, finding film work exciting.

During the long waits between scenes, she observed all she could or walked around talking to people. She charmed others on the set with her attentiveness. Being a stutterer all her life had taught her to be an excellent listener, leaving the talking to others. In quiet moments by herself, she kept her hands busy, knitting and crocheting; there was never an idle moment.

The most difficult part of the new routine was getting up at 5:30 A.M. to have her hair washed before facing the rigors of being made up. With the early schedule and general anxiety, she lost five pounds. The studio put her on a potato diet to fatten her up.

She was surprised at the techniques necessary to provide the screen with a totally unblemished image. She had always tried not to wear makeup, but in spite of her flawless skin, a good hairline, thick hair, fine teeth, a strong chin, natural long black lashes, and lustrous blue eyes, Hollywood had to make her over for the screen.

The camera photographed her face as excessively white—an eccentricity of the motion picture camera then—so makeup was necessary to darken her face. Jane went off to spend four days in the sun and returned to the set with a good tan. Too dark, cameraman George Barnes told her. She had to wear makeup after all. Accustomed as she was to using make-up theatrically, it was nothing like this. One side of her jaw was wider than the other and required extra shading, and one eye slanted upward and had to be taped down prior to the application of make-up.

Studio workers loved Jane. "I think Jane is the most attractive girl I've seen in years," said one. "It's because of her animation, her vivacity, I think—her face is so alive, it stands out in a whole roomful of people. Wholesome, magnetic, altogether lovely—and something you don't find in a carload of other women."

The wardrobe people also found her remarkable. "What a joy when you have to make clothes for her!" said one worker. "It's as close as possible to perfect." The papier mache and cloth model used for Jane's dimensions was used afterward as a standard by which models were judged for new movies, including *Colleen,* with Ruby Keeler, made by Warner Brothers in 1936.

Her golf game suffered on the huge courses in California. Her score, in the respectable 90s, rarely came in under three figures there. She took up tennis, instead, and took advantage of the Cantors' tennis courts as well as their swimming pool.

Once again, when the picture was scheduled to start, bad luck nipped at her heels and she contracted pneumonia. There were delays, but at last the film was made, and Jane did her part well. She spoke perfectly. Her press agent exuded delight: "You may consider it as another triumph for Hollywood. There is literally nothing Hollywood cannot do."

Stars Over Broadway previewed at the New York Strand Theater on November 14, 1935, to good notices. Most of the songs were likable tunes, but the critics did not find them

**Jane (right) with Jean Muir and James Melton in
Stars Over Broadway**

especially memorable. One of the film's highlights was Jane's deep-throated rendition of a blues song, "You Let Me Down," showing off her smooth lower register. Melton's solo, "September in the Rain," also rose above the rest of the score.

Although Busby Berkeley and Bobby Connolly had planned three big production numbers for the film, the only one that made it onto the screen was "At Your Service, Madam," done in exquisite art deco style. In it, Jane plays a society lady, with James Melton playing the butler who wins her away from an oily suitor. A second production number, "Broadway Cinderella," did not appear in the final cut of the film, for reasons unknown. Berkeley was not happy to see this number go, but his disappointment was even greater when the third never got off the ground. Berkeley had envisioned an elaborate forest of moveable silver trees set to the music for "September in the Rain," the one tune that was repeated throughout the film. The front office would not approve the added expense. It is doubtful that either of these added numbers would have made a bigger hit of the movie, which was entertaining but still run-of-the-mill for the time.

When Jane's work on *Stars Over Broadway* was completed, she was happy to return to New York. She always felt a little logy on the West Coast, instead of her usual bouncy self. She missed the opera and concert season. "I can't live without music," she said in a *Radio Stars* interview. She confessed to missing radio, too. ". . . I do love that old microphone!" she said. "I'm at home there. . . ." Along with another round of the picture houses she sang on one radio program after another, never wanting for a big sponsor.

When Bromo Seltzer sponsored *The Intimate Review*, featuring Jane and James Melton, singing with Al Goodman's music, they felt they needed someone to emcee the show. A young comic named Bob Hope auditioned for the job. With vaudeville on the way out, Hope had tried a comedy role on Broadway, but he and the show didn't make it. He revamped his vaudeville routine for the radio audience, borrowing jokes from entertainer Harry Richman and delivering them in a monologue. "This is the voice of inexperience, Bob Hope," he starts out. "Hope," he reminds listeners. "You spell it with an H, not a D." Bromo Seltzer liked him and signed him on, giving Bob Hope his start in radio on Jane's show on January 4, 1935, thrusting him into a new style that was to be the trademark of his lifelong career.

Jane sang the songs of Cole Porter, Rodgers and Hart, Howard Dietz and Arthur Schwartz, many from the heart of Broadway. Her voice, now a finely polished mezzo-soprano, brought to the songs the richness they deserved. People came to hear her, filling the theaters in which she played.

Cole Porter's *Jubilee* opened at the Imperial Theatre on

October 12, 1935, introducing the songs "Begin the Beguine" and "Just One of Those Things." Two days earlier, George Gershwin's *Porgy and Bess* had opened at the Alvin Theater, with a memorable score including "It Ain't Necessarily So" and "Summertime." The songs were perfect for Jane's voice, and she made them a regular part of her repertoire.

There was no one Jane admired more than Gershwin, whose songs she had sung for years at parties, in concerts and on the radio. She had met the young composer in February 1935 at a children's benefit in Palm Beach. He was still writing *Porgy and Bess* and, in his usual exuberant state, played his new music for Jane and other guests. She especially loved the lullaby "Summertime," and Gershwin promised her that if she introduced the song over the air, no other artist would sing it for a year.

George Gershwin

Jane sang "Summertime" on the radio before the Broadway opening of *Porgy and Bess*. Gershwin kept his word. "Summertime" became a big hit, as many of Gershwin's songs had before it.

Opera lovers watched Jane's career with interest—she was like one of the new "pretty" breed of singers who could sing opera, like Grace Moore, Lily Pons, Lucrezia Bori and Helen Jepson, and look like a movie star at the same time. Opera fans bemoaned losing her to popular music.

Jane never defended her love of American popular song or her choice of pop over classical. She simply put everything she knew into her music, and the results were superb. She was elegant. Her phrasing was exquisite. Her breath control was amazing. She knew technique but wasn't obsessed with it; the soul and meaning came through. For the music of Cole Porter, Vincent Youmans, George Gershwin, Irving Berlin, Harry Warren, Jimmy McHugh, Arthur Schwartz, and Richard Rodgers, there was no better interpreter. As new songs were introduced on Broadway—Rogers and Hart's "My Funny Valentine" from *Babes in Arms* or "Spring is Here" from *I Married an Angel*, for example—she brought them into her repertoire and was the first to present these works in "modern" concerts. The audiences loved her. Critics were in awe.

Ralph Lewando, one of Pittsburgh's top vocal coaches, picked up on this phenomenon in his column in the *Pittsburgh Press* on January 7, 1935:

> I might be going out of my realm in writing about a singer of radio-movie-stage show popular songs. However, attending the Stanley Theater show last evening, I was really impressed by the quality of voice displayed by Jane Froman. It was the first time I had heard her, but can fully understand why she is such a favorite with the vast public. In projecting her songs she seems to have lived every word, every phrase, every note, and the quality of tone, lovely in texture, creates an appeal that wins its way to the hearts. Would that certain singers on the concert & operatic boards could infuse such warmth and intelligence in their performances.
>
> Had Miss Froman chosen to make a career in concert and opera I feel certain that she would have created as much a furore as she does with her singing of "popular" songs. On the other hand, many singers would do well to emulate Miss Froman.
>
> —Ralph Lewando

Jane and Paul Whiteman had not let their past differences sully their relationship. When Whiteman's birthday party was aired on the NBC network on March 30, 1936, he invited many stars whom he had helped make famous— George Gershwin, Jack Teagarden, Mildred Bailey, Bing Crosby and Jane Froman among them.

In the summer of 1936 Jane appeared as a regular on KHJ's *California's Hour* in Los Angeles, where talented young people could make their debut on the air. They reminded Jane of how frightened she had been when she had first faced a microphone in Cincinnati, and she circulated among them giving out friendly words of encouragement. This generosity was a side of Jane's nature that many folks in show business came to know.

Hosts of radio shows were dazzled by Jane's personality as well as by her beauty and remarkable voice. Her stutter kept her from engaging in chatter, but they happily spoke about her instead. On the Radio Corporation of America's musical program, *The Magic Key,* narrator Ben Grauer introduced Jane with a tribute that was an eerie portent of what fate had in store for her.

"Winning one's way to the top," he proclaimed, "traditionally includes years of hardship and struggle." In Jane's case, he pointed out, she had had more than her share of both. He talked of her first opportunity to appear on radio, squelched by an emergency operation. He noted that on her way to audition for Paul Whiteman, she broke her ankle. (She still sang for him, then was rushed to the hospital.) And fate imposed another challenge when she was about to make a motion picture and contracted pneumonia just before the work on the picture was to begin. Grauer ended with the ironic note, "Then fate let her off, stopped tormenting her, and Jane Froman, for the first time, had clear sailing into the major stardom she so richly deserves." Little did he know.

In the summer of 1937, Jell-O, the producers of *The Jack Benny Show*, the most popular program on radio, had to find a summer replacement for the show. A radio season ran thirty-nine weeks. They needed a show that would carry the comedian's tremendous audience for the remaining thirteen. Auditions were set up. One hundred and forty shows competed, including one designed and submitted by Don Ross, featuring Jane as the singer and Don as the master of ceremonies, with Werner Janssen's orchestra, and a guest comedian each week. Don's show won the spot.

The style of *The Jell-O Summer Show* was light and breezy, with Don doing most of the talking and Jane speaking a few lines, nothing daunting. She added some "hot" rhythm numbers to her regular repertoire. Joe E. Lewis was the first guest comedian, and the Tune Twisters were hired as a supporting vocal group. The only problem facing Don during the run of the program was in cleaning up the acts of comedians he found for the show. Their blue material would never be allowed on the air.

The success of *The Jell-O Summer Show* was solid. Jane's picture appeared in *Radio Guide*. Walter Winchell mentioned her in his column. Once again, Jane was voted Number One singer in the nation in radio polls. Don, who got the Jell-O show on the air, received little attention.

That same summer of 1937, the death of composer George Gershwin shocked the nation. The composer, only thirty-nine years old, had complained of headaches for about a month, but it wasn't until the very end, when he was hospitalized, that he was diagnosed with a brain tumor. It was too late to operate.

Jane, who loved Gershwin's music, found the loss profound. He had broadened popular music, drawing from authentic musical sounds of America and exploring unusual rhythms, including jazz and ethnic music. She, like all singers and musicians, had been excited about the new challenges posed by his compositions.

The end of 1937 found Jane in Hollywood again. Although she couldn't understand it, her movie career was not over yet. It amazed her when Warner Brothers wanted her to make another picture. Her contract with Warners committed them to two pictures, but they were wary of her stutter. They loaned her to Paramount, who wanted Jane to play the part of Gwen Holmes in *Big Broadcast of 1937*, to be directed by Mitchell Leisen. Paramount's tests had satisfied them that Jane was able to perform, but just after shooting began, an outbreak of ptomaine poisoning hit the set, and Jane began to stutter so badly she had to be taken out of the picture. Paramount replaced Jane with actress Shirley Ross, who was later to be forever associated with Bob Hope, singing the duet "Thanks for the Memory," in another *Big Broadcast*—that of 1938.

Jane's removal from the picture was a huge blow to her pride. Now she had to accept the fact that her chance for a big movie career was over. Harder to admit was that her stuttering would not be tamed.

Warners, avoiding litigation with Paramount or Jane, was not about to lose their investment in the beautiful and talented singer. They took her back. This time, she was put under contract with RKO to do a comedy film, *Radio City Revels*, a story about a group of vaudevillian writers and performers and their interweaving love lives. The famed Rockettes, Radio City Music Hall's own chorus line, could not obtain a leave of absence to go to Hollywood to appear in the picture, but the movie showcased a galaxy of stars: Helen Broderick, Milton Berle, Ann Miller, Don Wilson, Jack Oakie, Kenny Baker, and Jane Froman. Jane's speaking part was kept to a few transitional lines between scenes. She sang two musical numbers, "You Let Me Down," a deep register blues song, and "Speak Your Heart," a tune set to a musical extravaganza by Busby Berkeley, in which Jane danced on screen for the first time. Her movements were somewhat stiff, probably due more to anxiety than lack of talent, but she looked ravishing and her voice was at its best. A lasting friendship with Milton Berle, then a young comic, was to come out of the movie. Over the years Berle, who got on the nerves of many in show business, proved to be a great and loyal friend to Jane, and she adored him.

Going over the script in **Radio City Revels**

Needlework was always handy for long waits

The film was released on February 11, 1938. Reviews credited it with a good cast and occasional good moments, but barely mentioned Jane's part in it, except to say she did a good job with the singing. Berle got a passing grade for an emotional scene that he played with Jack Oakie. The rest was tossed off as just another piece of fluff, an RKO B film of the star-studded variety.

Hollywood and the movies were not to court Jane anymore, but on radio, she remained as popular as ever. Her picture appeared on the cover of *Life* magazine. Famed photographer Alfred Eisenstaedt had captured her on film at rehearsal, seated in an empty theater, knitting, waiting for her next cue to sing.

Work in films and all there was to learn had kept Jane's mind off the unhappiness between herself and Don. She returned to radio work, finding comfort in its familiarity, in an environment where she was loved and appreciated, but it wasn't enough to mask the continual strain at home.

Don complained that Jane's career took up too much time for him to work on his own. His career, under the management of the William Morris Agency, was not as strong as Jane's. Jane was much more in demand, so hers was the career that was watched, not Don's.

Jane's loyalty to Don, for all that he had done for her in teaching her the craft of her profession, drove her. She tried everything to improve Don's mood, to make him happy with his work, but he would accept advice from no one, especially her. At last, frustrated, she stopped working in an attempt to give Don time and space to concentrate on his own career.

Don sometimes got jobs, but he didn't get along with other people in the business. Stubborn in his ways and arrogant about his knowledge, he lost his temper frequently and Jane had to cover for him again and again. Although he still got shows on the air, and they were good, he was out of work more and more, and then problems at home would resume. Whenever they began to go broke, Jane had to go back to work.

Desperate to make their partnership and marriage work, Jane drew Don into her career as her manager. For a while, it worked. He poured into Jane's work what he could not do for himself. He directed her career and was good at it, up to a point. Many times, to please him, she followed his advice even when she felt it was wrong or outmoded, yet she was unable to completely compromise her ideas. On tour, away from Don, she did things her own way, and she noted that the results were obviously good.

As Don got further away from his own career, he drank more and more, making him even more difficult as a partner in every sense. His was the final word on everything concerning Jane's career. He did not want anyone else to advise her and was resentful when they tried. It was a stifling existence for Jane. She channeled her energies into her only refuge, work, but again she slowed down so Don could spend more time on his career. She threw elegant parties, but even the gaiety of the parties could not mask the fact that she was unhappy. They needed money again, and Jane resumed her career.

Fan magazines noted Jane's withdrawal from show business at these times. Articles appeared, with teasing comments about Jane becoming a lady of leisure. Was a blessed event in her future? Fans who still saw Jane and Don as radio's happy young couple persisted; marital trouble was the furthest thing from their minds.

For a while, the relationship between Jane and Don improved. They moved to New York, into a penthouse apartment. Jane continued her numerous radio broadcasts, with her career hot and getting hotter.

Almost exactly a year after George Gershwin's death, on July 10, 1938, Nathaniel Shilkret, an American composer and conductor, assembled the finest interpreters of Gershwin's music to create a recording worthy of Gershwin's genius. Former music director at both RKO Pictures and MGM Pictures and one of the most popular bandleaders of the era, Shilkret rivaled even the great Paul Whiteman and had worked with Gershwin's music on records and radio. He hired Jane to be the lead female voice, supported by Sunny Skylar and Felix Knight. *Gems from Gershwin* still holds up as a remarkable representation of how Gershwin's music sounded as sung and played by his contemporaries. The album was later reissued at the peak of Jane's television career, in 1954, and again as a CD some years later.

Jane is in fine voice on the album, showing her amazing versatility, capturing the ebullience of "I Got Rhythm" and the youthful bounce of "Do, Do, Do," as well as her heartrending version of "The Man I Love," possibly never done better. Two of the songs that were to become her signature pieces, "Summertime" and "It Ain't Necessarily So," are also on this album, the latter song personally requested again and again in command performances by President Franklin Delano Roosevelt.

To be America's darling, dominating the radio waves one year after another, yet to be unable to make her marriage work, tore at Jane as she managed the difficult business of upholding her public image. Audiences who tuned in to her programs or came to see her in person at the picture houses deserved her best, and she, by nature, could give them no less.

In 1939, Jane did shows for Pontiac, Coca-Cola and Texaco. She starred on the weekly *Gulf Musical Playhouse,* Sundays on ABC, with Erno Rapee and his Orchestra and singer Jan Peerce. Jane was once again voted one of the nation's top female singers in the polls. She certainly was the busiest.

When the World's Fair opened in New York, history seemed to repeat itself as Jane was invited to sing at the Missouri Day program in a coast-to-coast hookup with a relay broadcast at San Francisco. Thirty-five years before, Jane's mother, then Anna Froman, had sung on the Missouri Day Program at the 1904 World's Fair in St. Louis. Of course, there had been no radio facilities then. Anna and William Hetzler were guests at the program, and once again Jane's picture was on the cover of *Radio Guide.*

Don, meanwhile, got a job as emcee of CBS's *Alibi Club,* on Sunday evenings, opposite Jane. As usual, he was in her shadow.

7

WAR CLOUDS
1940 — 1942

EXCEPT FOR OCCASIONAL rumblings in the press or on the air about a maniacal leader in Germany named Adolph Hitler, who had marched his armies into Poland as part of a master plan to take over all of Europe, the U. S. seemed to be at rest following a string of bad times. The country had endured the Great War of 1918, the stock market crash and the Depression that followed it, and then Prohibition. Europe could take care of its own affairs—Americans had enough to work on right here in this country. People wanted—needed—to believe there were good times ahead. They needed a break and, maybe, to have a little fun.

At a White House Correspondents' Association annual dinner on April 1, 1940, Jane sang a parody of the song "Careless" to urge President Roosevelt to serve for a third term. A mild fracas developed when a camera was thrust out from the opening in a stage curtain, aimed directly at President Roosevelt. Secret Service men rushed to the source to find Don Ross taking candid pictures of the President. Colonel Ed Starling, head of the White House detail, chewed him out for violating the rules about taking pictures but, fortunately for Don, Jane intervened and the flurry died down. With all their success, Don's arrogance continued to mar relationships.

Roosevelt won the reelection and became the first president in history to have a third successive term in office. He did his best to keep the economy going and to put people back to work again. He started his "fireside chats" on the radio to let the public know that things were being done and that their patience would pay off.

Inexpensive entertainment was an art every family learned. Bathing at public beaches was a popular pastime. Hot dogs were a dime. The country played Monopoly, went to the movies, and listened to the radio. Ventriloquist Edgar Bergen, with his wooden dummy, Charlie McCarthy, had the biggest show on the air. A hit song of 1940 was "The Woodpecker Song," with the rat-a-tat-tat hammering of the bird in the lyrics. Walt Disney's Pinocchio was stealing the hearts of children, while little Shirley Temple still captured those of the grownups.

On Broadway, a new Rodgers and Hart musical, *Pal Joey*, played to record crowds at the Ethel Barrymore Theater, while over at the Broadhurst Theater, Jane appeared in the musical comedy *Keep Off the Grass*, starring Jimmy Durante, Ray Bolger, and an eager young newcomer named Jackie Gleason. Music was by Jimmy McHugh, including "Clear Out of This World" and "Look Out for My Heart," lyrics by Al Dubin, and choreography by George Balanchine.

McHugh had persuaded Jane to join the cast, writing several romantic numbers with her in mind. She could hardly resist being the first to sings his songs, varying in mood and spanning a range from high soprano to low contralto.

Once again, she skirted the stuttering issue by landing a choice role in which she had few speaking lines. Excited by the theater world, and its "intriguing, fascinating sparkle,"

Jane was happy to be a part of it. Even a streptococcus infection during the first few days of *Keep Off the Grass* could not keep her from the theater. She sang with a temperature of 102 degrees, losing 16 pounds in the first three weeks of the run.

The show closed on June 29, 1940, after only 44 performances. The play itself was not memorable, but one person never forgot the experience.

Jackie Gleason had been struggling for a foothold in show business and when he was offered a part in *Keep Off the Grass,* he brought his usual rough ad lib style to the part. The rest of the cast was friendly to the newcomer, but Jane was especially kind to him, spending time with him, sitting and talking show business, sharing some of the knowledge and insights she had learned from Don and Fanny that had taught her how to take wide or crude gestures and turn them into style and grace. Gleason, more familiar with a barroom crowd than a Broadway audience, never forgot her kindness.

Years later, when Gleason had become one of the biggest stars in television, Jane was a guest on his show. One night while Jane was rehearsing, a messenger came around with a large box of flowers. She opened it, and there were her initials in white orchids. She was stunned. The messenger stood there grinning. "Don't stop now," he said.

"What do you mean?" she asked.

"There's a tray. Lift it out."

She lifted the tray out of the box and underneath was a silver mink stole. The card read: "Because you were so nice to me—*Keep Off the Grass*—Jackie."

Offers came in from small clubs. Fascinated, Jane considered them. This was an aspect of entertaining that she had not yet explored, one that could suit her style of intimate singing. The money was good, too. Once again, she and Don were broke.

With the repeal of prohibition, night life had once again become respectable. Bootleg liquor and smoke-filled dens inhabited and abetted by underworld thugs were a thing of the past. New clubs emerged, brightly lit and lavishly decorated. A few were flashy, like the Latin Quarter with its chorus girls and tropical decor, and others were more tastefully executed, but they all brought in headliners like Sophie Tucker and Joe E. Lewis. By the early 1940s, the clubs were an elegant date, or an excellent place for a rendezvous. As Jane recalled, "The food was good, the drinks always had been good, the entertainment was great, the take was high. The patrons were the most sophisticated in town."

Don did the scouting and negotiating, and Jane did her first tour of the clubs, taking on only the most lucrative and elegant of them. At the money game, Don excelled. He took a salary from Jane's earnings.

The first club Jane played, in August of 1940, was the Bon Air Country Club in Evanston, Illinois, run by Abe Lyman. Reviews were good. The *Chicago Tribune* had this to say:

> [Jane Froman] is the only performer in the Bon Air history . . . ever able to still the big room's dinner clatter. She does it with that rich, deeply colored voice that sells "Louisiana Purchase" with as much éclat as "Summertime." Torch songs, swing songs, Gershwin art—the fluid voice transfigures 'em all. And the lady knows what the music means.

The Bon Air led to many other clubs: the Versailles in New York, the Riverside in Milwaukee, and the Royal Palm in Miami. The Chez Paree in Chicago kept her on for two months, where she shared the bill with Joe E. Lewis. She was a great success.

Jane's charm was not only in her voice. She had a look that was different from other night club performers, a combination of sophistication and the American ideal of youth and beauty. The Froman image, from the head held high and the streamlined shape to the long gowns and evening gloves, presented a picture of uncommon good looks and fine taste.

Jane's gowns were becoming a part of her image. Always canny about her appearance on stage, she had replaced the sequined numbers of the past with classically flowing gowns, especially designed for her. She had four particularly dramatic jersey creations by Valentina—two in white and two in red. She wore each with fresh carnations, delivered nightly to her dressing room—red for the white gowns and white for the red ones.

Another gown had a white crepe veil that floated from the back of her head around to the front of her dress, where it was fastened in place with red gardenias.

For broadcasts, she had Sophie of Saks Fifth Avenue design her clothes. Of them all, Jane was particularly fond of a royal blue velvet princess gown trailing to the floor, topped by a tiny velvet hat of the same material, no bigger than a saucer, and a veil which fluttered to her waist. Creating an image was all part of the game.

"Dressing for singing has its tricks," Jane said. "For night clubs or small houses, a gown can be slinky, svelte, subtle. In the huge picture houses, however, fluffy, picturesque gowns are best." She dressed for the last row of the gallery.

Jane and Don had moved to a beautiful house on a remote, eighty-acre estate just outside of Nyack in Rockland County,

New York. Neighbors were actress Helen Hayes, actor Burgess Meredith, and Maxwell Anderson, the playwright.

Jane settled into country life, gardening in old work clothes, planting beans and corn, chatting with the neighbors, and cooking. She hoped that they would have their next Thanksgiving there. Jane thought the cozy house and countryside surroundings were a good place to be snowbound, and talked gaily of "retirement," although she was at the peak of her career. More likely, it was yet another attempt to rationalize staying out of the spotlight while Don attempted to catch up on his career.

In 1941 wartime fears and anxieties had taken over the country. Although the United States was not yet in the fray, news of the devastation in Europe arrived over the air waves. France fell to the Nazis in June, casting a pall on America. People mobilized to do their part. Wherever a crowd could be gathered, stars of stage, screen and radio appeared to ask for household pots and pans, fats, blood, or whatever would help in the war effort. Gas rationing went into effect, and radio programs reflected the patriotic fervor of the day.

Jane joined the Civil Air Patrol service, made up of civilian volunteers whose task it was to patrol the coastal areas and watch for enemy craft. They worked under army regulations just as though they were part of the armed forces. She began flying lessons in preparation for her duties, which might be as navigator, pilot, spotter or ground crew, but before she could accomplish this, events led her in another direction.

The wheels of war were turning. Young men were drafted and gathered in army camps far from home to be trained for overseas duty should our country enter the war.

People still remembered stage star Elsie Janis, who during

World War I sponsored a club for servicemen in a New York brownstone, and later dedicated herself to providing entertainment for boys in the service at home or overseas. The first camp show was produced at that time, and the morale of the troops was notably lifted. Now President Roosevelt called on the show business community again to provide live entertainment for the GIs sitting in camps around the country, facing another big war.

Jane, one of FDR's favorite performers, was among the first to be asked, and accepted without hesitation. In May, 1941, she performed in the first camp show of World War II at Fort Dix, New Jersey, produced and promoted by the great entrepreneur, Billy Rose. When asked to name the ten best female singers, Rose had once remarked, "Jane Froman . . . and nine others." The camp show also starred Betty Bruce, Bill Robinson, Fifi D'Orsay, Ginger Harman, and Jane's old pal from the movies, Milton Berle.

Berle was to reappear in Jane's life many times during their long careers, not only sharing a spotlight or a stage, but his friendship as well. When his broad humor might put others off, Jane was there howling with laughter, slapping her knee in delight. She loved to laugh, her voice as resonant in laughter as in singing. Over the years many comedians found in Jane an appreciative and responsive audience— Berle, Jimmy Durante, Danny Thomas, Joe E. Lewis, Jackie Gleason—and, of course, her beloved Fanny Brice.

Other shows were held in camps at Fort Belvoir in Virginia, where Jane sang for 7,000 soldiers, and at Fort Meade, Maryland, with Ed Wynn. A veteran camp show performer, Wynn had been an entertainer in the first camp show of World War I, two decades earlier.

The truck shows, as they were called, were a big hit, playing to the scattered GIs in military camps around the country, from upper New York State to Florida and from Arkansas to Wyoming. The big red and chromium trucks made it to camps that were far from bright city lights, carrying troupes of professional entertainers and their costumes and props. When they pulled into place, they opened into mobile stages. Jane, with top billing in some of these shows, did many a show from a truck stage.

Entertaining for the draftees filled Jane with pride and affection. "Those boys are so fine," she said. "They're starved for music. It's a thrill to sing for them."

Canada, close neighbor of the United States and part of the British empire, was already deeply involved. Celebrities pitched in to help in various causes for the war effort. Just three weeks prior to the attack on Pearl Harbor, in November of

Camp shows, some on the backs of trucks, were a big hit

1941, Jane accompanied composer Richard Rodgers, his wife Dorothy, lyricist Lorenz Hart, and orchestra leader André Kostelanetz to a Canadian War Savings Drive in Toronto. They were shocked to cross the border and see a country in the throes of a war that had not yet touched the United States directly. The group visited army camps from seven o'clock in the morning to late at night. Around midnight, as they walked through the station to catch their train back to New York, they were exhausted. Jane, so tired that she leaned on Rodgers for support, suddenly burst out laughing. "You know, Dick," she said, "if we were getting paid to do this, we'd all raise hell!"

On Sunday morning, December 7, Jane was alone in the upstate New York house. Gas rationing had forced Don to move to an apartment in the city to avoid long commutes. It was the maid's day off. The temperature had dropped to ten degrees below zero and the furnace was acting up. Jane made a fire in the fireplace, but the fireplace smoked. It disturbed her, like a bad omen. She turned on the radio for a weather report and heard the news: Japan had bombed the United States military base at Pearl Harbor. President Roosevelt had declared that America was at war.

Hundreds of thousands of young men from every city, town, and village in America signed up or were inducted for service. Women took their jobs in factories and defense plants. Troops were sent to several areas in Europe and to North Africa.

Americans drew together in a fever of patriotic activity. Although most of the attention was focused on the European theater, a growing number of people were agitating to open a second front in Russia. The Allies were alone to fight a strong Nazi deployment around Moscow.

Celebrities were called on to help. Performers were wanted to entertain troops overseas, much as they did in the camp shows at Fort Dix and elsewhere around the country. Those GIs were lonely, scared, and very far from home. General John Pershing had declared in World War I that he preferred a thousand soldiers who were occasionally entertained to ten thousand who never were. President Roosevelt agreed that it was a good idea. The United Service Organization, or USO (a conglomeration of social, recreational, and spiritual service organizations such as the Y.M.C.A., the Y.W.C.A., the National Jewish Welfare Board, the Salvation Army, the Knights of Columbus and the Travelers' Aid Association of America) was incorporated in 1941. Its purpose was to provide live entertainment at the various camps around the world wherever American servicemen and women were stationed. The President called on the most logical person in the entertainment world to run it—Abe Lastfogel, chairman of the board of the William Morris Agency.

Lastfogel was the brilliant successor to William Morris, founder of the powerful agency that represented the major talent in show business. More than just a talent agent for many of the stars of that day, he was also a fine human being. Although barely five feet tall, Lastfogel was a giant among his clients, who loved him dearly and treated him with the utmost respect and intense loyalty. It was a standing joke among show folk that when Abe had an audience with the pope, people asked, "Who's that guy with Abe Lastfogel?"

Stories about Lastfogel's integrity and devotion to his clients at the William Morris Agency are legendary. Danny Thomas, a struggling night club comic in the early days of World War II, could not afford to make the

**Singing over the Armed
Forces Network**

USO tours without pay. Lastfogel promised him that if he took minimum scale—what the USO paid to performers who couldn't afford to go for free—he would get him only well-paying engagements after the tour. Abe kept his word, and Thomas went on to become one of show business's most successful comedians.

Lastfogel could not ignore the request to head a unit to entertain the troops, although he received no salary and paid his own expenses. He would be responsible for hiring professional entertainers, briefing and dispatching them in troupes to wherever servicemen needed them. It was to be a strictly private enterprise, with no government or military funding. When he saw how big the job was—it was called the most gigantic and far-flung enterprise in the history of the entertainment world—he left his position at William Morris, and was not to return for several years, then to serve as the agency's president.

The USO got off to a good start with the help of private contributions equaling $33 million. A generous portion of that was made by Prescott Bush, the USO chairman, who later became a United States Senator and the forebear of two United States presidents.

Jane continued her club dates and radio work, but also appeared at war bond drives, whistle stop tours, and in other activities to aid in the war effort. Recalling it later, she wrote:

> I remember doing a broadcast in Times Square to help the aluminum drive. I sang beneath an enormous sign which read, "Give Your Aluminum." Pots and pans—stew pots, coffee pots, frying pans, roasting pans—all were piled in one vast heap in the middle of Times 135
>
> Square, with me on top waving enthusiastic congratulations to the housewives for ransacking their kitchens.

Between engagements, Jane gave concerts in her home town to boost the sales of war bonds, or to sing for the servicemen—whatever she could to boost morale. She gladly did a series of "Victory concerts" at three Columbia campuses—the University of Missouri, Christian College and Stephens College—in the spring of 1942. She became acutely aware that she had not seen a single black face in any of the audiences at these concerts, and looked into it. She learned that blacks were not permitted in the auditoriums, and that was that. Columbia was as segregated as any place in the south in 1942, but Jane insisted it was simply unacceptable that these young men, ready to go off and fight for their country, should be deprived of a concert because of their skin color. What were they fighting for, anyway?

At her own expense, she gave a fourth concert for black servicemen, hiring a band and the Frederick Douglass High School auditorium, and printing up flyers and programs on her own. Management was furious, but she didn't care. Only a woman of Jane's stature, respectability, and grace could get away with it. The town swallowed its pride. Years later, when

**Special concert in
segregated Columbia**

Jane retired to Columbia, several black people came up to her and thanked her for the concert they remembered so well, at a time when it was socially anathema to mix races.

Jane was as busy as a young performer could be that summer of 1942. On Sundays she starred in the CBS *Texaco Star Theater,* subbing for Fred Allen, who was on vacation. She dropped in twice a week at the Stage Door Canteen in New York, where lonely GIs on leave came for refreshments and conversation. She appeared at drives to sell war bonds and stamps, and still maintained a home for herself and Don. Then she took on another Broadway musical. The busier she was, the less time she would have to spend thinking about her marriage. Unable to give up on it, frustrated, she found relief only in work.

Laugh, Town, Laugh was written and produced by comedian Ed Wynn, with whom Jane had performed in the camp shows and who would star with Jane in the production. The show opened at the Alvin Theater on June 22, 1942.

Performances were seven nights a week, with matinees Wednesdays through Sundays. A third show was sandwiched in on Sundays. The show was good, according to the critics, but its lighthearted theme came at a poor time. The public was preoccupied with war.

Jane was booked into the Paramount for the ninth time in seven years. It softened the blow when *Laugh, Town, Laugh* closed on July 25.

In Rockland County, Jane worked along with her neighbors for the war effort. Helen Hayes was among those who helped mount a benefit for Russian War Relief, staged in South Nyack at the Yorktown Country Club. Kurt Weill, Lotte Lenya, Will Geer and Ed Wynn appeared in the show. Years later, when the physical war was over and the cold war with Russia began, aspersions were cast on anything vaguely Russian, and Jane's work for Russian Relief would come back to haunt her, as the FBI looked into her activities for some sign of subversion. They soon gave up, but it gave Jane a certain wicked pleasure afterward to talk about the time when she was investigated by the FBI—even more thrilling than being watched by the mob during her days with the Chesterfield program.

Meanwhile, Don spent little of his time at the Nyack house. He had started a new venture with a cosmetics company, which kept him busy, leaving Jane alone.

Abe Lastfogel was priming his new organization for action. A telegram arrived from USO headquarters. Jane was one of a hundred entertainers asked by Lastfogel to go overseas. She adored Abe and wired him back within the hour to accept the job, making her the first USO volunteer. She was placed on a list of available entertainers and asked to stand by. Given no other information about the tour, including her destination, she had to keep up a normal existence while waiting for the call.

Jane was still drawing crowds at the Roxy and she sang as well on the popular radio show, *Stage Door Canteen*. The rest of her time was spent entertaining in hospitals and appearing in Washington at the request of President Roosevelt for the induction of all reserve officers. Here she met General Marshall and all the big brass, many of whom gave her their stars, which she added to her growing collection of Army rank insignia, begun at the training camps. She committed to co-star with Milton Berle in the new Ziegfeld Follies and signed for her own radio show.

At the top of her profession, a star of radio, night clubs, and Broadway, Jane was in constant demand, having to turn down offers that didn't fit into her schedule, but the war was going badly. Soon boys would be sent overseas; those already there were sitting on a powder keg as the war escalated. Singing for them might help lift some of the stress of being away from home and facing combat. She had to give what she could to help, and her talent was the best she had to offer.

Lastfogel had Jane briefed for her tour by Kay Francis, Martha Raye, Carol Landis, and Mitzi Mayfair, who had done a preliminary tour to better understand what lay ahead for the entertainers. The experiences of the four actresses were later written into a screenplay for the movie *Four Jills in a Jeep*.

The Army alerted Jane to await her call for embarkation. She journeyed to Brooklyn for shots, packed a duffle bag—which could not exceed 55 pounds—with song arrangements, personal belongings, and two evening dresses that were practical but feminine. Her bag stood ready at the door of her apartment.

She had just opened at the brand new Riobamba* night club on East 57th Street in New York, taking a large cut in pay to open the small but very smart club. She was a smash hit, and people lined up for blocks trying to get in. Old pal Milton Berle wisecracked, "I leaned down to tie my shoe and a waiter threw a tablecloth over me."

To keep herself available for the USO tour, the call for which might come at any time, Jane refused many new stage and club dates. Single appearances were safer, so she happily guested on Berle's radio show, or sang at various benefits and lunches.

The offers kept coming, even from the movies. She could not explain her refusal, because her mission was top secret, but her career was hot. She was held over and over at Riobomba, all the time knowing that each show might be her last. To keep her mind off that phone call that could come at any time, she played golf. At a New Jersey golf course she managed to get her score down to an 88, her best score ever.

Finally, in February, 1943, the call came. She was to leave at once, destination unknown.

---

* During her Riobamba engagement, a young composer wrote a specialty song for Jane, "Riobamba," for which she paid him $50. The song was forgotten, but its musical theme was worked into a ballet by its young composer as he collaborated with a dancer from the American Ballet, who choreographed it. The ballet *Fancy Free* premiered on April 18, 1942, bringing the composer, Leonard Bernstein, and the choreographer, Jerome Robbins, to the attention of the musical world. Bernstein further developed "Fancy Free" into the hit musical, *On the Town*.

8

THE CRASH
1943

J ANE ARRIVED EARLY on the morning of February 21, 1943, at the Marine Terminal of New York's La Guardia Airport, where she joined the troupe of entertainers assigned to her tour—Grace Drysdale, a puppeteer; Gypsy Markoff, an accordionist; dancers and comedians Lorraine and Roy Rognan; singer Yvette Silver; and actress Tamara. Looking glamorous and carefree, they posed for publicity photos.

Saul Abraham, their USO Camp Show coordinator, was also there. No one but Abraham knew just where they were going. Wartime travel was cloaked in secrecy. The Army's Special Services Division in Washington had called Abraham, who booked the talent for the tours and took care of travel arrangements. They asked him for a unit of seven performers to go overseas to entertain the troops, and this was the group he called. For security, he was to keep their destination a secret until they were ready to board the plane. All he could tell them was to prepare for a three-month trip, and where and when to meet.

Abraham was pleased with the group of seven entertainers. All of them were eager to make the journey, had proven to be popular in local camp shows, and all used music in their acts. Music was the easiest entertainment to provide at military bases. Enlisted men and women overseas liked hearing the popular songs being sung and played in the States—it brought them closer to home.

Tamara Drasin, star of stage and film, who used only her first name professionally, was known for her role in Jerome Kern's *Roberta* as a refugee Russian princess working as the manager of a Parisian couturier business. It was she who had brought the beautiful ballad "Smoke Gets In Your Eyes" to the public for the first time when the show opened on Broadway in November of 1933.

Accordionist Gypsy Markoff was a close friend of Tamara's. The two entertainers shared a Russian heritage, although Markoff's background was also part Egyptian. She had appeared before heads of state and performed regularly at the Waldorf-Astoria Hotel in New York and at Shepheard's Hotel in Cairo, as well as in vaudeville theaters and night clubs.

Lorraine and Roy Rognan, a dance team known professionally as Lorraine and Rognan, had been together since shortly after they met in 1936. Roy had been a vaudevillian—a former circus clown and acrobat—and Lorraine was a comedienne and dancer. They had performed in vaudeville, nightclubs and films, and managed to remain happy as a couple throughout the stresses of performing together.

Grace Drysdale, considered one of the best puppeteers in the business, had appeared at theaters and sophisticated night clubs in the New York area from the Roxy to the Waldorf-Astoria.

Yvette Silver was a nineteen-year-old singer who performed in nightclubs and radio, singing in French and English. She, too, used only her first name professionally.

Saul Abraham held the tickets for the seven performers, still not revealing their destination. He had picked them up

The full USO tour group at the airport: (clockwise from front left) Jane, Tamara Drasin, Yvette Silver, Roy and Lorraine Rognan, Grace Drysdale, and Gypsy Markoff

from Pan American's ticket office on February 19. He lined up the entertainers at the processing desks, and placed the appropriate passport and ticket in front of each one. Clerks checked them through and passed the tickets and passports down the line to the customs inspectors. At the end of the processing, all the tickets and passports were handed back to Abraham. He handed out passports and boarding passes to each member of the troupe, but only at the last minute, when the plane was ready for boarding, did he hand all seven tickets—showing their destination—to Roy Rognan. They were on their way to Foynes, Ireland, by way of Bermuda, the Azores and Lisbon, Portugal. From there they would change flights for their journey to England and, eventually, to North Africa, to complete their tour.

At nearly 9 A.M. the group boarded the *Yankee Clipper,* a Boeing 314, one of Pan American's remarkable "flying boats." The plane had been developed especially for transatlantic flight, with the capability to land in water. Constructed of aluminum alloy on a central frame of steel, it had a walkway inside each wing that enabled flight engineers to reach all four engines in case in-flight repairs were needed. Its predecessor, the *China Clipper,* a Sikorsky-42, had made its first flight over the Pacific in 1935, beginning an era of transoceanic flight. By 1939, the bigger and more powerful Boeing 314, the largest plane of its day, was developed for transatlantic flight. The *Yankee Clipper* had been christened by First Lady Eleanor Roosevelt in Washington on March 3, 1939, using a bottle of water gathered from the seven seas. The plane had made 240 flights without an accident.

Twelve crew members were on the flight—Captain R. O. D. Sullivan of Sanford, North Carolina, a former Navy flier in World War I who had recently completed his one hundredth crossing as a Master Ocean Pilot; First Officer Stanton Rush, the copilot; two backup pilots; two navigators; two engineering officers; two radio officers; and two stewards. The double crew enabled them to work in shifts on the long flight. Although government regulations required that pilots undergo a physical examination twice a year, Pan Am's own stringent rules required that pilots have a physical examination before every flight. Captain Sullivan and the rest of the crew passed their physicals with no problems.

Besides the USO troupe there were twenty other people on board—including military officers, State Department officials, war correspondents for newspapers and radio networks, diplomatic couriers, and businessmen on wartime missions.

The accommodations on the *Yankee Clipper* were equal to those on luxury ocean liners, and as impeccable as Pan American's safety record. There were soundproof compartments that held ten passengers each in the lower level of the 109-foot fuselage, as well as sleeping berths and separate dressing rooms for men and women, a spacious lounge that doubled as a dining room, and a well-stocked bar. A deluxe cabin in the tail section could even serve as a bridal suite. Connecting the passengers' level to the crew's quarters and cargo space above was a spiral staircase. The cockpit and cabin were enormous—larger than in any airplanes before. A large conference table sat at the rear of the cabin.

Fourth Officer John Curtis Burn, blond and quiet in his

The Yankee Clipper

manner, was making his first Atlantic crossing since joining Pan Am a few months earlier. It was his job to move among the passengers, explaining procedures and safety measures and informing them from time to time of the plane's altitude, speed, and estimated time of arrival at the next stop. He recognized Jane among the passengers, having recently seen her at the Roxy, but did not speak to her directly, although he did explain their need to fill out a document required for landing in Bermuda. Jane remembered being amused at Burn's shy manner and how his cheeks flushed pink as he spoke.

They landed at Bermuda at 2:10 P.M., refueled and processed mail, and took off again at 4:10 P.M. The *Yankee Clipper* flew through the night, as the passengers slept soundly in their comfortable berths. They arrived at the beautiful harbor of Horta, in the Azores, at 10:14 A.M. the next day—Monday, February 22, Washington's Birthday. They were there for about an hour and a half, just time enough to stretch their legs in a stroll around the famous harbor, and then took off for the next portion of the flight, to Lisbon.

The passengers amused themselves in conversation and song during the seven-hour flight. At 4 P.M. Lisbon time, the plane's radio officer sent a coded message to Lisbon that they were expecting to land in approximately three hours. Pan Am's ground crew sent out its launch to lay out the string of lighted buoys that served as a runway for flying boat landings in the Tagus River.

At around 6:15 P.M., passengers were asked to take their seats for the landing. Jane and Tamara, seated in a rear compartment, did as they were asked, but Tamara inadvertently took Jane's seat, facing forward, instead of the one she had been occupying, facing the rear of the plane. It didn't seem to make any difference. Jane took Tamara's seat.

Fourth Officer Burn was in the roomy cockpit, watching Captain Sullivan make the landing. It was twilight. They were making a descent from 7,000 feet to 600 feet to meet wartime regulations. Planes had to fly low to be clearly identified as they approached. First Officer Rush spoke to the launch crew by radio phone and was given instructions on the landing. Nothing was out of the ordinary; no one sensed any danger.

The plane headed up the Tagus River, passing the monastery that had been built by King Manuel I to commemorate the opening of the passage to India by Portugal's great seaman, Vasco da Gama. Jane saw the lights of the city of Lisbon going on, and noticed flashes of lightning in the distance. The plane banked to the left. She wondered whether it was more dangerous to take off or to land. Sharply, the plane banked again. A wracking jolt tore the plane apart as its left wing hit the water, flipping it over on its back. Those who were thrown clear of the plane grabbed on to anything they could to stay afloat. Gypsy Markoff was injured but alive, terrified because she couldn't swim. Yvette, a good swimmer and unhurt herself, found a pillow for Markoff to cling to until she was rescued, saw to it that a few other survivors had some part of the wreckage to hang onto to stay afloat, then swam the two miles to shore.

Jane came to in the icy water. A skilled swimmer, she attempted to swim to the surface, but her legs wouldn't kick. Her right arm hung helplessly. She pushed herself to the top with her one good arm and flapped with her left hand to keep her body on the surface.

Nearby, in the dark, someone was cursing angrily. She called to him for help.

"Fourth Officer Burn at your service, Ma'am," came the reply out of the darkness. "May I be of assistance?"

Burn swam over and tried to swim with Jane, but that didn't work as she had only one good arm. As debris from the wrecked plane drifted by, he grabbed some of it and they clung to it. When Jane wanted to examine her leg to estimate the extent of her injuries, Burn tried to stop her, expecting her to become hysterical, but she insisted and he let her. She took in the fact that bones were sticking out of her leg matter-of-factly.

Around them, others were hanging on to seat cushions, pieces of wood—anything they could to keep themselves from drowning. Some, in their desperation to save themselves, pushed away others who were seeking their help.

Burn knew they were far from the main wreckage where the rescue boats were searching and hoped to keep their minds off their predicament by starting a conversation. Jane caught on and joined in, making small talk as they hung on for dear life to pieces of the wrecked Clipper.

"I saw you at the Roxy," John told Jane. "I never thought I'd meet you swimming in the Tagus River."

"You've got blood all over your face!" Jane said and splashed at it with her good hand.

"Cut it out!" he cried, shocked by the cold water.

They laughed, and continued to talk about their backgrounds, their childhoods. She asked him about flying. He had only recently started training with Pan Am. Before that, he had been a ferry pilot, delivering military aircraft from factories to war zones. He asked her about music. She had been singing since she was a small child, singing arias at bedtime with her mother. She was thirty-five; he was twenty-four.

For forty-five minutes they talked like old chums, hanging on to each other amid the wreckage of the plane.

At last, a motor launch arrived, beaming its searchlight on them. Two Portuguese boatmen attempted to grab Jane. One of them leaned over too far and fell into the water. The second one lunged for the first and fell in too. The helmsman yelled at the clumsy boatmen and in his excitement, stalled the boat's engine. The launch floated away. Jane and John laughed hysterically. They continued their conversation.

It was another twenty minutes before a small motorboat came along. Jane knew her left leg was in such bad shape that it could be torn off in the rescue as they hauled her up into the boat. She reached down with her good left hand and held onto it until she was safely in the boat.

On the dock, the remains of Jane's clothes were cut off. Her coat, blouse, shoes and stockings had been torn off in the impact of the crash. They wrapped her in a blanket. She and other survivors were taken to the tiny San Jose Hospital, a small emergency facility in Lisbon.

At the hospital, she was placed in a bed in a crowded room with the other injured and given sedatives to ease her pain. She could not move. The doctors around her talked mostly in Portuguese with a little smattering of English now and then. She knew they were discussing what to do about her. Their tone was heavy as they discussed and pointed to her right leg.

John Burn, the young Fourth Officer who saved her life, was in the next bed. As the doctors moved on to him, examining his x-rays, Jane sensed their dire prediction. "He probably won't live through the night, so there's no point in operating on him." They moved on to the next bed, leaving Burn to sweat it out.

Where was Tamara? And the rest of the troupe? How badly were they injured? For hours, Jane could find out no more, and lay in a state of dark fear, waiting, wondering.

In the grim hours as she lay there, she was paralyzed. Not even her eyelids worked. A heavyset woman came by—a nurse? an aide?—it wasn't clear. She was large and smelled of garlic. She held Jane's hand and talked to her in words that were incomprehensible, but Jane had never felt more grateful for human contact than she did with this simple act of kindness from a stranger.

Hours dragged on. Utterly alone and stripped of everything she possessed, even her identification, it seemed to Jane that she was being born again, helpless, into a strange and frightening world. All that was left was that which she carried inside herself.

Her thoughts drifted to Mama, the center of her life, who had struggled without complaint to make a decent life for them when *her* world had collapsed; Grandma Barcafer, who traveled west in a covered wagon, raised thirteen children, yet still managed to be a successful artist; Aunt Pearl, who, with mulelike determination, always managed to find time in her busy life to teach knitting or crocheting to a lonely little girl. The legacy of those dauntless Barcafer women, who with their immeasurable determination and pride had built their lives on pure grit, would help her through this.

At last, around midnight, doctors surrounded her bed. She could tell by their faces and their hushed tones that they were concerned about that smashed right leg. To her relief, one of the doctors, who could have been an East Indian, spoke English—with an Oxford accent. Jane overheard him asking whether they were going to amputate her leg. Calmly, she said, "Don't cut my leg off—but if you have to, please tell me first." She did not want to come out of the anesthetic to find it gone. He said they would.

A young man came up to her cot as she lay there. He spoke English, introducing himself as Glen M. Stadler, State Senator from Oregon. He had just arrived in Lisbon when he had heard about the Clipper crash and ran right over to the hospital to see what he could do. Glad to have someone to speak to and for her, Jane asked him to talk the doctors out of cutting off her leg. He spoke to a young Portuguese doctor in French, asking him if they planned to amputate. The doctor shook his head and said, "no." The intervention calmed her. When it was finally her turn for the operating room, the young senator helped wheel in her cot and held on to her hand.

Although Jane was unaware of it, the Senator had asked the doctor to answer "no" no matter what decision they had made.

Jane had no idea how close to death she was, but refused ether, afraid that if she lost consciousness, the Portuguese doctors would take her leg off. She remained on the operating table for three hours. At one point, she nearly died, but was given a blood transfusion, said to have come from a Portuguese sailor. In and out of consciousness, Jane succumbed to the rigors of the surgery, not knowing if she would have a leg when she woke up.

Jane was out of danger, but her injuries were serious: her left leg had been nearly severed below the knee, and the right leg was even worse, with the bones crushed. She also had several broken ribs, a dislocated pelvis, and a right arm fractured in several places. Her body was covered with bruises and cuts where bits of steel and wood from the plane had become embedded in her skin. The Portuguese doctors had saved her right leg, but guessed that it would end up being shorter than her left. Had she not been a professional stage performer, they told her, they surely would have amputated.

John Burn, meanwhile, had survived the night. The doctors had been wrong, and in the morning, when they saw Burn had not died as they had predicted, they performed emergency surgery on him. His back had been broken and he had a fractured skull.

In the United States, news of the Clipper crash appeared in headlines across the country.

CLIPPER CRASHES AT LISBON;
FOUR DEAD, 20 MISSING

JANE FROMAN HURT IN CRASH

LISBON SEARCHERS PROBE FOR
MISSING PERSONS

Nobody knew for sure yet the number of fatalities or whether Jane's condition was good or poor—only that she was alive.

A reporter talked to Jane two days after the crash. She had blacked out, so did not remember the actual crash. She remembered coming to the surface and not being able to swim very well—both legs and her right arm did not work. She remembered the young crew member who had stayed with her, in spite of his own injuries, who kept her talking and afloat until the rescue boat came for them.

Don was notified immediately but, because of the war, travel to Europe was impossible without special permission through either the President or the War Department. He sought President Roosevelt's help. As channels were cleared for him to fly to Lisbon, word reached him that his father, the Reverend F. E. Ross, had died in Columbus, Ohio. Don left for Ohio, instead.

In Columbia, Missouri, Mama also received a wire. It told her simply that Jane was injured but would live. Mama's husband, the mayor, was gravely ill; she had been nursing him when the news came. She sent a cable, signed, as required for security reasons, with the name of the Secretary of State.

> YOU'RE IN MY PRAYERS EVERY NIGHT.
> MAY GOD TAKE CARE OF MY BABY.
>   LOVE, CORDELL HULL

News of the other survivors—only fifteen in all, out of 39 passengers—trickled in. Tamara, who had switched seats with Jane, and Roy Rognan, of the Lorraine & Rognan dance team, were gone. Gypsy Markoff, Lorraine Rognan and Grace Drysdale had been badly injured. Yvette Silver, the young singer who swam to shore, was the only one of the USO troupe who escaped without a scratch. Apart from the USO troupe, courier William Butterworth, first secretary of the American Legation, survived, managing to walk from the rescue launch to a waiting ambulance. Newspaperman Ben Robertson, foreign correspondent for the New York *Herald Tribune*, had been killed. So had athlete Frank Josef Cuhel, who had won the silver medal for the United States in the 1928 Summer Olympics in the 400 metre hurdles.

Jane was sent to a convalescent home, the Casa de Saude de Benefica, a sprawling mansion set on a hill in Lisbon. John Burn, in a cast from his neck to his waist, was also a patient at the home.

Casa de Saúde de Benfica
Lisboa - Portugal

The convalescent home where the long recovery began

Already acquainted through their desperate struggle in the waters of Lisbon harbor, Jane and John Burn met again at the home. They saw each other almost every day. As soon as he was allowed to get out of bed, Burn went down the hall to visit Jane. Getting to know one another—to speak in English—helped as they let their broken bones mend and their spirits recover. Neither of them seemed to hurt as much when they shared stories and laughter, so far from home.

John's background had made him mature and responsible. His father, an ex-naval officer, had died when John was ten, so he had become the man of the family for his sister and mother.

It wasn't long before Jane and John realized that they were strongly attracted to each other. John later said that he fell in love with Jane in the Tagus River. Their mutual respect kept their feelings in check. Jane's loyalty to Don was unyielding. No matter what the circumstances, including her unhappy marriage, she felt obliged to stick with it and try to make it work. John honored her commitment.

Stanton Griffiths, later to become U.S. ambassador to Argentina, was in the area and visited Jane. When he returned to the United States he contacted Don and told him that Jane must be brought back in order to receive proper medical attention. Otherwise, she would not survive.

Don finally flew to Lisbon on another Pan America Clipper. It was just about a month after the crash. He found Jane covered from head to toe in plaster.

Normal crossings had been curtailed by the war, but Don secured passage for them to return home on an 8,000-ton Portuguese freighter, the *Serapa Pinto,* on April 14. It cost an exorbitant amount of money—$2,000—but they had to get home, where Jane could get proper medical attention.

John Burn was not at all happy to see Don, and Don sensed something about the young pilot, but did not pursue it. John left his bed to say goodbye to Jane. They parted, but both he and Jane were aware of a powerful bond between them.

Sailing across the choppy Atlantic was bad enough, with Jane in a body cast, strapped to a board the whole time, and often seasick, but to make it worse, they were torpedoed twice by German submarines, one missile narrowly missing the freighter. The trip took more than two weeks.

When they arrived in Philadelphia, on May 2, 1943, Jane had the stretcher bearers lower her so she could reach out and touch a kiss to the ground. An ambulance met them and drove them straight to Doctors Hospital in New York, where everyone spoke English. She asked for cold white milk and white bread. When they were brought to her, she broke down, crying violently, hysterically. All the anguish of the previous two months came pouring out. It was the first time she had cried since the crash.

Mama arrived in New York to find her daughter just skin and bones, with her right leg in horrible shape. She thanked God for sparing Jane's life.

The endless rounds of operations began immediately. The emergency surgery in Lisbon had saved Jane's right leg, but the damage was so great that doctors concluded that she would probably never walk again. First, the New York doctors corrected what had been done to her in Lisbon, saving both legs and Jane's right arm from certain amputation.

Then she needed an extensive bone graft. Don engaged an orthopedic surgeon with an excellent reputation but old-fashioned techniques. The surgeon's method involved making a splint by taking a large piece of bone from another part of Jane's body and grafting it to her right leg where bone was needed. In operations like this, infection often invaded the site of the union, however, and if that happened, and the bones failed to fuse, the entire procedure would end in failure and have to be done over again. It was a grueling ordeal to endure once; repeating it would be unbearable. Newer techniques were now used, involving more than one grafting site, allowing more chance of success. Jane wanted to try that method, but Don insisted on keeping the traditional surgeon against Jane's better judgment.

In August, she had the operation. It was not successful. When she was strong enough, she would have to have it done over. Mercifully, President Roosevelt intervened again on her behalf to provide her with the new drug, penicillin, which was not yet available to the general public. So far it had only been used for the military. The penicillin probably saved Jane from further spread of the infection that could have cost her the leg.

Recovery from the second bone graft was slow, complicated by error. A three-inch piece of wood embedded in her right arm had been overlooked. The wood was removed this time, but the arm did not heal well. She would be left with an arm that would need serious rehabilitation and, worst of all, with a deadly infection, osteomyelitis, that had invaded her right leg. Osteo, as Jane learned to call it, thrived on injured bones, and she had plenty of those.

Jane wanted another orthopedist's opinion, but Don insisted on managing things, and he stuck with the present doctor with his impressive credentials.

Through every operation, that terrifying fear that they would cut off her leg nagged at Jane. Doctors were gloomy in their predictions. In her unfinished memoir, Jane writes of this grinding fear.

> Twenty top doctors tell me I'll never walk again. I know raw fear, terror and despair.
>
> I'm told I'll have to lose my leg, that right foot that tapped its way so gaily to the rhythm of song. The furies take possession of my soul.
>
> I try desperately to keep my leg and to keep my faith. I lose all my belief, but somehow I manage to hold on to my leg. But I'm crippled in spirit as well as body. The fight goes on—physical, spiritual.
>
> I struggle to find a reason for it all. There must be, there has to be some great purpose behind all this. What is the reason for this gnawing pain and agony of mind?

Why was I alone spared of all the people in that section of the plane? Why did that lovely girl Tamara insist I take her seat just before the crash? Why is she dead and I'm alive?

I've got to know! Why? Why should I suffer like this? Why should this happen to me? I'm bitter, rebellious, resentful. I'm terribly, terribly angry.

I struggle to understand why everything has been taken from me, everything I'd worked for when voluntarily and with no recompense of any kind I had left eagerly a life of excitement, glamour and success to answer a call that I felt I must obey.

Stripped of everything right down to the bone—some of the bone included—gradually, so so gradually I begin to find the reasons.

Invariably, they came to her through music.

PART II

9

RECOVERY
1943—1944

LYING FLAT ON her back in Doctors Hospital in New York, Jane looked squarely at her situation.

She had had it easy until that day, seven months ago, when the plane she was on crashed into the Tagus River. Born with good looks and talent, provided with an education in music as well as in academics and a good upbringing, she found success easily. With vocal coaching from her mother, an excellent musician in her own right, a few important lessons in stagemanship, and regular work in radio and on the stage, she had become a star in great demand. From her first radio job as a conservatory student, she had never lacked for work. Audiences responded to her deep rich voice, her youth, her beauty, her charm. In polls across America, she had been voted among the most popular girl singers several years in a row.

She had known difficult times, too. Her father had left her without a goodbye or an explanation. Being a faculty member's daughter, she had to be a model of deportment at school. A powerful stutter gave her a stultifying shyness that kept her apart from others—and from having a movie career. She was stuck in a loveless, dependent marriage. All this she bore with no complaint; this is what was expected of a member of the Barcafer family. Everyone had their troubles and she had no reason to expect to be spared her share. So why now did fate deal her this terrible blow? She had to find answers.

Stripped of all that she had, all that she knew, where would she go from here? She stubbornly refused to feel sorry for herself. Those tenacious forebears of hers had met their challenges without a whimper: Grandma, giving up the world she knew to ride west in a covered wagon, then raising her own brood while pursuing her art; Mama, left on her own with a small child to raise, giving voice and piano lessons to support the two of them. What did *she* have? What could *she* offer?

The only possession of hers recovered from the crash was a little gold cross. It had been sent to her by a young fan from Syracuse, and Jane, always a bit superstitious, had packed it in her bag for good luck. Was its recovery a sign? What did it mean?

She took stock of what she had left. Her legs were maimed, one nearly useless. One of her arms was pretty far gone, too. For all the physical damage, however, her face had been spared. She had to ask herself why. She dared to wonder, too, about her voice. What if that were gone? Her whole life had been music. All she ever wanted to do was sing a good song. It had been a long time, lying there in the hospital, since she had even tried to sing.

A popular song at the time was "Sleepy Lagoon," with lots of long oo sounds in it. "A sleepy lagoon, a tropical moon. . . ." She opened her mouth and let out a long oo. The voice was still there! What a thrill to hear it, to feel it! Her spirits soared. She kept going: "and two on an island; A sleepy lagoon and two hearts in tune. . . ." The voice box was intact.

What kind of tone could she hope for? She opened up with full voice. Nurses came running. Hospital aides stared at her like she'd gone crazy. Had the pain, finally, driven her mad? She kept singing. The thrill of finding she still had her voice had made her wild—with a desperate need to sing.

Every day, she vocalized. The breath bellows was unimpaired. The timbre, she thought, never sounded better. Her voice became stronger; her incredible three-octave range had not diminished at all. The urge to go back to work was unbearable.

Encased in a hundred pounds of plaster casts and flat on her back, what could she do? How could she begin? Her useless right arm left that hand extremely weak. She asked for needles and wool and began knitting, crudely at first, and slowly, but with a vengeance—socks, mittens, sweaters, ties, scarves—anything to keep her hands moving. She silently thanked Aunt Pearl many times over for teaching her to knit when she was a little girl.

She was used to movement—fairly athletic, she had always hurried everywhere, kept trim. Without exercise, she would get stiff. She did leg lifts from her bed, plaster cast and all. She could work on the rest of herself while her leg healed.

Friends cheered her on, wanting to see her rally and get well. Abe Lastfogel called regularly. Danny Thomas gave his time and talent to make her laugh. Milton Berle, her old buddy from *Radio City Revels*, was now a hot night club performer, and came to the hospital to give bedside performances, going through his whole routine for her. Fans who listened to her on the radio, celebrities who worked with her on stage, screen, and radio, poured out their love and compassion in the letters and flowers she received.

Toots Shor, whose restaurant on West 52nd Street was a favorite watering hole for famous athletes, ambitious politicians, and Broadway stars, sent hampers of beef from his restaurant. Reuben's, famous for its celebrity clientele as well as its cheesecake, sent baskets of delicacies. The devotion of friends only underscored the deep loneliness she felt when Don was off pursuing his own interests. Alone at the hospital on Christmas, Jane shared a Chinese dinner from Lum Chung with songwriter Vincent Youmans, a fellow patient in the hospital, whose songs she had sung many times.

A surprise visit from John Burn lifted her spirits. Burn had been one of the last survivors of the crash to return from Lisbon. He stopped by to see how she was doing. As they had discovered in the waters of the Tagus and in the convalescent home in Lisbon, they could talk easily and even laugh and wisecrack together.

Jane needed to work. Spurred by her enthusiasm, even the doctors approved the idea. Work could be good therapy. Don, smelling a show business venture, talked to Lou Walters, owner of the popular night club, the Latin Quarter, about a show in which Jane would star. Walters, an astute businessman as well as a show business icon, wanted Jane, and in order to get her, he agreed to sign on Don as well. True to his nature, Walters ignored the doomsayers who predicted it would never work and took a chance.

Don Ross and Walters co-produced a musical revue in two acts, starring Jane, with Don writing most of the script and dialogue. The lyrics and music were supplied by Dan Shapiro, Milton Lascal and Phil Charig. Milton Berle, one of Jane's most ardent show business fans, wrote a song for her to sing in the show called "Let's Keep It That Way," but, for reasons that are unknown, it was not used in the final production.

Rehearsals began for *Artists and Models* in Jane's hospital room in Doctors Hospital on September 29, 1943, just seven months after the crash. Jane's right leg and right arm were still in plaster casts.

When word got out and people seemed concerned, Jane put them at ease, as she always did. "My leg will still be in a cast, but don't worry. I'll be camouflaged in ruffles," she told a reporter for the New York *Daily News*. "It's all fixed so I won't have to walk around and you don't need crutches to sing." Crutches backstage, along with a nurse, were replaced on stage by a chariot, a throne and a bed. "I ought to be really good in that bed scene," she said. "I've had a whale of a lot of practice."

The consuming thrill of being able to work again left no room for doubt. Jane gave it everything she had. Don's script

Rehearsing for Artists and Models

had the unmistakable tone of a vaudeville production, from its corny comic touches to the use of dozens of pretty show girls to cover the fact that the show did not have much depth. What it lacked was the crisp, witty dialogue and memorable music that Broadway productions were known for. Jane, in the euphoria of returning to the stage in a big, new production, tried to look past the weaknesses.

Midway through preparations for the show's Boston preview, the wound in Jane's leg opened up. A doctor was called in. They had to fix it immediately. A hundred and eighty people were depending on her, including the young Jackie Gleason. While rehearsals continued, Jane underwent her thirteenth operation to close the wound. She was fitted with a new cast—this one with a walking heel.

Since her accident, Jane's weight had gone from 127 pounds to a fragile 85 pounds. The new cast on her leg weighed 35 pounds. The cast was removed from her right arm before the production, but her arm was still useless and she had to put her makeup on with her left hand. A maid was hired to dress her, and Don lifted her from her bed or couch or into a bath.

Gowns were designed to disguise Jane's scars, casts, and the hardware that would hold her up, yet they were feminine—billowy skirts with low-cut bodices, beads or flowers worked into the fabric, long sleeves. Her brunette hair, pinned back with ribbons or flowers, cascaded to her shoulders. The effect was one of unflawed beauty.

No one saw the stagehands carrying Jane on and off the stage. Nor did they see the slanted board against which Jane leaned in some scenes to appear upright, or the wheelchair hidden under enormous satin pillows when she was seated. Once

***Performing in* Artists and Models**

in a while the curtain was slightly delayed. The stagehands fumbled and she slipped from their grasp. Jane's good nature kept such moments from unnerving the crew. They propped her up, she straightened her dress, and no harm was done.

Interviews with Jane were prized. Her story was remarkable, and the public could not get enough. One reporter asked what made her determined enough to do a show after all she had been through.

First, she replied, there was the spiritual lift it gave her to be working at the job she loved best. And in the second place, there was the physical lift, "of drawing a good breath, giving it a good healthy support, and opening up on good, free tone. The sheer physical rightness of good singing does something to the entire body." The money must have helped, too, as hospital and doctors' bills were adding up.

Artists and Models previewed at the Boston Opera House on October 11, 1943, just eight months after the plane crash. The afternoon of the opening performance, Jane received word that her stepfather had died of a stroke. In keeping with show business tradition, the show went on.

The audience that night was comprised of 3,500 service men and women. When the curtain opened, they all stood and whistled and applauded for a solid twenty minutes while Jane struggled to maintain her control. Even the rest of the cast slipped momentarily out of their roles and applauded along with the audience. Not an eye was dry.

Stagehands lifted her and moved her on and off the stage twenty-two times at each performance — forty-four times on matinee days. As long as her leg was enclosed in plaster, it continued to heal, whether she was in the hospital or on a Broadway stage. When the curtain came down each night, Jane returned to her hospital bed, where she was under constant care.

"Pieces of steel, pieces of bone, pieces of wood were oozing out of me." she said. "Fortunately, my voice was spared. 'It's a pleasure to look down your throat,' the doctors would say when the rest of me was all crushed."

The company traveled to New York by train for the Broadway opening. Getting Jane on and off the train in her cast was tricky. Fellow entertainers from the show placed her on a stretcher and two of them attempted to slide her on the stretcher through a window. They lost control and dropped her, cracking her cast. Emergency repairs were made and the show went on.

Artists and Models opened at the Broadway Theater in New York on November 5, 1943. Telegrams poured in and flowers filled the dressing room. Helen Hayes, Jane's Rockland County neighbor, sent a single flower in an antique vase.

Jane sang two solos in *Artists and Models,* "Your Romance" and "My Heart Is On a Binge Again."

She looked lovely on stage with all the illusion of costumes, props, makeup and lighting, but recalls the reality of it in her memoir:

> There was Don Saxon. . . . Don and I sang a duet, accompanied by the appalling smell of putrefaction that went with osteo—the bone infection in my leg that simply would not heal. It's hard to describe the agony of my embarrassment when the heaviest perfume proved useless once the heat of the footlights began to get in its work. There was poor Don, singing me a love song. How could he pretend to ignore the poisonous reek? He didn't. He didn't try. Instead, right in the midst of my part of the song, he bent lovingly toward my ear and breathed, "Mmmm, leg smells pretty powerful tonight." I gasped, but managed to go on singing. Then, when he was singing, I murmured back, just as lovingly, "Stinker!"
>
> The impossible had happened. I was able to joke about something it wasn't even polite to mention, and I was no longer embarrassed.

The show was weak but reviewers loved Jane and praised her looks, her talent, her performance. Burton Roscoe of the

New York World Telegram noted, "There are plenty of models in it—but with the lone and notable exception of the beautiful, lyrical and gallant Jane Froman, no artists . . . ." Burns Mantle, the reigning Broadway critic, wrote, ". . . the show should have been called 'One Artist and Models.'"

Two days after the New York opening, radio fans were thrilled to hear Jane's familiar voice on the Andre Kostelanetz show, *The Pause That Refreshes,* for Coca-Cola. Jane, in a wheelchair, sang two songs from *Artists and Models,* plus "The Man I Love."

Even Jane in all her radiance could not save a weak show. *Artists and Models* closed after twenty-seven performances. Offers rolled in, however, for Jane to do a high paying radio series, stage appearances, night clubs and an MGM movie. Meanwhile, the Riobamba owners were threatening legal action over leaving her engagement so abruptly in February. They insisted on ten days of Jane's singing and Jane's doctors fought them off. Asked for her reaction, Jane said, "Ah, but it was very gratifying to hear them battling over me again. I could make a fortune in taxes for the government, but my husband and the doctors won't let me."

The war in Europe continued to rage. On Christmas Eve, 1943, Dwight D. Eisenhower was appointed Supreme Commander of the Allied Expeditionary Force for the inevitable invasion of Europe.

In Doctors Hospital, New York, Jane Froman was fighting another kind of battle. In January, 1944, she went into the hospital to have a piece of bone removed that was found working its way out of her body. As usual, codeine was prescribed to relieve her pain after surgery. Codeine, the strongest pain killer known at the time, had brought hours of relief to

Jane's suffering, but it had become her constant companion. She could no longer get through a day without it. Her dread of losing her leg was always there, but even greater now was her fear of this dependency. Doctors had told her that habituation to the drug was inevitable, but that the situation could be reversed later if it became a problem. Jane knew the time had come. She refused drugs for total withdrawal.

The ordeal was as rough as anything she'd been through so far. When, still in the hospital, she heard the news that she had to have another bone graft, she knew drugs would once again be a problem. She had the operation this time without anesthesia.

Free of drugs for the first time in a year but thoroughly exhausted, Jane returned to work in the familiar environment of radio, where she received a warm welcome. For the small studios where the broadcasts originated, it was fine to sing while remaining seated. In larger studios, she insisted on underplaying her injuries. Theaters were darkened while she walked onstage on crutches, and again as she walked off.

Medical expenses were mounting daily; her savings were depleted and she had to make more money. Night clubs paid best, and were also short-term, in case she had to have another operation. She loved the intimacy of the clubs, moving among the tables, being physically close to her audience. How could she do that with her leg in a brace up to her hip, unable to walk without crutches? Playing on the audience's sympathy—appearing in a wheelchair or using crutches, or even revealing the heavy brace on her leg—was out of the question. Too many others had given much more in the devastating war than she had for her to take advantage of her own misfortune.

She and Don sought a solution and Don came up with a radical plan. Drawing upon his theatrical knowledge of craft and illusion, he made sketches of a platform on wheels. He found builders who could follow his plans and between them they came up with a contraption that could move about the floor, carrying a piano, an accompanist, a microphone and Jane.

The platform on wheels ran on a small electric automobile motor, with the batteries stored under the piano bench. The piano player operated switches under the keyboard and a rod near the foot pedals to move and steer the platform around the floor. Jane would be propped upright, standing on her left leg and chained to a brace so she wouldn't fall over.

The first performance using the moveable platform was at the Mounds in Cleveland. Before she made her entrance, the room was blacked out completely. A voice introduced her and a spotlight hit the stage. There she stood, next to a piano, in a flowing pink net gown and elbow-length evening gloves. Her hair was swept back and upward, elegantly styled. The audience stood up and applauded.

As the lights were turned up, the audience could see the platform-on-wheels and Jane, the back of the upright providing a backdrop for her. The accompanist sat on the other side, at the keyboard.

Slowly, the accompanist moved the platform around the room, bringing Jane close to her audience, a vision of loveliness and grace. In this intimate setting, moving among her audience with a portable microphone, she was at her best; the audience was under her spell. *Artists and Models* had well taught her the safety of illusion. After all, it was all part of the theater to make things appear as you wished them to be.

**Performing on the moving platform—with an
exuberant GI, no less (at right)**

A feature of Jane's routine was to draw a guest from the audience to come up and sing with her. Inevitably, it was a young man in uniform. The routine involved some singing, and a little conversation. Jane had learned that she could handle spoken bits like this in her act without stuttering, using the same rhythms as she used in singing. The audience loved it.

More offers came in and were accepted. The motorized platform was packed in special cases and shipped from one city to another.

How did she feel about going out on the floor this way? She was scared, afraid she would make a fool of herself. Having those enormous medical bills helped. If they hadn't forced her to get out and work, she might too easily learn to lean on others, and that could lead to feeling sorry for herself. She had no intention of doing that. It was up to her to make money to pay her debts; she had to go out and behave like a normal person, and that made her feel like one, too.

The Chez Paree in Chicago booked her in October and kept her for two months. She captured the hearts of her audience, looking "like a picture from a page in a romantic novel," said one reviewer. She appeared in her usual manner: a voice introduced her in a blackened room, and a spotlight hit the stage where she stood, already propped by the piano, which then started to move around the floor. Her hair was swept up into curls and she wore a pink ribbon, a touch of the feminine that she hardly needed. Her voice seemed to be even better than before—haunting, some people said, with better tone. Her extraordinary charm reached the toughest theatergoers, as she remarked after one song, "Ah, but that song was too sad, wasn't it?" and shifted gears smoothly to slide into a more upbeat one.

In the audience one night were Lorraine Rognan and Yvette, two of the Lisbon survivors. Rognan, whose partner, Roy, was lost in the crash, had injured her leg so she could no longer dance, but the two women had joined another USO unit and spent eight months overseas entertaining servicemen.

Scheduled next for the Copacabana, Jane returned to New York, but just before opening, she strained her vocal chords. The show was postponed until January. She went to Florida to recuperate, under doctors' orders not to talk for two weeks. That was fine with Jane. Basking in the sun was her favorite therapy.

10

FINISHING THE JOB
1945

JUST SHORT OF the second anniversary of the Lisbon plane crash, on February 9, 1945, Jane found herself at the center of a most unpleasant controversy. Republican Representative Marion T. Bennett of Missouri rose on the floor of Congress and angrily charged that the Purple Heart was being distributed with "reckless abandon"—that dogs and blues singers were receiving them—and made reference to one awarded to Jane.

V-mail poured in from devoted soldiers and sailors, defending their gallant Jane. Actors Equity and other professional associations protested. A resolution was adopted expressing disapproval of the congressman's assertion, condemning "in the strongest terms the statement by Bennett belittling the services which these performers have given and especially directed at that fine actress Jane Froman."

Jane needed no one to fight her battles for her. She sent off a sizzling wire to Bennett herself.

> The most striking example of "reckless abandon" is displayed by you with regard to the truth. . . . I have never received the Purple Heart. I have furthermore done what you failed to do—check into the facts. . . . No other performer injured or killed in Army camp tours has ever received the

Purple Heart. As a result of the unfortunate plane crash, I have spent the better part of two years in hospitals. You might be interested to know that I paid all my own hospital and doctor bills. I have never received any compensation, awards, rewards, and have never requested or desired them.

The contributions of the theatrical profession (in this war) will make a brighter page in our history books than your record as a member of the House of Congress.

Jane had never spoken about the crash, or jobs she had turned down going overseas for the USO, or the weary months in hospitals when she feared amputation of her leg at every turn, but her dander was definitely up when others were attacked. Show business itself had been slurred.

On April 12, 1945, President Franklin Delano Roosevelt died suddenly of a cerebral hemorrhage while sitting for his portrait. The country was in shock and everyone was in mourning. Harry S Truman, from Jane's home state of Missouri, took the oath of office, shouldering the enormous responsibility of finding a way to bring the war in Europe and in the Pacific to a swift end. In June, allied troops under the command of General Eisenhower had invaded Normandy, and while the invasion had effectively broken the enemy's defenses, the final days were still playing out. Mussolini was killed at Lake Como on April 28; Hitler's suicide in a German bunker was announced on May 1, but fighting continued in all the war zones.

In her own life, things looked no less bleak. With no hope left for a happy home life—not even for the temporary uplift she had had from John's visits—Jane took refuge, as usual, in her work. It had always pulled her through; there was no shortage of it—she had plenty of offers coming in for night clubs, stage appearances, radio shows and concerts. Something was missing, but she didn't know what it was until she was working at the Capitol Theater in New York.

The Capitol Theater on Broadway, built in 1919, was truly majestic, with a 5,300-seat theater and an expansive lobby featuring a white marble staircase. Jane was the principal attraction in a stage show at the luxurious theater, accompanying a spy movie with Marion Davies called *Operator 13*. She had to climb one hundred steps at each performance— five times a day—to a platform on the stage to do her featured number. It occurred to her—if she could do that, she could finish the job she set out to do for the USO when she was interrupted by the crash. The idea thrilled her.

Don was dead set against Jane's going overseas. The orthopedic doctor was also opposed. For heaven's sake, he argued, she was on crutches. Unknowingly, he had hit the nail on the head. That is precisely why Jane wanted to go— *because* she was on crutches.

She phoned Abe Lastfogel. He was all for it. Although the war in Europe was officially over, thousands of servicemen were still deployed there, many of them wounded and battle weary. Entertainers were needed as never before. Jane would help enormously in boosting the morale of the troops. She described how she felt in an interview.

> I'm convinced that I can do a tremendous amount of good for the wounded boys, especially those who have been seriously hurt, the ones who have lost the use of a leg or an arm. You see, I've been through what so many of them will have to go through, with hospitals, operations, and casts, and

I'm sure I can bring them hope. At least, I'm going to try. Honestly, that little word "hope" has become the most important word in the English language to me. The doctors now tell me that it might be two more years before I'm able to walk again, but I've got that little word tucked away firmly in my mind and in my heart and it makes the waiting a lot easier. If I can get this thought over to the boys I'm going to see, I'll be a very happy girl.

The Army medics gave her the okay, and on June 18, Jane and Don left for Europe with their USO unit. The Allied invasion of Europe had effectively led to Germany's surrender. There was still work to be done, and the morale of servicemen and women was at a low point. Troops wanted to come home but were awaiting orders, possibly for deployment to Japan, where the war was still going on. The USO sent over its largest contingent of entertainers at that time, to boost their spirits. Actress Celeste Holm, who also entertained for the USO, called it the "cockeyed time" between the fall of Hitler and the sobering triumph over Japan.

Jane and Don sailed for France on May 10, 1945, arriving in Le Havre and going on to Paris. There, they found conditions were primitive. Housing consisted of a shower, a latrine and an ironing board for the entire troupe, which included a GI band, a dancer, Joyce Brooks, an accompanist, a comic, Don and Jane. There were times when Jane bathed out of a soldier's helmet, as the GIs did—but she took it in stride.

The shows could be on a makeshift stage or the back of a truck. It didn't matter. Wearing a fifty-pound cast from her hip to her toes, Jane took the stage on crutches to perform. From others before her, Jane had learned a few tricks. Margaret

Whiting said to leave off the perfume—it would drive the boys crazy.

They had no transportation, so at a party, Jane engaged General Paul Hawley in conversation, and the next day they had a car, said to be none other than General Eisenhower's private car, with a trailer hooked up to it to carry their equipment.

Young Sgt. Robert Paulson, who had been

Jane in Paris, 1945

General Eisenhower's limo

Sgt. Robert Paulson

in the ETO for four years and had earned a chest full of medals, including the Purple Heart and the Bronze Star, was one of Jane's drivers. He had nothing in particular to go home to in Wisconsin, so he stayed on and was put in charge of dispatching limousines for the big brass. When he got a call for a driver to pick up Jane Froman at her hotel, he was the only one available and there was only one car—this time it was King George's big limousine. Paulson had never heard of Jane, and saw her for the first time at the hotel when Joyce Brooks, the tap dancer, opened the door. Jane was sitting in a wheelchair inside. She invited him to sit down and they had coffee.

When it was time to go, Paulson wheeled Jane downstairs, got her into the limo and took her out to one of the camps set up in huge tent cities that had gone up on the outskirts of Paris to house the troops when the fighting in Europe stopped. At one of these camps he and other soldiers helped get Jane up on stage. Joyce Brooks did her tap dance and Jane sang the popular "Accentuate the Positive" to get the show off to a rousing start. Sometimes she stood up to sing, supported by her crutches.

After one show, Paulson drove Jane back to the hotel and, as usual, she invited him in for coffee and they talked a little. Jane took a liking to the young sergeant and the next day, asked the brass if she could have him as her regular driver. They said she could.

As they drove from camp to camp—"Old Gold," "Pall Mall," "Chesterfield," etc., each one named after a different brand of cigarettes—Paulson got catcalls from other soldiers, who thought he must have the softest job in the army. They couldn't see, as he sat behind the wheel, his many decorations.

"Why don't you sit on some books so they can see your medals?" Jane suggested. He tried that, and the taunting ceased.

At each camp, Jane found a sea of young faces before her looking to her for some reminder of home. Hearing the songs

Jane and Don on the USO tour

In spite of her own injuries, she sang for 30,000 GIs.

they loved sung by a pretty girl in a lovely gown did wonders for them. When she sang, a hillside filled with young men and women in uniform was as silent as a church.

With her background, Jane could include any songs the GIs requested—even a little light opera if they wanted it. Her range was broad and her voice was so well supported that it carried far into the crowd without the aid of a mike. Her memory was excellent too; she could sing about two thousand songs by heart, a practice left over from her experience at WLW, when she was called on to sing for days on end without resorting to sheet music or repeating a number.

Jane knew the songs to sing for any audience. War called for songs with bounce, to keep the GIs' spirits up, but for every rhythm tune there had to be a ballad. She chose songs that spoke to the hearts of young couples apart for long periods, with the possibility of permanent separation always in the air.

She sang for the occupation forces and she sang for the wounded. When they got to Rheims, Jane sent her mother a letter from a chateau with bomb holes in the roof. Her singing had a wonderful effect on the wounded men, she wrote.

On August 11, 1945, radio personality and columnist Dorothy Kilgallen received a letter at her New York *Journal-American* office from a young corporal, Joseph P. Lewassar, who saw Jane perform at Rheims. Kilgallen printed it in her column.

> I am writing this letter in the interest of a wonderful star who presented a U. S. O. show yesterday afternoon. The lady is Jane Froman.
>
> All the boys were given inspiration by her performances. It has proven to us that there are still some in the world who satisfy themselves by giving benefit performances and are not there for the sole purpose of their own welfare and the gain of filthy lucre.
>
> She arrived on the stage with a smile on her face and a dazzling pair of sparkling eyes. She sang the songs we wanted to hear, and in the way we wanted to hear them, until she was almost exhausted.
>
> Would you please, through your column, give Miss Froman some recognition for her wonderful work, and tell how greatly we appreciate it?
>
> For our money she is terrific and can sing for us any time and any place.
>
> Sincerely,
> Cpl. Joseph P. Lewassar

The soldiers ate it up.

Like Kay Francis, Martha Raye and some others, Jane approached her job differently from Bob Hope, Bing Crosby, and other big stars who played for the big audiences. Her style, as in night clubs, was intimate, personal. She went to remote areas where small units could easily be overlooked and the men were starved for live entertainment. She had left her mobile piano at home for just this reason. She wanted to reach every young man waiting to go home, or lying afraid and alone in a hospital.

"I want to sing in the wards and go from bed to bed and talk to the boys and I get along fine with my crutches," she said. "Anyway," she laughed, "they'll help me to keep the wolves away."

During her tour, an army Finance Office clerk who cashed a check for Jane said to her, "Jane, none of us guys have ever had a chance to hear you." Then and there, she staged an impromptu show, out of schedule and just for the special benefit of the friendly clerk and the boys who quickly gathered around.

Jane's appearance had an electrifying effect on the wounded servicemen and women, who identified with her. She talked with the wounded men in the hospitals about their injuries, and they knew she understood, because she had been there. Jane did her best to look good so they could say, "If a girl can do it so can I."

Maybe she did too good a job. At one performance, she noticed four young men in the front row with crutches, casts, splints, and slings, wearing red bathrobes. At her next performance in another camp, up front, there were four men—with crutches, casts, splints, slings, and red bathrobes. They were at the next camp, too, and the next one. This group had gone AWOL to follow Jane wherever she went!

When Jane had to move on to more distant camps and had to part ways with her driver, she said, "Sergeant, if we make it, after the war, you come to California and be my guest."

Jane's tour diary mentioned meeting several young men from her home town of Columbia, Missouri. She saw Odon Guitar in Frankfurt, and in Luxembourg she met Carl Bacchus, former football star at the University of Missouri, now a colonel in the Air Force. Another hometowner in the audience at a USO show was Rowland H. Smith, a newspaper man who was a supply officer with the Office of War Information in Bad Nauheim, Germany.

"I don't remember too much about meeting her," he said later. "I saw the show and met her and others on the tour at the hotel bar." During the show, when Jane asked "Is there anyone here from my home state of Missouri?" his buddies urged him to volunteer but he refused. "I felt a soldier should go," he explained. "I was a civilian with an assimilated rank."

While some soldiers were waiting to be sent home, others feared deployment to Japan, where the fighting continued. Jane found herself somewhere near Neustadt, in Germany, on August 15, 1945, when news of victory over Japan was received. That night, she gave an unforgettable performance to a bunch of happy GIs who just that afternoon had been training with howitzers in the woods to get themselves and their equipment battle-ready. Sitting on top of a piano in a borrowed auditorium somewhere in Bavaria, Jane warbled joyfully one popular song after another for the GIs.

In September, after driving over three thousand miles of bombed-out roads across half of Europe and performing ninety-five shows, Jane's body rebelled under the stress and she dislocated a bone in her spine while mounting the platform to sing. Her tour of duty was over.

She and Don found themselves stranded in London. President Truman had decided to drop the atomic bomb on Hiroshima on August 6, and another on Nagasaki on August 9, to prevent more loss of American lives. Japan surrendered, signing surrender terms aboard the battleship Missouri. The troops were going home in huge numbers, aboard whatever transport could be found, including the *Queen Elizabeth*. That put all nonessential travel on hold.

Jane was finally able to book passage on the *Queen*, but she needed Don's help, and his passage was not included. It looked impossible under the circumstances, but on September 8, desperate, she wired President Truman from London.

LONDON NFT SEP 8 1945
THE PRESIDENT
WASHINGTON D. C.

DEAR MR. TRUMAN:

I HAVE BEEN IN EUROPE FOR 3 MONTHS
SINGING FOR 300,000 GI'S. I AM SAILING ON THE
QUEEN ELIZABETH FROM SOUTHAMPTON SEP-
TEMBER 13 SINCE I AM STILL ON CRUTCHES
DUE TO THE LISBON CLIPPER CRASH IN FEB-
RUARY 1943, I NEED A PRIVATE CABIN IN WHICH
I CAN HAVE MY HUSBAND WHO IS WITH ME
OR A PRIVATE NURSE ON THE RETURN TRIP I
WAS PROMISED THIS WHEN I LEFT THE STATES
BUT CANNOT ARRANGE IT HERE. COULD YOU
PLEASE ARRANGE FOR ME.

GRATEFULLY,
JANE FROMAN

The President arranged for the accommodations Jane
needed. On September 13, as Jane sailed home, she wrote a
letter of thanks to President Truman.

Tuesday September 25, 1945

Dear President Truman —

Thank you so much for arranging it so that my husband and I could be together coming back to the states on
the *Queen Elizabeth.* The only place where I am almost helpless is on a boat—because of the roll—and the crutches—and
I must have someone to steady me in order to move off my
bunk. I had gone through all the regular channels in the
army, trying to arrange passage, and only as a last resort, did

I bother you with it—as it was imperative that I get home. Thank you so much.

I had a wonderful tour of Europe, singing to the wounded. It is great morale work and I feel so proud that I could be a part of this tremendous undertaking.

Thank you again and continued good health and happiness. We of Missouri (my home is in Columbia, Missouri) are particularly proud.

> Sincerely,
> Jane Froman

On the *Queen Elizabeth* with Jane were the 271st and 272nd Regiments of the Sixty-ninth Division, Air Force ground crew troops, Navy personnel, nurses, WACs, war correspondents and personnel of the Office of War Information, Office of Strategic Services, United Service Organizations, and the American Red Cross. Jane was thrilled to be coming into New York harbor with 15,000 GIs, who did not make a sound as they passed the Statue of Liberty.

News reporters were there as the *Queen Elizabeth* docked at Pier 90 on September 20, 1945. Dorothy Kilgallen was one of them. Kilgallen reported seeing Jane, a dark-haired girl leaning on crutches, coming down the gangplank among the thousands of soldiers, and posing for a photo with the Fighting 69th.

Stories and articles appeared regularly about the gallant singer. Even hardened reporters were awed by her. To the eye, Jane was as beautiful as ever, her slim figure attired in a silk blouse and tailored slacks, her bright blue eyes flashing as she spoke.

In 1945, I kept the date I made in 1943. For three months I sang in hospitals in France, Germany, England, Belgium,

Jane with GIs

Austria, and Czechoslovakia. I sang in PX's, bombed out houses, open fields. It worked in every room. As I flung the crutches away, boys flat on their backs, boys in casts up to their chins, boys who hadn't spoken a word in months, screamed, yelled, clapped and joined me in singing. It was worth much more than pay. I felt so good—braces, crutches and all. My idea was that if I could go over there for the boys who were hurt, it would help them—and it did. I had the time of my life.

Kilgallen invited Jane to be on her show, to talk about her trip. When asked to sing one of the songs most requested by the boys she had visited, Jane sang the Gershwin tune, "Embraceable You."

On October 6, the American veterans of World War II named Jane Froman and Bob Hope "honorary GIs" for doing more for the morale and welfare of American service-men than any other entertainers.

Orthopedists helped Jane with her back, but a bigger problem lay ahead. Her loyalty to Don had run out. Their marriage was empty, just a routine in which she produced the income and Don managed it and made all the decisions. His drinking had become serious, leaving her alone most of the time and smothering in the dreariness of her existence.

In December, an examination revealed that seven tumors had to be removed from Jane's leg. She went back into the hospital to battle once more to save her leg. Once again, Jane's desire to see a new orthopedist was squelched by Don's belligerent attitude, insisting that he knew best.

Newspapermen had voted Jane the most courageous entertainer of the year at their Annual Page One Ball; she left the hospital to go to the Ball, sang a song with Duke Ellington's band, received the award and returned to the hospital that same night. Surgeons removed the tumors the following morning. As she came out of the anesthesia, Jane called for John.

11

SHOWDOWN
1946—1947

THE CLUBS WERE hot and friends from show business were performing around town. Jane could not bear to sit by while life—the lively, gay life she loved—passed her by.

Inside its heavy plaster cast, her leg slowly healed. There was little Jane could do to it with that body armor on, so she treated it like a portable hospital. She calmly got out of bed, slipped on her clothes and took a cab over to the Copacabana to attend Joe E. Lewis's closing night. At two in the morning, she was back in the hospital again.

Recovery was taking its toll. In the three years following the accident, there had been not only the grueling bone grafts but repeated bouts with osteomyelitis, the insidious infection that thrived on injured bones. Filth picked up in the waters of the Tagus River could be complicating matters. She had been near death three times due to shock and physical exhaustion. Frustrated at all the time that had elapsed without making any progress, Jane wanted to see another doctor, but Don violently objected.

Don was not there when she most needed his support, emotionally as well as physically. With her leg once again keeping her housebound, she felt afraid and helpless when he left her alone. What if there were a fire? Not used to being unable to fend for herself, she felt frightened, trapped.

She lost weight. Alone, facing an uncertain future, she realized that her marriage no longer existed. For the first time, she fought against the fierce loyalty that had bound her to Don. She made her decision to leave him.

John Curtis Burn

John Burn had completely recovered from his injuries and was flying again for Pan American Airways. He had continued to visit Jane and was in awe that, for all that had happened, she was not bitter. Even the hospital surroundings, which could have been so grim to her by now, were accepted as just a home away from home.

Jane's doctors, seeing that John's presence buoyed her spirits as nothing else could, encouraged his visits. The staff conspired to let him in through the back door of the hospital at all hours to visit Jane, bypassing the usual visiting hour regulations.

If there had been any change in Jane at all, it was that she loved life even more than she had before the crash. Being so close to death so often, she had a keener appreciation of people and fun and being alive. Simple pleasures brought her enjoyment, like rereading *Alice in Wonderland* and other old children's classics or listening to music on the small record player John had brought her as she lay in her hospital bed.

Her love of fun shone through a world dominated by doctors, hospitals, medical charts, dire predictions. She could not take life so seriously now, or be a tragic figure. Her sense of humor, like her voice, was intact. One morning she broke up the entire staff of orthopedists by playing the Grand March from *Aida* as they paraded into her room for their daily visit. It took them a while, but the doctors finally smiled.

The attraction between Jane and John was undeniable and grew stronger every day. They both knew it was natural, after all they had gone through together. They paid no attention to the age difference; it didn't seem to matter.

On her own now with medical decisions, Jane saw several orthopedists, who took more x-rays. She heard with consternation that the last bone grafts were not mending properly—again, there had been no union.

When she got out of the hospital this time, Jane felt certain she was going to die. She went directly to Florida, taking a maid with her. If she was going to die, she just might as well do it in a nice warm climate. Mama left behind her busy life in Columbia to join her, and they rented a tiny apartment in Coral Gables. For the next round of bone grafts—a necessary ordeal if she was ever to walk again—Jane had to build up her health. Exercising every day would keep her leg limber and her muscles strong. The tropical heat had always been good for her healing bones; it would be good for her disposition as well. Sweetening the decision even more was the prospect of seeing John, who had arranged with Pan Am to be transferred to Florida.

Everything but her personal possessions had been left with Don. Low on cash, with medical bills mounting alarmingly and facing still more operations, she had no choice. She had to work. "I didn't die," Jane said. "I just went broke."

Jane turned to George Wood, her agent at William Morris. He called on a couple of the famous headliners he had booked into Florida's Colonial Inn, Sophie Tucker and Joe

E. Lewis. When they learned of Jane's plight, both performers canceled their dates so Jane could have their jobs. She drew crowds for two months straight.

Ed Sullivan, columnist for *The Daily News,* saw Jane's performance at the Colonial Inn and wrote in his column,

> Like those who have had to live with pain, she has developed a philosophy that is not found in many performers. There is a quality in her face, in the carriage of her head, the cut of her jaw and in her very blue eyes that reflects the things she has gone through. Standing there on the floor of the Colonial Inn, braced against the auto-piano, which can move her around the place, she easily is the most arresting looking of the current show stoppers.

Jane's grace astonished many. Myrt Wertheimer, owner of the Colonial Inn, remembered one night when Jane had a fever, but insisted that she'd go on. "After the first show," he recalled, "she was so sick that I ordered her back to her hotel. A few days later, on payday, she telephoned me. She said that some mistake had been made, that she'd received her full week's salary, that the auditor hadn't deducted the midnight show she missed. You just don't expect performers to act like that. But this one has class, loads of class."

When she returned to New York, with things clearly over between herself and Don, she and her mother moved out to Atlantic Beach on Long Island. She still needed money. She signed a contract to play the Copacabana.

The Copa was a tremendous success. For two months, she performed three shows a night. Still in demand after two months, she was asked to stay on, but a brownout curtailed the shows. It was a relief for Jane, who found the heavy schedule extremely taxing. From this experience, she learned another important lesson. When she signed with night clubs in the future, she had it written into the contract that she would do just two shows a night. Owners complained, but Jane stood firm and got her way, paving the way for other grateful performers to adopt the precedent-setting clause for their contracts.

The Froman voice was better than ever, but she had to leave show business for a while to return to the hospital for another try at the bone grafts. John begged Jane to get a divorce from Don and marry him before going into the hospital again, but she refused. She could not be sure she'd keep her leg—or even her life. How could she make a promise to John until she knew how the operation turned out?

Jane went back into the hospital for the bone grafts. She would not give up hope, even though doctor after doctor offered no encouragement. If this were not successful she knew her years of patience and grueling pain would be for nothing.

According to Jane's mother, that year, 1947, saw Jane at the most critical point in her life. She had endured twenty operations on her leg, yet most of the doctors were doubtful that she would ever be able to use it again. They still recommended amputation. Then Jane met one surgeon who did not say "amputate."

That doctor was Mather Cleveland, head of Orthopedics at St. Luke's Hospital in New York. Cleveland had spent the war years as senior consultant in orthopedic surgery in the European Theater of Operations. Nobody knew more about current orthopedic procedures than Cleveland. He used the modern technique of grafting several smaller pieces of bone, so that if infection set in at some of the sites, the others would still have a chance to bond and all would not be lost.

"You want the truth?" he asked. Jane said she did.

He explained that five operations were needed and warned of the poor odds. Cleveland had to lay open the leg, get down to the bone and determine once and for all if the infection that threatened her injured leg could be ended. Her bones might not heal. Amputation might be necessary; there was a mere 40 to 60 percent chance that she'd keep her leg. He also warned of the probability of addiction to narcotics again.

Dr. Mather Cleveland

Jane put herself in Dr. Cleveland's hands. She had nothing to lose. She asked the doctors, as she always did, to let her know first, if they decided to amputate.

Through the hot summer of 1947 Jane lay absolutely still in St. Luke's Hospital, allowing for the slow process of healing as the bones grew together. Don called several times in the wee hours of the morning, drunk. Doctors no longer allowed him to visit. John, meanwhile, arranged for a temporary transfer to New York, where he could spend time with Jane when he wasn't flying. Jane made her decision about herself and Don final:

> It is impossible to keep a normal home or a normal marriage going when one of you is so badly hurt. I was wearing a 48-lb cast most of the time. I was in pain. Debts haunted me. I had to work myself out of them. He helped me. He got jobs for me. But I couldn't be the same girl I had been. I had changed. Things that used to be important simply didn't matter to me.

She filed for a divorce.

The grafts, finally, were successful, although Jane nearly died from shock during one operation. The joy of the grafts' success was soon overshadowed when osteomyelitis set in again. Even dear Dr. Cleveland felt defeated this time; he agreed with the other doctors that hope was gone and the leg should be amputated. Jane, defiant, stubbornly refused to let them cut off that leg.

As the money gave out again, she was torn with worry. She could not afford any further surgery, but without it, how could she hope to keep her leg, have a future? If she could not pay her way, she could end up in a ward of a state hospital, where she would certainly lose her leg. You had to have money to choose your hospital and doctors who would fight for you. She did not know which way to turn.

Abe Lastfogel, aware of Jane's predicament, wrote to her at St. Luke's Hospital.

Abe Lastfogel
Rockefeller Center
1270 Sixth Avenue
New York 20, N. Y.

February 20, 1947

Dear Jane:

I have reviewed our commission account with you, and on behalf of Bill Morris, Johnny Hyde and our associates, have decided that we would readjust this account to the extent of $8,501.73, which are the total commissions we earned from you last year. We have instructed our accounting department to credit your account with this amount and we will not countenance any change. However, we would like to have your approval of this adjustment even though we will not deviate in any respect from this, our final determination.

Words cannot express my personal gratitude to you for the great spiritual help and stimulation that I have received from our association and your unusual good cheer, which always makes me feel so much at ease in your presence, and beyond everything else, my admiration for you in not permitting any bitterness to creep into your heart, which might so easily happen.

With all my love and affection,
Abe Lastfogel

Miss Jane Froman
St. Luke's Hospital
Amsterdam Avenue & 113th Street
New York, N. Y.

Enclosed with his letter was a check for $8,501.73. Jane was overwhelmed; all that she had heard of Lastfogel's devotion to and support for his clients had not prepared her for this generous move.

Jane had the operation needed to remove infection from the bone. Mama took an apartment nearby, refusing to believe, even to herself, that Jane was to be crippled, or even left with

Abe Lastfogel

scars and braces. She kept her usual stiff upper lip, and came daily to the hospital. Between visits, she took music classes at the Julliard Foundation.

For some reason, the doctors had been wrong about Jane's leg. Sydney Kanev, Jane's osteopath, told the *New York Times* that a final successful operation had been performed by Dr. Cleveland and added, "She will be able to walk without cane or crutches soon."

Dr. Kanev was to become a fixture in Jane's life. For one thing, he had studied under Dr. Cleveland. For another, he was considered vital to many show business people. He used a technique, apparently devised by him, in which he would take an artist who had the most terrible kind of throat problem—a bad cold, flu, almost anything—and he would pack their nose and spray their throat, and it would be enough for them to go through a performance.

Jane remained in St. Luke's Hospital in New York for eight months—two months longer than anticipated—to clean out all infection. Shortly after she was released from the hospital, she returned to her tiny Florida apartment to recuperate near plenty of ocean and sunshine. A nurse was with her at all times and John was a regular visitor.

Jane's triumph over her injuries and her gallant struggle to return to work had gained her a reputation for courage that moved people profoundly. President Roosevelt had awarded a medal to the heirs of Carole Lombard after she died on a war bond trip for the Treasury Department, and Froman admirers tried to get a medal awarded to Jane for her work for the soldiers in time of war. Jane sought no special recognition for herself, but she did enjoy the nickname "soldier in greasepaint," that had been used to describe her and other entertainers who worked for the USO in times of war.

In December, Coca-Cola sent Percy Faith to Coral Gables to see if Jane could sing again. It was the first time anyone had questioned it. She had done the tour in Europe, a Broadway show, night clubs. She sang for Conductor Faith and was offered a show beginning in January.

Finally, she could give John her answer.

Jane on the Percy Faith Show

12

AT LONG LAST LOVE
1948

JANE WAS BACK on the air, flying to New York weekly to star
in Percy Faith's *The Pause That Refreshes* for Coca-Cola on
CBS. She stayed at an apartment in the Hampshire House
for the Sunday night broadcast at 6:30, then flew back to
Florida. She dreaded getting on the airplane each time;
whenever the plane did anything out of the ordinary, she felt
every eye was on her to see her reaction.

"On my last trip down from New York the Miami airport was hidden by mists," she told a reporter. "In circling, we
banked—and banking is what really gets me.... I was scared
to death. When the pilot finally found a hole and we landed,
I never was so relieved in my life."

As with everything else Jane did, she intended to master
her anxiety with dedication and hard work. She would not
let fear rule her life.

Her openness and down-to-earth good sense and humor prevailed. Once, during a broadcast, the announcer said,
"Miss Froman will next sing the theme song of the Society
for the Prevention of Cruelty to Animals—'River Stay Away
From My Door.'" Then, sotto voce, he added, "If it doesn't
it's going to drown a lot of wolves." That got her laughing so
hard she couldn't sing.

The public adored the gutsy singer and wanted to hear

A jubilant Jane on her wedding day

Wedding kiss

more about this amazing star who had gone through an unimaginable physical ordeal and bounced back with her spirit and her sense of humor intact. How could she not be bitter about all that had happened? Jane Froman had become a living symbol of courage and faith. Magazines and newspapers sent their reporters to get stories about her.

Interviewers found a gracious but vibrant and witty young woman, without a trace of self-pity, who could joke about the mad shoes she would buy once she could give up the sensible black oxfords she was now forced to wear, and who referred to the ever-present crutches as her "pogo sticks." Always quick to put people at ease, Jane led conversations away from talk about her troubles.

The romance between Jane and John flourished as they spent time in the Florida sun. Jane's divorce from Don Ross came through in late February, 1948, and her wedding to John was set for March 12. The press anticipated the storybook ending. It made every newspaper in the country. "Jane Froman to Be Bride of Pilot Who Saved Her," the *Los Angeles Times* announced.

The wedding of Jane Froman and John Curtis Burn took place in Coral Gables in front of a picture window at the home of Henry Chapin, a writer friend of John's. Both mothers were present. Mama played the wedding march as Jane swung easily down the aisle on her crutches. Her floor length dress of pink organdy and lace concealed her leg. She wore a picture hat of pink tulle trimmed in lilacs, and managed to carry a muff of pink lilacs despite the crutches. As "something new," Jane wore a new steel leg brace.

The Reverend Dr. Nevin H. Schaaf, a Presbyterian minister, officiated. During the ceremony, Jane put aside

At home with John in Coral Gables

her crutches for the first time in five years and stood unaided for fifteen minutes.

Jane and John spent the next two weeks honeymooning at Pirate's Cove in Key West. Jane rationalized taking the train. She went wild on her trousseau, she said, and wound up with so much luggage that no plane would accept the load. "I hope John's job is a steady one," she quipped, "because he's taking me broke."

The newlyweds moved into a five-room fieldstone and brick house in a wooded area in Coral Gables. Jane, still recovering from her injuries, had a full-time nurse in attendance, especially important for the times when John was away. A copilot now, he was flying Pan Am's Caribbean–South American route.

Happier than she had ever been, Jane settled comfortably into the role of Mrs. John Burn.

When John was called for a flight and Jane was between

broadcasts for the Coca-Cola show, she followed the advice of her doctors, baking her healing bones in the tropical sun.

Wasn't she worried about John's flying? people asked. After all, they had both been through a terrible accident. No, that wasn't how it was at all. "After all, I wouldn't have met him if he weren't a flier," she would respond, "so I can't start objecting now on those grounds."

No longer able to play at any of the sports she loved, she nevertheless maintained a regimen of strenuous exercise to keep in shape. She continued the leg lifts she had started when her leg was first encased in plaster, and she walked. She joked about the great shoulder muscles she had developed using crutches.

One of the few outdoor sports Jane could still master was deep sea fishing, which she had done when she went to Miami in the wintertime. Now she got John interested. They fished off the Florida Keys, where Jane caught the world's smallest marlin—at fourteen pounds, a scale model of a full size marlin.

Deep sea fishing

Later in the year, after one of her commutes from New York by rail, Jane stepped off the train in Miami without crutches. She had practiced for days in New York to surprise John.

In time, she exchanged the large steel and leather leg brace for a smaller one. Although her right leg was a mass of scars, and was to be at least an inch shorter than her left leg, a lift in her shoe would correct the difference. She knew she would probably never walk without some kind of support, but she was determined to walk as normally as possible on her own. She tried raising one hip and lowering the other as she walked, practicing until her walk became a glide that let her move gracefully and rhythmically, without a limp.

Once in a while John's mother came to stay with the Burns. John recalled that sometimes he would find Jane curled up on his mother's lap, and his mother would say something like "There, there, child, take it easy," or "Yes, dear, it's in the past."

This was the kind of relationship Jane had never had with her own mother, who, loving as she was, did not display affection so readily. Mama never could get used to the open affection and playfulness John and Jane exhibited with each other but took it in her stride as she did all things.

In August, Jane opened at Bill Miller's Riviera Club in Fort Lee, New Jersey, standing unaided before an audience for the first time since her accident. The room was jam-packed. Singer Tony Bavaar led Jane by the arm down two steps to the stage and the moment the audience saw her, they rose with a burst of applause. Earl Wilson, popular *New York Post* columnist, reported:

Standing, unaided, at the Riviera Club

A great ovation greeted her as she was led down the steps sans crutches and sang "Begin the Beguine" beautifully. She followed it by holding a small mike, whirling gracefully around the stage and singing "Steppin' Out With My Baby."

As the show progressed, she slid into a couple of old favorites from Irving Berlin—"It's a Great Life" and "Millionaires

A visit home had to include a game at Tiger Stadium.

Don't Whistle," selections which summed up how she felt. From Jane's choice of songs and the joy with which she delivered them, it was clear that she was in high gear, stubbornly and proudly climbing to the top once again.

To the audience, she confessed she wasn't too scared coming out to sing here tonight; after five years and twenty-five operations, this opening couldn't be so bad.

In November, Jane's home town bestowed a new honor on her, dubbing her their first "coming home" queen. The Missouri Tigers had always followed the tradition of having a homecoming queen, but after following Jane's progress through the years of her recovery and aware that she had recently abandoned her crutches, they created the title for her. Jane responded with great joy as she took part in the energetic rallies alongside the homecoming queen, both wearing their tiaras.

When an invitation to President Truman's Inaugural Ball came from the White House, Jane accepted. It was one of several visits to the White House for her, but this time John was with her.

It was actually daughter Margaret, a budding singer herself, who had befriended Jane, from the time they were first introduced to each other by Eleanor Roosevelt. Truman had been Vice President at the time.

The ball was held in the National Guard Armory in Washington, where the room was set up like a gymnasium, with tiers of seats all around. Jane and John were escorted by an officer of the Marine Corps to the President's box, where the President's family was seated—his wife, Bess, and Margaret, their daughter. As Jane and John arrived, Truman turned to Margaret and said, "Margaret, your friends are here." Then, as the president watched his daughter gather her ball gown together to rise from her seat, he added, "Margaret's having a problem with her dress . . . there's too damn much of it."

The atmosphere that evening was festive, unlike the last inaugural, in 1945, when Franklin D. Roosevelt was president and the country was still at war. Jane performed, along with many stars from the theatrical world who came to entertain the new president, and afterwards she and John danced among dignitaries and friends of the Trumans.

The evening ended memorably for the Burns, too, when John fell and broke his arm, having to be rushed off to the hospital. It must have been painfully amusing to Jane and John, after the number of bones they had broken between them.

13

BATTLE FATIGUE
1949

PUBLICLY, JANE WAS a symbol of courage, a woman who had triumphed over unimaginable odds, inspiring in her struggle to overcome the injuries suffered in the Lisbon crash. Although maimed and scarred, she was determined not to inflict her troubles on others, to remain positive and upbeat.

Genuinely uncomfortable hearing about her courage, she did understand, from stories written about her in newspapers and magazines and letters that poured in, that she seemed to give people courage to go on when they were facing their own burdens, not unlike the hope she had brought to thousands of wounded GIs.

In one interview with *Etude* magazine, she said, "I have sung 'In my Father's house there are many mansions,' about 2,000 times. Sooner or later, I'll start on the third thousand. Perhaps I realized during the last five years that I was passing through one of those mansions on my way to others. Perhaps it was that that helped me to come back."

On the sixth anniversary of the crash, February 22, 1949, a luncheon was held in Jane's honor at New York's Pierre Hotel, marking the observance of Brotherhood Week, under the auspices of the National Conference of Christians and Jews. Jane was presented with a scroll praising her "... abiding faith and courage, her determination to overcome physical handicaps, and her inspiration to women of all races and creeds."

Night clubs where she appeared continued to be packed. In January, she appeared again at the Broadmoor Hotel in Miami Beach. In March, at Miami Beach's Copa City, she was met with deafening applause and rave reviews. The buoyancy of Jane's spirit lifted audiences to new heights. She held them spellbound by her elegant gowns, her brunette hair pulled back with a flower, her flawless skin, her gliding motion across the floor, so that they forgot that under the long gloves and the bouffant gown were terrible scars and a heavy leg brace.

While outwardly all was well, or at least under control, Jane dealt privately with the reality of constant pain. Without drugs, the suffering would have been unendurable. For a while she was on chloral hydrate, a strong sedative, and she was, for all practical purposes, unconscious for most of the day. She moved on to codeine, the most potent pain medication available.

Trained nurses had to administer the drug, so a live-in nurse was necessary. The nurses Jane hired were generally good practical companions; some were even cheerful and encouraging. They did their jobs well and managed to maintain a professional hand as they took care of Jane's medical needs. John was grateful for the companionship the nurses offered Jane when he had to be away on a flight.

It didn't take long for the steady doses of codeine to create another full-blown dependency. It was one of the side effects that was expected from extended use. Doctors agreed that once Jane was well again, she would come off the drug in a controlled manner.

When John's route was changed, they moved to an apartment on East 80th Street in New York. Coming home after one of his flights, he sensed that something was wrong. Jane was demanding and argumentative. It didn't take long for him to figure out that the problem stemmed from the current resident nurse, who seemed to have her own way of doing things.

This particular nurse withheld the drug until Jane had endured all the pain she could stand and then had to beg for it. This cruel method encouraged Jane's dependency on the nurse as supplier as well as the narcotic drug. Not only had Jane become habituated, predictably, but she had her own personal coach, and it was legal.

It was difficult for Jane to accept the idea that she was an addict. She did not want to hear that at all. It was all necessary medication to relieve the incessant pain. John found the nurse's hold over Jane intolerable. The doctors advised him to stay out of it because the problem could end up in a choice between him or the nurse—and it could be bad for him—but John didn't buy that. Fed up with the situation, he confronted the nurse.

He told her he did not approve the method she was using; it was creating more harm than good. Jane was not the woman he knew. The nurse protested, using her profession and claiming her position as her defense. John ordered her to leave. She refused to take orders from him; only Jane could fire her, she argued. The woman underestimated John's determination. Later, as the nurse dozed, he startled her by coming into the room shouting. "You're ruining Jane's life and mine. You're leaving the house now!" As she started to argue, he picked up a heavy glass ash tray and deliberately threw it above the woman's head, scaring her half to death. The nurse left with no further argument.

After the Coca-Cola program went off the air in early 1949, Jane took the opportunity to focus on eliminating the drug problem. In May she checked into Columbia Presbyterian Hospital in New York. She was given nerve blocks to improve the circulation in her right leg and reduce the pain. At the same time, she withdrew from drugs. The plan went awry when the codeine was withdrawn too rapidly, and the experience was ghastly. Still, Jane kicked the drugs and was as proud as could be that she had succeeded.

She came home from the hospital in June. The summer of 1949 was very hot, and the aftereffects of the codeine withdrawal were worse than anyone had anticipated—stomach cramps, headaches and muscle pain—and she was terribly dehydrated and weak. The Burns took a house on Fire Island for the sun and sea air. Mama moved in with them along with Jane's new nurse, Marie Kenney. Kenney, as she came to be known, was as good and endearing as the former nurse had been controlling and disruptive. She was tough as a boot, in John's words, but with a heart of gold. He adored her. Jane began exercising as much as possible, pushing herself to regain her strength. Under Kenney's care, the drugs remained in control and Jane's health and outlook improved.

Work, always a tonic, appealed to Jane once more. With renewed optimism she signed on to do her first television appearance as a guest star on Milton Berle's popular *Texaco Star Theater*, which had recently taken the country by storm. Berle, known as "Mister Television," was seen by everyone who owned a TV set in 1949—and by their neighbors, who came over to watch the show on Tuesday nights. People loved

"Uncle Miltie." Jane was pleased to be working with her old friend again. She sang a couple of old favorites, "I Get a Kick Out of You" and "Begin the Beguine," and participated in some of the comedy sketches as well.

When she did her first television shows, if standing in one place proved too much for her, a portable metal cage was erected around her so she could be braced upright on the stage, and she wore a pouffy gown that fit over it. Illusion had once again made it possible for her to be back to the "normal" life she was after—and that included being able to pay off her enormous medical bills.

A fabulous offer came in from Charles Hughes, founder of the famed Detroit Athletic Club, to appear at their thirty-fifth anniversary celebration. The DAC, one of the finest private clubs in the country, was known for its Albert Kahn design, inspired by Rome's Palazzo Farnese, as well as its amazing dining, dancing, and club facilities. Among the luminaries who had been ushered through its doors were U.S. presidents Teddy Roosevelt and Woodrow Wilson, John Philip Sousa, Henry Ford, Billy Sunday, and other celebrities from war heroes to famous athletes. Actor/comedian Frank Fay and pianist Adam Carroll were to appear with Jane. She accepted happily. The event was booked for the following spring.

It was a shattering blow when her leg reopened and she had to be rushed to St. Luke's, terrified that the ruthless osteomyelitis had come to plague her again. Was she never going to see an end to this?

Indeed, an abscess had formed, but this infection was quickly brought under control. The shock, however, of her leg becoming infected again, just when the future looked good at last, was more than she could handle. There had been no warning. It had been six years and twenty-five operations since the crash. Half of that time had been spent in hospitals. Could all this suffering and pain be for nothing? Once again, the horrible feeling that she might yet lose her leg, or never walk normally, terrified her.

She knew she was losing her grip. Falling into a deep depression, she even lost the faith that had sustained her through the previous six years. A crackup was coming, and she knew it. Jane just couldn't fight on her own any longer and realized she needed professional help.

More than one doctor had told her about a clinic in Topeka, Kansas, known for pioneering work in the treatment of behavioral disorders. Dr. C. F. Menninger and his sons, Doctors Karl and Will Menninger, had cofounded the Menninger Foundation and had established a school there in 1946 to train psychiatrists to meet the growing demand among military veterans returning from World War II. Mental illness was still something no one talked about openly, although a couple of movies—*Spellbound,* in 1945, about the relationship between a doctor and her patient during psychoanalysis, and the groundbreaking *The Snake Pit,* in 1948, showing the horrors within a state-run mental institution—had at least brought it to the public's attention. Public awareness of emotional and mental illness had definitely increased after the war. Dr. William C. Menninger himself had served as Chief of the Army Medical Corps' Psychiatric Division, being promoted to brigadier general in 1945.

The clinic seemed to be the ideal place for a girl suffering from her own form of "battle fatigue." In one of the most important decisions of her life, Jane decided she would go to Menningers.

"At first, I wouldn't listen," Jane said. "You could say I was like all the other people who talk about psychiatry in hushed voices. And I was frightened at the idea that some of my problem could be the result of an emotional disturbance. But I didn't know where else to turn. Reluctantly, I went to the clinic." At her weakest point, she found her greatest strength.

On September 24, 1949, Jane's osteopath, Dr. Sydney Kanev, released a report to *The New York Times* that Jane would be spending some time at the Menninger Clinic "for the rest and physical buildup made necessary by her exhausting surgical experience of recent years."

He added that she had had a final successful operation on her leg by Dr. Mather Cleveland, head of orthopedics at St. Luke's Hospital, and soon "she should be ready to resume her professional career with no handicaps whatsoever."

Stories about Jane still excited a response. A *New York Times* editorial followed Kanev's announcement, praising Jane

**Dr. William C.
Menninger**

for her courage and inspiration to all those who might give up too easily. Jane received over 12,000 letters following the appearance of the editorial.

Jane and John stopped to visit Mama, now back in Columbia, then went on to Topeka, arriving at Menningers in late September. Kenney went along.

They were greeted by Dr. William C. Menninger, known

affectionately by friends and associates as "Dr. Will." He was to become Jane's valued and trusted friend, and she admired him greatly.

At Menningers, Jane rebuilt her physical and psychological strength. With her personal therapist, Dr. Ruth Barnard, she broke through some of the difficult obstacles in her emotional life. Acknowledging that she needed help was the first step to recovery. She went on to deal with fears that had plagued her throughout her life—being apprehensive of strangers, for one.

Before the crash, Jane's stuttering had ruined many opportunities for her. Her difficulty with speech had forced her

Jane with Dr. Ruth Barnard

to avoid certain situations and become more introspective. She wrote more letters than the average person, partly because she had always loved writing, but it was also easier for her. Due to her strong public persona, few people guessed that she was painfully shy with people until she knew them well. She had millions of fans, but only a few really close friends.

"I desperately tried to keep people—all people—from getting too close to me," she said. "I guess I really was afraid of being hurt." Perhaps this was a subconscious defense that protected her from loving someone too much, as she had her father, only to be hurt deeply, as when he walked out of her life.

Understanding her fears and where they came from was key to her mental health. With the kind of treatment Menningers was known for, intensive and individualized, Jane began to heal. She related to the emotionally disturbed children of the Southard School, the children's division of Menningers, and spent a great deal of her time there visiting them.

As she worked with Dr. Barnard, facing her problems and coming to understand them, the stuttering that had plagued her became less brutal. She opened up about the new set of values that the accident had given her. She talked at length about how the stuttering became less important in the light of what really mattered and, as a result, it bothered her less.

While in treatment, Jane began painting as therapy. Although she had never had a lesson in her life, she found she had a natural talent. It was something she would pursue with great joy even after her stay at Menningers. She played ping-pong and danced. For the first time since the crash, she slept long and well. Her birdlike appetite vanished, and she began to eat three squares, plus assorted snacks, malteds, and hot dogs.

The psychiatric guidance Jane received at the Menninger Clinic helped her regain a healthy perspective, and she learned how to lead an active life without persistent anxiety about further injury or infection. She learned that she did not have to pay the penalty of exhaustion and shattered nerves to return to a normal existence.

In three months, Jane's physical condition was vastly improved. She could walk without her crutches and cane. She began to play golf again.

She had changed emotionally, too. She was more at ease, more understanding, easier to know and like. Even her singing voice was warmer. Her outlook on life had changed; she had regained self-confidence and was no longer haunted by her fears. Friends were astonished at her relaxed and happy demeanor.

Her first visit from John was at Christmas. He was astounded by what he found. He noticed first of all a great calm. Jane's self-assurance was intact. She was happy, with an optimistic attitude toward life. Her stutter was barely perceptible.

In February, she made a trip home to Columbia for a visit—the first trip she had made alone in seven years. It was a time of great joy. Life no longer was a painful trial but a delightful existence.

Ruth Barnard was good medicine for Jane. Trained in psychiatry at the Menninger Clinic, she was not only an excellent therapist, but had a great sense of humor. Jane loved that, and enjoyed telling the story later on about one of their big breakthroughs concerning the public image Jane had built up around herself over the years—that impenetrable facade that kept her somewhat insulated from others. This "Froman myth" created a barrier—a person beyond reach, too perfect to touch. With great glee Jane recalled how Dr. Barnard ended their last session with "And that will be all, *Myth* Froman."

Jane returned to New York for good in March, after six months at Menningers, without crutches. She emerged with her vitality restored, eager to get back to the energetic life she loved, and to spending time with John. Her experience at Menningers had broken down all the fears and anxieties about psychiatry and taught her the good it could do, but her compassion for the emotionally disturbed children at Southard School left her with a deep determination to help mentally ill children somehow.

To maintain her independence from drugs and unnecessary anxieties, Jane sought help on a regular basis with Dr. Lawrence Kubie,* a most extraordinary and unorthodox psychoanalyst who had been recommended to her by the Menningers. Kubie was an authority on the use of narcotics, During the war, he had been in the Air Force, and had done a lot of work with wounded air crews. He became convinced that the traditional approach to narcotis withdrawal—giving patients a minimal amount of a drug so they watched the clock for their next dose—was all wrong. It made narcotics become terribly important. He believed that if you knew your business you knew how much a person needed to keep

---

* Lawrence Kubie was perhaps best known for his thesis that homosexuality was both pathological and treatable. He presumed to analyze Ernest Hemingway, whom he had never met, in an aborted article for *Saturday Review,* over which Hemingway threatened a lawsuit.

them comfortable, and when the day came when they didn't need it anymore, the doctor would know, and stop it. That was not the approach taken with Jane. Her doctors had used a very stingy approach, and that had a lot to do with her getting caught by the narcotics.

Back at work, Jane's spirits were high. At the Detroit Athletic Club she was a sensation. Adam Carroll loved working with her. "She always left the audience clamoring for more," he said.

As a result of the DAC performance, Jane received fabulous offers to appear at the Flamingo in Las Vegas and the Mocambo on the Sunset Strip in Hollywood, and she asked Carroll if he'd go with her. He did, and Jane was sensational.

Abe Lastfogel flew out to see her act at the Flamingo and invited her and Carroll to dinner afterward. Carroll remembered that this was when Jane learned from Abe about Twentieth Century–Fox's offer to make a movie of her life, with her in the starring role.

"I'll never forget the startled expression on Jane's face," said Carroll. She was dumbfounded, he said, but after a thoughtful moment, confessed that her physical condition would not permit her to play herself. She could sing, however, all the songs that would be used in the film. Abe asked if Jane could recommend anyone who could portray her in the film. With little hesitation, she answered "Susan Hayward."

Carroll, whose recollections were written from memory in 1965 at the urging of a professional colleague, may not have captured the scene as accurately as it happened, but does provide a delightful glimpse of a dinner and conversation that might have been quite similar to this.

The Mocambo was another fantastic success for Jane. Charles Mornessao, proprietor of the club, kept singing birds in cages at the rear of the Jammer Room, where Jane performed. At every performance, when Jane sang, the birds chimed in. This delightful detail was not overlooked by reviewers. One club critic wrote, "Jane Froman was sensational with her audience asking for more. Even the birds loved Jane and sang with her, their obligatos sounding like angels singing."

Next on the schedule was the epitome of night clubs: the Persian Room at New York's elegant Plaza Hotel. Jane was ready.

14

WITH A SONG IN MY HEART
1950—1951

THE MAGNIFICENT PERSIAN Room of the Plaza Hotel was regarded as the height of New York style and sophistication. The room boasted service that became the exemplary model for all of New York's fine clubs. It had been conceived in 1934 by the same Joseph Urban who had created many Ziegfeld Follies sets, and featured breathtaking murals by Lillian Palmedo. The room had recently been redesigned by Henry Dreyfuss, who had created interiors for the luxury liners *Constitution* and *Independence* as well as the symbols of the New York World's Fair, the Trylon and Perisphere. No other night club had ever surpassed the style and class of the Persian Room. Jane Froman was the perfect performer for this magnificent venue.

Her opening was a triumph. Physically and emotionally strong, she had the added confidence of being able to talk for the first time, and incorporated many speaking lines into the new act she had created for the occasion. Her voice, with its rich texture and mellow timbre, lingered in minds and hearts. The audience delighted in Jane's charm as she swept through her routine. Among the guests that evening was Dr. Mather Cleveland, the man who had saved Jane's leg. Jane wrote in her memoir:

... Dr. Cleveland is present—with the tears rolling down his cheeks, saying over and over again, "My God, I would never have believed it." In his exuberance and in his cups he keeps singing at the top of his voice, that great old hymn, "Will There Be Any Stars in My Crown?" Oh, I'll say there will, Dr. Cleveland. There simply won't be room for more stars in that crown. . . .

Reviews announced that Froman never looked or sang better. She put on a great show with terrific substance and style and the audience adored her. Night clubs from one end of the country to the other eagerly signed her up—from the Saxony in Miami to the Flamingo in Las Vegas. Once again, her career was flying high.

During her engagement in Miami, a benefit was going on during the day for the Damon Runyon Cancer Fund, with the boardwalk serving as the stage and the beach given over to the audience. All the performers who worked the clubs at night appeared for the benefit during the day. Jane, the Ritz Brothers, Jack Carter, Milton Berle, Al Jolson, and several others were scheduled one afternoon. Jane Froman and Al Jolson, who was a superstar before the term was created, were on the program back to back. Jolson spotted Jane and called her out.

Jolson's enormous ego was legendary in show business. He never missed a chance to show off. He asked Jane to do a duet with him of "Swanee River." Before he began he threw away the mike, as he always did in the theater. Most singers would blanch in such a moment but Jane shrugged, took a deep breath and sang out, reaching the farthest areas of the beach. Her concert training gave her a volume and range very few pop artists had. The mighty Jolson had been thwarted.

Playing the night club circuit again after a long time away, Jane was encouraged by good attendance and great reviews. She saw Milton Berle in the audience at Copa City and, in her low-cut gown, leaned over to greet him. "Please, please," he begged, "bend up!" In August, when she opened at the Mocambo, the West Hollywood hot spot on Sunset Boulevard, Fanny Brice was in the audience. Her presence melted Jane's heart.

Dear Fanny! . . . Hollywood was agog when she made one of her rare appearances as, still limping badly and with steel braces, I opened at the Mocambo. Fanny, who never went anywhere at night and never went to night clubs, had recognized my plight as she had so many years before and was there to spur me on once more.

Jane and John took Fanny to dinner whenever they were on the West Coast. Jane, who could not tolerate anyone who put on airs, found Fanny's earthy manner refreshing and honest, and John found her intelligent, easy to be with. Fanny adored them both. Once at the Brown Derby, when she was nearing sixty, she whispered to John, "Johnny, dance with me, or people may think I'm getting old."

During Jane's visit to the Coast, her story became a major topic of conversation among the movie studios. Paramount, MGM, Warners, and Twentieth Century–Fox all courted her, talking with her about a motion picture based on her life.

This time there was no playing golf in the sun-drenched countryside while offers escalated. A wiser performer as well as clever business woman now, Jane liked the idea of having a movie done—she wanted to reveal her battle with drugs, talk about it, expose it, and show her struggle to overcome

With Lamar Trotti on the set of With a Song
in My Heart

it, because that could help others kick their habits. Most of
the studio people she met were insensitive or too commercial; she wanted to work with someone whose feelings on the
issues were kindred to her own. When she met writer and
producer Lamar Trotti of Twentieth Century–Fox she found
in him the man of integrity she was looking for.

Trotti had begun his career as a journalist but had soon
moved to screenwriting. He had been with Twentieth
Century–Fox for twenty-one years. In the latter part of those
years, he produced several films as well. Trotti's movies were
commercially and critically successful. He had done bio-
graphical pictures before—of Lincoln, Alexander Graham
Bell and Woodrow Wilson—but this was to be a departure.
Jane, despite her classical training, was a popular star.

All the studios had wanted to do a musical, but Trotti's
vision went beyond that. He felt that people, especially the

men and women who filled the beds of the VA hospitals, would gain hope from the story of Jane's fight to overcome her injuries and return to her career. He understood Jane's desire to reveal her drug problem so that it might bring hope of recovery to others. Trotti was talented, tender, and wise. Jane agreed to do the picture with him at Twentieth Century–Fox.

When Lamar Trotti first discussed the script with Jane, she found that he knew more about her than she knew about herself. For her part, she was to sketch out the story of her life. At the end of it, John added this postscript:

> It would seem as though every possible obstacle were interposed between the girl and the thing she sought to attain, as though she were being submitted to a trial, infinite in its severity. She accepted such conditions, further, she imposed the strictest of ethics on herself. She must fight at all times honorably, ask little of others, and at the same time fulfill every obligation in a fuller measure than is asked of those not burdened as she.
>
> I think you may search back through the years, through history and legend, and never find an example of humanity at its best that will stir your heart more profoundly or give you greater pride in mankind.

The contract was signed and Jane and John went back home only long enough to pack for their stay on the coast. They took Mama along for those periods when John would be flying, and moved into the lovely Garden of Allah in Beverly Hills, along with some of the cast.

The Garden of Allah, a famous apartment complex on Sunset Boulevard, had been built as the lavish home of silent screen actress Alla Nazimova, who sold the property when her career was over and she needed the money. It had become a magnet for visiting celebrities like Errol Flynn, Greta Garbo, F. Scott Fitzgerald, Clark Gable and Marilyn Monroe. The swimming pool was one that Marlene Dietrich loved to swim in—naked. It had been quite the place to stay in the Golden Age of Hollywood, and it was still not too shabby in 1950, when Jane, John and Mama moved in.

One of the finer pleasures of living at the Garden of Allah was taking a swim in the pool at one o'clock in the morning. At that time of night there were fewer people around to gawk at her badly scarred leg. A publicity release for *With a Song in My Heart* announced that Jane was in a very jubilant mood during the filming of her movie biography. "For the first time in eight years, the songstress went swimming," it read, "an inspiring feat for a woman whom doctors predicted would never walk again."

Jane was appointed technical director for the film, then called *The Jane Froman Story*. She wanted the film to be entertaining but also wanted people to be inspired by it to conquer their own fears and overcome their dependency on drugs. She observed every detail for accuracy, but also learned where literary license could get them out of a jam.

For example, instead of showing the actual succession of nurses who had assisted Jane from Lisbon to New York, one nurse, a composite of all, was written in as a character, a tough old bird named Clancy, played by veteran actress Thelma Ritter. To explain why Clancy stayed with Jane, a fictional element was added to bring a comic touch to the story: she had left Brooklyn to escape her relatives, but now that they were coming overseas, she was going back to the States with Jane.

Hollywood in the early 1950s was not yet ready to tackle

the drug problem . . . at least not with someone who had an image of elegance and good taste, and who was loved by so many. Even Lamar Trotti's sensitivity couldn't break through the studio executives' final word on the subject: there would be no mention of drugs. There was great resistance to portraying Jane, a woman greatly admired for her heroism and grace, with an addiction to drugs. Like mental illness, drug addiction was an unspoken malady, not discussed in polite society. The disappointment to Jane was huge. Some years later, Betty Ford, wife of President Gerald Ford, did what Jane couldn't do in the 1950s: show the truth about substance abuse and reveal her own addiction to get the message across to the public, where people could learn from her ordeal and be encouraged to get help. Little did Jane realize that her story, even without the drugs, would accomplish what she had hoped for.

Other aspects of real life received the Hollywood treatment too. John, blond, with thinning hair and quiet, was played by tall, dark, and glib Rory Calhoun. The studio's first choice, Dana Andrews, had asked for too much money. John said later he took a lot of kidding from his flying buddies about the casting.

Illusions were part of movie-making and Jane had become a master of them. She walked with a jaunty step, a conscious swing from the hip, to give the appearance of a confident stride rather than a cover-up for her limp. She wore long gowns that bellowed out to conceal the brace on her right leg that was attached to specially made sensible oxfords instead of the dainty high heels that she had so loved for her tiny, size three feet. Long evening gloves covered the deep trench in her right arm, left from the removal of a piece of wood that had lodged there in the crash. She memorized

Director Walter Lang with Jane and Susan Hayward at work

lines of dialogue the way she memorized music, to trick herself into speaking without a stutter. The most amazing illusion of all, however, was to see herself come to life through Susan Hayward's acting.

Hayward admired Jane enormously and had wanted desperately to play this part. The studio had chosen Susan, and Jane could not have been happier with their choice. In her words:

> She looks like a singer. Every singer knows that when you breathe—it shows. Susan breathes. She understands how to stand, to move, and that gestures must mean something. She

didn't copy me slavishly, either. She had tricks of her own up her sleeve.

As a child, Susan had been in a serious accident in which a car ran over and fractured both of her thighs. Doctors believed she might not live, much less walk again, but Susan was walking in six months. Her grit seemed to be a good match for the Froman story.

Ten days before they went before the cameras, Susan walked up to Jane in the commissary and asked if she could make a date to talk with her.

"How about now?" Jane said. The two met half an hour later in Susan's dressing room and spent the whole afternoon and far into the night going over the script, scene by scene. Susan asked about Jane's childhood, her mother and father, her grandmother. She wanted to know what kind of clothes Jane wore, what her drives were, her tastes, interests, hobbies. Susan asked her questions.

"Immediately after the Clipper crash and you found yourself in the water, how did you feel?"

"Numb," Jane told her. "In shock."

"Not afraid?" asked Susan.

"No, not afraid. Not then. Not yet."

"What did you and the Clipper's copilot, John Burn, talk about all the while he held you up in the water, saved your life?"

"Trivialities . . ."

"What exactly were your injuries and John's?"

"I had a compound fracture of the right leg, left leg nearly severed below the knee, two broken ribs, and my right arm fractured in several places. John suffered two fractured vertabrae of the spine and a fractured skull."

"How did you feel when you knew there was a chance of losing your leg? Did it floor you? Or did it put fight into you?"

"Before, and for a long time after my first operation (which I was positive would be the only one), I was quite hopeful. After that, after each successive operation, I felt deepening doubt and a little bitterness."

"What, in all that time, was your greatest and gravest problem?"

"To have to go out and make dough again after the 25 operations in order to pay for the pain. . . . The real fight, the real problem was not to hate all human beings."

Susan's performance captured, masterfully, the singer's style and bearing. Day after day she sat on the set, three and four hours at a time, watching every move Jane made as she sang.

Jane did all the singing for the movie, dubbing twenty-six musical numbers. When she began recording the sound-track, Susan was in the studio, absorbing every detail.

The title of the movie changed. For a while it was called *You and the Night and the Music*, but ultimately that title, too, was rejected. The final title, *With a Song in My Heart*, came from a song written by Rodgers and Hart that had appeared in the 1929 Broadway musical, *Spring Is Here*. The song became not only the title of the movie, but its big production number as well.

Hollywood moviemaking often involved changes to the script during shooting, and studio head Darryl F. Zanuck was known for his talents in reshaping movies as they were being made. His insightful notes show that he, along with Trotti, had the perception to keep the movie from becoming sticky sweet or melodramatic. He let Jane's story, as it really happened, do the job, and suggested omitting some of the numbers or reducing them. He also suggested toning down Jane's histrionics, as first written into the script. It was Zanuck's vision that Jane be heard but not seen in the opening to keep up the suspense. The audience at this point did not know that she was able to walk again after her injuries.

Jane and John watched the completed picture for the first time alone in the projection room. "We couldn't have anybody else around," Jane said. "It was a great emotional experience seeing my whole life like that. And then living through the crash again. The two of us sat there crying like babies."

Jane and Susan on set

Jane couldn't get over how Susan had *become* her on the screen. At first, it seemed to Jane that Susan's mannerisms were not right. She didn't raise her head like that, or lift her chin when she started to sing. She stood in front of a mirror and sang a few numbers. In the mirror she saw the raise of the head, the quick lift of the chin, the mannerisms which were so much a part of her she was not conscious of them until she saw them played back to her in the mirror of Susan Hayward.

During the production of the movie, tributes kept pouring in for Jane. She managed to get away long enough to accept many of them. One in particular she would not miss for the world. The Cincinnati Conservatory of Music awarded her an Honorary Doctor of Music degree for her "accomplishment in music." It was conferred by Maxwell Powers, Director of the prestigious Greenwich House Music School. Jane felt she owed an enormous debt to the conservatory and accepted the degree with great pride. Mama also walked in the procession in cap and gown, the triumphant smile on her face revealing her satisfaction that, at last, her talented daughter was being recognized seriously for her musical accomplishments.

Jane took another short break to return to Columbia for the Christian College Centennial weekend, an event she could not miss. She took Mama with her. On a clear moonlit night she held an informal concert on the steps of St. Clair Hall for 4,000 eager listeners who had gathered on the front lawn. Franklin Launer, director of the Conservatory of Music at Christian College, acted as master of ceremonies. The crowd cheered and went wild when Jane, looking radiant, introduced her mother as "my first and best accompanist." Anna Froman Hetzler joined her daughter to sing "I Love You Truly."

Jane receiving her honorary Doctor of Music degree from the Cinncinnati Conservatory of Music

In Hollywood, work progressed on the movie. Mama became the belle of the movie set. She had her picture taken with Jane and Susan Hayward. Everyone found her utterly charming. Half the fun of making a movie, it seemed, was meeting the cast members off the set and getting to know them as real people.

One afternoon, a few of them were sitting around the pool at the Garden of Allah. Thelma Ritter, who was perfectly cast as the tough but big-hearted nurse Clancy, kept them all amused with her wisecracks and sardonic humor. Her children were playing in the pool when suddenly her son popped over the side and said, "Mom! I can stay under water thirty seconds!"

"It's been a long, hard day," said Thelma. "Can you make it thirty minutes?"

During rehearsal of the scene in which Thelma Ritter as Clancy and Rory Calhoun, playing John Burn, are sitting at a table talking, Calhoun drummed his fingers on the table.

"Stop it!" cried Thelma.

"Why?" asked the actor.

"You know how big your hand is going to be on the screen? Nobody will see or be aware of anything else but your fingers bouncing up and down."

"You mean I could steal a scene like that?" Calhoun returned.

"Yes, and I'll break your arm if you do."

He stopped drumming.

Jane heard a familiar voice on the set one day singing "I Like the Likes of You." Sure enough, it was Brice Hutchins, who had been in the Ziegfeld Follies with Jane and was now famous on the screen and on TV as Bob Cummings. The reunion was a happy accident for both of them.

The final revised script was sent to the Breen Office. From the 1930s, the Breen Office had enforced the rigid Hays Code, which watched over the morality of moviegoers, looking for signs of indecency. Every movie was under the same scrutiny. Even the script for *With a Song in My Heart* felt the heavy hand of the Breen Office when it came back with this note: "We urge you not to play this marriage with anything of a comedy flavor. . . . Such a flavor, we feel, tends to cheapen marriage." Several changes were made to bring the dialogue into line. This was the 1950s, after all.

Susan brought her twin boys, Timothy and Gregory, to the set the day she did the scene in which she lip synched the film's title song while a recording of it was played on the sound track. The lyrics include the phrase "... heaven opens its portals to me...." The next day, Susan reported that the boys were going around the house screaming, "With a song in my heart, heaven opens its portholes to me...."

Jane and John were invited to dinner at the home of producer Lamar Trotti. After dinner, they wound up playing poker. John was ill at ease when he learned that a chip was worth ten dollars. Everyone in the room probably made a lot more than a pilot's salary. He could be working for these people the rest of his life!

Jane was a sharp poker player, a little too daring for John's taste. That night, however, he was grateful for her skills. As it turned out, none of the others could play poker, so he and Jane trimmed their sails and, by the end of the evening, John had won close to $2,000. That's when he learned that, according to Hollywood protocol, the chips were actually worth ten percent of face value, but just like everything in movieland, the stakes were hyped up a little to increase the drama.

"I was furious," he said, laughing. "I sweated blood for a hundred and fifty dollars, to play with those clowns!" It was obvious that Jane and John had a good time.

After the rush of making the movie, there were many TV appearances. Jane appeared on the *Goodyear Revue* with Paul Whiteman, Ed Sullivan's *Toast of the Town,* the *Voice of Firestone,* the *Jackie Gleason Show* and Milton Berle's *Texaco Star Theater.*

Berle continued to feature Jane on his show as a guest. She loved performing with him; he put her at ease and she could have pure good fun. She even danced, to everyone's amazement. An article in the May 1952 issue of *McCall's* described a rehearsal in which Jane danced:

... when she tried the step for the first time in a street length dress which did not conceal the brace, the effect was electric. The hard-boiled professional people, most of them connected with the show, sat sniffling and gulping as though they were seeing a four-handkerchief movie.

On Berle's show she sang a medley of songs from the movie—"It's a Good Day," "Embraceable You," "Tea for Two," "With a Song in My Heart"—and closed the show singing "God Bless America" with the chorus and another guest star, teenage idol Eddie Fisher.

Her confidence renewed by her success on TV, Jane got out into the active life of a star again. On Tuesday, October 16, 1951, Judy Garland opened at the Palace Theater in New York. It was the biggest party Times Square had known since D-Day. Celebrities walked the regal red carpet laid from the curb to the entrance under revolving kleig lights. Forty-seventh Street and Broadway had a noonday glare. Two hundred mounted and foot policemen patrolled while wooden barricades held the throngs back. Celebrities arrived: Jimmy Durante, Jack Benny, Irving Berlin, Marlene Dietrich, Billy Rose, Moss Hart, Sophie Tucker. Jane was among them.

Jane and John had been married nearly four years. John, now a Pan American World Airways captain, was flying the route from New York to San Juan, Puerto Rico. They had bought a house on East 93rd Street on New York's upper east side, a five-story brownstone with a steep flight of stairs up to the front door. Friends cautioned Jane to consider those stairs, but she remained undaunted.

"I love to walk up and down those stairs," she said. "For me—it's *something*!"

There was an elevator inside the house, but she never used it. John put his foot down when it came to frigid weather and icy streets. He refused to let Jane come to the airport on blustery nights when he took off on a flight. For company while he was away, John gave Jane a dachshund puppy, with whom she fell in love and promptly named Til Euelenspiegel, after the mischievous title character in the Strauss opera of that name.

Jane and Til

In the eight and a half years since the accident, Jane had spent thirty-six months—three full years—in hospitals. She kept on working and singing, sometimes even when she was a patient in the hospital. Financial necessity drove her; she had to pay every cent of the $350,000 that all those operations had cost. Now, at last, she was back, with money again for the things she could enjoy. And she was well, thanks to her stay at Menningers. "All the way well," in her words.

In great physical shape, her emotional problems behind her, Jane was in the thick of life again. Starting the family she had always wanted seemed to be the next logical step. She had never been happier.

15

THE FROMAN APPEAL
1952

THE WORLD PREMIERE of *With a Song in My Heart* was held at the Miracle Mile Theater in Coral Gables, Florida, on April 4, 1952. Seated close to Jane at the black-tie event was noted comedian Eddie Cantor.

"Jane, your voice really made the picture," he said.

She smiled. "Having Susan Hayward's face to go with it didn't hurt a bit."

Cantor said later that he couldn't get over such a remark coming from one of the most beautiful women anywhere.

With a Song in My Heart almost immediately gained millions of new fans for Jane as the film was released halfway around the world in Europe and Australia. Her inspiring story reached the hearts of people who found in it a renewal of their own faith, or had their courage bolstered as they faced their own crises. People wanted to know more about this woman, to hear her voice, to thank her for what she had done for the wounded in battle, and for them.

Sentiment was still not embarrassing in the 1950s as it would be several decades later, and there was plenty of that: the tender love story, the struggle to overcome great odds to walk again, the patriotism and fervor of the country during World War II. The script may have been somewhat schmaltzy, as some reviewers said, but it captured people's

Popular Jane has an orchid named after her

hearts and minds. The public wanted to see and hear more of Jane Froman.

Capitol Records, meanwhile, had produced the sound track album from *With a Song in My Heart*, which was proving to be a best seller. With Susan Hayward's picture on the cover in the dramatic fire and brimstone musical number, "Get Happy," and Jane doing all the singing, the album was a winning combination.

The sound track had been recorded with the Fox Studios orchestra in California, but a couple of the songs had not been treated fully in the movie: "That Old Feeling," written by Lew Brown and Sammy Fain, and "I'm Through With Love," written by Matty Malneck, Jay Livingston and Gus Kahn. They set up a date at Capitol's New York studios to re-record those numbers. Sid Feller was the arranger and conductor. Feller recalled that first meeting with Jane. He called it "love at first sound."

The musicians were all in their places as the clock showed that the recording session had officially started. The recording artist had not as yet arrived at the studio, so I started rehearsing the orchestra. The arrangement we started on was "That Old Feeling."

A few minutes later I glanced up and saw a group of people arrive in the control room of our studio. Amongst them were the president, two vice-presidents, and two top recording directors of Capitol Records. They were in deep conversation with a beautiful young lady.

Just then the recording engineer opened the speaker in the control room and the sounds of the orchestra playing in the studio started drifting into the control room where the music hit the ears of the female member of the group. She politely interrupted the conversation and announced, "I hope you'll excuse me, but with all that beautiful music playing out there in the studio I just have to join in and sing!!" And with that she happily left the control room and came out into the studio where I met for the first time the finest singer and person I have ever known—Jane Froman!!

Jane and Sid liked each other instantly; it was the beginning of a beautiful friendship. The two musicians found in one another perfect working partners. Gert Feller, who was in the studio that day when Jane met Sid, summed up that first meeting. "Hearts know hearts," she said. "Jane was so kind and loving, she made you feel that if she didn't see you today, she'd be upset."

With a Song in My Heart was nominated for five Academy Awards: Susan Hayward for Best Actress and Thelma Ritter for Best Supporting Actress, as well as Best Musical Score,

Best Costume Design in Color and Best Sound Recording. Alfred Newman won for Best Musical Score, beating out *Singin' in the Rain.*

As the movie was distributed around the country and started to break box office records, word came in from a theater owner in Florida that there was a problem. During the movie's main production number, Richard Allan waltzed Susan Hayward around the sound stage, Hayward reached up to Allan for a lift and for a split second, her left breast popped out of her gown. It happened so fast very few people had caught it—including the folks at the intimidating Breen Office.

Actor Robert Wagner went into the projection room with Walter Lang and Lamar Trotti to check it out, but they couldn't find it. Finally, they caught it when they showed it in the Movieola. It was just a couple of frames, in a distant shot, but this was too risqué for the 1950's; a decision had to be made. They took a chance. Too many prints would have to be recalled at great expense, plus it would bring unfavorable attention to a popular family movie. The theater owner got a fresh edited print; all the rest were left alone. To this day, most prints of the film still have the unexpurgated version, and it has become a cultish treasure for some film buffs who dwell on the trivia of movies.

Awards and tributes to Jane's courage abounded. At a luncheon at New York's Waldorf-Astoria given by the USO-Camp Shows, Brigadier General Charles W. Christenberry awarded a Citation of Honor to her. Abe Lastfogel spoke of Jane's extraordinary will to contribute to the activities of the USO, even after the Clipper crash. He recalled the times he had visited her in the hospital.

Receiving the USO award

Feeling the responsibility of having sent Jane to Europe upon my first visit to the hospital I expected to find her bitter and resentful—to my great happiness I found no bitterness. I visited with Jane countless times during her hospitalization to cheer her up, but the amazing thing was that when you left Jane you were the one who had received the spiritual uplift.

Jane's old friend, Helen Hayes, unable to be at the luncheon, sent a telegram calling Jane "the darling of our country." The honor bestowed on Jane by the USO was entered in the Congressional Record for Wednesday, April 9, 1952.

Cruel fate was not finished with Jane Froman. Within days of the movie's release, as Jane was at home sewing on an Easter dress, Pan American Airways called her. John's plane had gone down into the sea off the coast of Puerto Rico.

The shock was seismic. She broke down at the news but composed herself quickly while Pan American left the line open until they could inform her of John's condition. He was alive, though injured.

Immediately, Jane flew to Puerto Rico, accompanied by Carl Gregg, John's good friend, also a pilot with Pan American. Tense and drawn, she grappled with the odds that this could be happening to them again.

The bare facts came in: John had been at the controls of a DC-4 four-engine jet leaving San Juan, Puerto Rico, for the United States when two of its engines went dead. He was returning to San Juan for an emergency landing when the plane crashed into the sea and sank.

Limping noticeably as she arrived at Presbyterian Hospital in San Juan, Jane leaned heavily on Gregg's arm. When officials told her that she could not see John, she was furious. What could they possibly mean, keeping her from John?

"You had better call somebody or I am going to raise hell," she shouted, her voice shaking.

John was under police guard, she was told; no one was allowed to see him. It was the custom to place crew members of crashed planes under technical arrest to facilitate inquiries.

Jane turned to Gregg. "Put in a call to the White House," she said, holding back angry tears. "Call President Truman and find out who's running the country."

Pan American lawyers argued with police and tried to contact District Attorney Zoilo Dueno. Newspaper reporters scribbled excitedly in their notebooks, as a crowd of patients, nurses, doctors and visitors gathered in the narrow hallway.

Once again, Jane found herself in the headlines: JANE FROMAN FLIES TO SIDE OF HERO-HUSBAND read a typical headline.

Jane argued heatedly with authorities for four hours before Dueno was found and was persuaded to amend his order. She could visit with John for an hour before attorneys and officials talked to him.

John appeared all right—a bruised right shoulder and a burned right hand. He said he felt pretty good. He had been treated for shock and exposure. Guards let her stay an hour and three quarters in exchange for posing for pictures. Jane sat beside John, who was propped up in bed, while cameras clicked away. She remained at a nearby hotel until John was able to leave.

The toll of the crash was tremendous. The plane had split in two. Of the sixty-nine passengers, only seventeen had survived. The water was teeming with sharks, making rescue attempts more difficult. Passengers reported that John launched four life boats before the forward section of the plane sank. He also saved the life of passenger Salvador Ayala, who was not wearing a life jacket. John, who wore one, kept Ayala afloat until help arrived. Many of the passengers were so frightened that they refused to leave their seats and went down with the plane.

"I began forcibly throwing people out the main door into the sea," Burn said. "I had removed all of the people in the vicinity of the door and was about to go for people further down the aisle when the door slammed shut . . . then it was flung open by a violent swell and I was thrown into the sea."

The true effects of the accident would not catch up with John for years. When released from the hospital, he seemed fine, and returned home with Jane to their East 93rd Street home. At a hearing before the Civil Aeronautics Board in

New York John was charged with a degree of pilot error called "questionable flying technique." He fought the charges vigorously, refusing to be the scapegoat for someone's mechanical error, but it was not until July 1953 that all charges against him were dropped and he was flying again for Pan Am. The long and tedious process took a terrible toll on him, physically and emotionally.

Jane's popularity was already soaring following the opening of *With a Song in My Heart*. She hired publicist Aileen Brenon, and found in her a good friend. Aileen was to see Jane through her new television career, which had made her a top star. The attention she received at this time only increased the public's devotion to her. Once again, in the face of disaster, she had come through with grace—and guts.

When the album from the movie became the third-best-selling album in the country, Capitol Records saw an opportunity to make Jane a recording star, to take her place among the top female vocalists. She had come from radio, in a time when that alone was prime exposure; records had been a secondary source of exposure and revenue. She had recorded some, but not until now had anyone thought to make her a part of the industry that turned out hit records. Since disc jockeys didn't play individual songs from albums, Capitol wanted a single they could release for commercial success. The songs they chose were "With a Song in My Heart" by Rodgers and Hart and "I'll Walk Alone" by Sammy Cahn and Jule Styne.

Sid Feller was again brought in to work with Jane. Feller, like Froman, excelled in all aspects of his art. He could make eight strings and a trumpet sound like a full orchestra. If a problem arose that nobody else could solve, Sid could find a solution. He could score a piece of music in minutes that took others hours and days to do, and his arrangement would still come out better. Feller, who would later be remembered best for his thirty year association with singer Ray Charles, for which he was honored with a place in the Rock and Roll Hall of Fame and the Smithsonian Institution, brought out the best in artists, without letting the orchestration show, overwhelming the singer.

Jane Feller Tolland with the baby dress Jane knit for her

When the Fellers had their fourth child, a girl, they asked Jane to be her godmother and named their daughter after her. As a gift to her little goddaughter, Jane knit a baby dress that was so exquisite, it is now framed and on the wall of Jane Feller Toland's home.

When CBS offered Jane her own TV show, she gave it serious thought. TV was an arena she had not yet explored. She had done guest appearances, but a show of her own was entirely different. She would have control over the musical content and the image that played to the public. She could bring to television everything she had learned from her early musical education through radio, movies, night clubs and the stage. Possibly, she could bring Sid Feller to the show, too.

CBS had its own staff of musicians and conductors, but agreed that Jane could have her own arrangements made. If for any reason the regular conductor could not be there, Sid would be brought in.

Ruth Barnard, formerly Jane's psychotherapist and now her good friend, worried about Jane's stutter on a regular show. It had been under control, but what if the excitement of the lights and the script caused it to resurface? The show would be live, as was most TV in 1952. Jane was confident and signed with CBS.

The network saw Jane's show as an opportunity to challenge the competition of NBC-TV's popular *Your Show of Shows* with Sid Caesar. With Irving Mansfield and Byron Paul, one of CBS's top producer-director teams, in charge, *USA Canteen* was born, using the format of Jane singing to servicemen in uniform as she had done overseas and in army camps during World War II.

The pride and idealism of America's role in World War II was still within recent memory. Jane's show provided a welcome association to the USO's role in the morale of servicemen fighting on foreign soil, and the audience loved it.

The logo for the USA Canteen

In *Timesquare Reporter,* Shirley Eder wrote, "In my opinion the Jane Froman television program is the finest variety show on the air. It has class and heart and it is great entertainment."

Jane hosted the show, with Alfredo Antonini leading the orchestra, and featuring guest stars from the military. The Department of Defense sought out talented servicemen who could appear on the show. Singer and teenage idol Eddie Fisher lit up the first show, appearing in uniform. Subsequent shows featured young comic Jack Carter and singing star Vic Damone, also in army khaki. The drill team from Fort Dix appeared. Jane stayed on at the close of every telecast to sing for men and women in the audience who were in the armed services.

USA Canteen was televised at CBS Studio 52, which would later be renamed the Ed Sullivan Theater. It was the same studio where Jane had sung on radio as "the Chesterfield Lark" many years before. The studios had been converted for TV, but there were still old radio studios in the basement.

The show was an immediate success when it aired on October 18, 1952. One segment of the show was devoted to Jane, seated at a desk, writing a letter to someone in the armed forces. She spoke the words as she wrote, telling the news from home. Inevitably, this led to a ballad. The Froman appeal was a natural for the early years of live television. To the delight of those like Ruth Barnard, who waited and watched with their hearts in their mouths, Jane did not stutter once.

Aileen Brenon went to work with press releases, publicity photos and setting up interviews. Stories and photo essays appeared regularly in the fan magazines.

Jane continued to choose songs from the best American

Bouffant gowns cleverly concealed Jane's brace . . .

songwriters. Her version of "You'll Never Walk Alone," from Rodgers and Hammerstein's 1945 musical *Carousel*, was the first song to become a nationwide hit after being featured on TV.

Many people who saw Jane for the first time on *USA Canteen* had been left with the impression from the movie of her life and stories they had read in the papers and magazines that Jane could not walk unaided, so when Peter Birch, the show's choreographer, took her and whirled her around the stage, the audience gasped and broke into spontaneous applause.

In a ball gown, wearing long evening gloves, Jane was the epitome of grace and beauty. Her eyes sparkled in the strong TV lights. Her welcoming smile made viewers feel at home.

Before a show, there were the inevitable jitters, as Jane fussed with her gloves or paced back and forth. Nerves were

***but sometimes the writers came up with
other interesting ideas.***

a part of the game, as Jane knew well, but something like
a friendly smile and conversation from CBS makeup artist Pat Darrell could always put her at ease. The audience,
meanwhile, was warmed up by newcomer Dick Van Dyke
or another young comic. When the show finally began and
she got her cue, Jane was transformed, secure in her role. She
confessed that being keyed up before a performance gave her
an edge that served her well once she stepped onto the stage.
She never took her talent for granted; with so many people
depending on her, she could not give anything less than the
best possible performance.

Jane paid tribute to many people on her shows, but anyone in uniform—or anything representing the armed forces,
for that matter—had her foremost interest. When the Army

ran a contest for a song that was as catchy and as memorable as those for the Marines ("The Halls of Montezuma"), the Air Force ("Off We Go Into the Wild Blue Yonder") and the Navy ("Anchors Aweigh"), it was a natural for Jane to introduce the song on her TV show. The winning song, "The Army's Always There," written by Sam H. ("Don't Sit Under the Apple Tree") Stept, had the verve and clamor of a rousing marching song, but for some reason it never did catch on.

Jane's show moved many people who had lost sons and daughters in this new war in Korea. The mother of a boy killed there wrote a letter to Jane in which she said she had nothing to show for her son's death except that routine wire from the Department of the Army. Wasn't it a pity somebody did not write something that would reaffirm the faith that gave the only real meaning to life? Producer Irving Mansfield turned the suggestion over to Ervin Drake, Irvin Graham, Jimmy Shirl and Al Stillman, the show's team of writers.

The writers went to work. At the end of the day, Irving Graham had to leave—he was hired for special material, to get around Jane's physical problems, and had another job to go to where he was writing special material for someone else. Al Stillman had to go to his job at Radio City Music Hall, where he'd worked since the Depression. Ervin Drake and Jimmy Shirl stayed and wrote the song. The four writers had an agreement, based on their experience of surviving in a cutthroat business, that no matter what they did separately or in pairs, they would share the outcome, so all four writers are credited with writing this song.

The next day, as the cast and crew rehearsed the show, the four young writers burst into the studio, excited about what they called "a new piece of special material." Everyone listened as Ervin Drake (the only one of the four who could sing) sang the song for Jane:

> I believe for ev'ry drop of rain that falls,
>> a flower grows,
> I believe that somewhere in the darkest night,
>> a candle glows. . . .

When he finished, he asked if she liked it.

"Liked it? Darling, I love it." She pulled back the sleeve of her sweater. "Look. Goose bumps." She asked him to sing it again. He did, and asked her again what she thought.

It gave her the chills, she said, pulling back the sleeve again. "Look. Goose bumps on top of goose bumps!"

A few changes were made in the script, and "I Believe" went into the show that very night, which happened to be the Thanksgiving show, making it the first song ever introduced on the new medium of television.

Response to the song was enormous. The song seemed to speak not only to those whose faith was intact but to others who doubted. The words of "I Believe" revealed to the world why Jane was able to cling to life when so much had been against her. The song reaffirmed the public's belief in some force greater than themselves.

Mansfield saw an opportunity to boost their Nielsen ratings. They might even use it for the theme song, instead of "With a Song in My Heart." He suggested to Jane that she record the song. Jane said it would never work. The song was not commercial, although it made good special material for TV. Besides, she wasn't exactly a big recording star; she had never had a popular hit on the charts.

When Mansfield heard that Jane didn't want to record the

song, he told the writers to go over to his friend, record producer Mitch Miller, at Columbia. No one mentioned this to Jane. Drake took the song to Miller, who liked it but wanted to add a girl and boy last line. It sounded like a church song, he said.

"Mitch—it's not that kind of song!" Drake explained, knowing that the addition would change the meaning of it completely.

Okay, Miller said. He was looking for another song for his protégé, Frankie Laine, and decided this was it. They would use a soft guitar strum as his accompaniment. They went to work recording it almost immediately.

When Jane heard that Frankie Laine was recording "I Believe," she was furious. It was *her* song; Drake had no right to take it to a competitor. Quickly, she alerted Capitol executives and in no time she had recorded the song herself. With Sid Feller's arrangement, Jane's recording of "I Believe" for Capitol Records earned Jane her first gold record for selling a million copies. Frankie Laine's recording of the song went

Jane being presented with her first gold record for "I Believe"; Sid Feller is on the right

on to become the bigger commercial hit because of its head start, but Jane's version remained among the top twenty in the country for several weeks, and over the years, it came to be as much associated with her as "With a Song in My Heart."

The song also resonated with people of faith—any faith. The story of how the song was born came to the attention of the Rev. James Keller, head of the Christopher Movement and a man who believed steadfastly that a single person can change the world. He decided that the mother of the dead soldier, the catalyst for getting the song written, rated the Christophers' monthly $100 award, but, sadly, she could not be found. Her letter was lost, and none of the people concerned could remember her name or her home town.

In spite of its success, *USA Canteen* never became the blockbuster show CBS had hoped for. In December, CBS decided to switch *USA Canteen* from a half-hour show on Saturday night, opposite Sid Caesar, to a twice-weekly show renamed *The Jane Froman Show,* which aired Tuesdays and Thursdays from 7:45 PM to 8:00 PM. General Electric picked up the sponsorship.

GE had been involved in commercial television since 1948, with Young & Rubicam producing musical variety and quiz shows in which to sell its appliances, electronics and lamps. It was not until GE switched to Batten, Barton, Durstine and Osborn (BBDO) advertising agency in 1951 that they began to garner the reputation they had sought as sponsors of "outstanding entertainment." It was in this period that they took on *The Jane Froman Show* in its biweekly format, shared with Revlon.

There were complaints about the change from reviewers and loyal fans who expected the quality of the show to deteriorate, but the show in its new time frame still captured a vast audience, thanks to Jane's appealing voice and style. The homey theme might be graduation day or a June wedding, but Jane also honored the songwriters she loved—Richard Rodgers, Arthur Schwartz, Noel Coward, Cole Porter. Byron Paul directed the show, and the orchestra was under the baton of Hank Sylvern, with Peter Birch and his troupe providing the dance routines.

To the audience's delight, Jane continued to dance on her shows. Peter Birch taught her to move in a way that took advantage of the swing of her leg. She was thrilled. "When I'm dancing, I forget about operations and braces," she said.

The show's new format did not depend on guest stars, but Jane did enjoy, occasionally, having a special guest. One of these was Gypsy Markoff, the accordionist who was a fellow survivor of the Clipper crash. Markoff had worked hard to regain some use of her fingers which had been damaged. Another guest was golfer Jimmy Demaret; Jane was an avid golfer and

Dancing with Peter BIrch

had recently learned to swing a club again. The most special guest of all appeared on the Christmas show in 1953.

Mama was in town, and Jane brought her along to a meeting with Irving Mansfield, who planned the programs with Jane.

"How would you like to be on the Christmas show?" Mansfield asked Mama. She said that would be fine.

Apparently Jane forgot about it, but Mama didn't. Irving Mansfield didn't either. A few weeks before Christmas he called Jane and said "How about your mother on the show?"

Jane sent Mama a professional telegram.

CBS WILL PAY ALL EXPENSES FOR YOU TO APPEAR ON THE JANE FROMAN CHRISTMAS SHOW. WHEN IS SCHOOL OUT FOR VACATION AND WHEN CAN YOU GET HERE?

The answer came back right away.

SCHOOL'S OUT THE TWENTIETH. I'LL BE THERE ON THE TWENTY-FIRST.

Nearly eighty years old now, Mama still taught voice and piano at Stephens College in Columbia, where she had been on the faculty since 1945. Jane wrote:

> Mother bought a new dress for the show. Right before the program, she was as nervous as a cat, but when the show went on and my mother walked out, she was like a show business veteran. She sat down at the piano and she and I did a duet. Every one of Mama's silver curls was in place, and her voice was still strong.

After the show, Mansfield told Mama, "In case Jane ever wants to retire, I know who I can get."

Jane had never worked harder. She found the TV show an exciting challenge, one to which she could apply everything she had learned: bearing and gait; hand and arm movements; stage posture and facial expression when on camera. She was

With Mama on the Christmas show

determined to use whatever she had to give a darned good show. She learned the television business—camera angles, microphone techniques, staging and timing—just as she had in radio, night clubs and movies.

Her gowns, so much a part of her image, were created for the show by designer Florence Lustig, a friend of producer Irving Mansfield and his wife, author Jacqueline Susanne. Spectacular creations, almost invariably strapless with yards of tulle poofing out from the waist over many crinolines, the billowing skirts concealed the leg brace and gave Jane a look of feminine charm and elegance. Jane added elbow length gloves, tulle stoles, or scarves to camouflage the deep scar on her right arm, completing the illusion.

Some gowns were cut too low in the bosom for Jane's taste, but remembering her days in the Follies and many a backstage repair job under Fanny Brice's coaching, Jane kept needle and thread and extra tulle on hand to sew into the dresses to avoid showing too much cleavage. Jane was not a prude, but she was a smart businesswoman. Too much bosom might offend some of those who counted on her to maintain a particular image of propriety. It was with this same sensibility that she shrewdly steered away from sponsors that would be unbecoming to her image.

As the show took over more of Jane's time, she had had to hire a secretary. She had also bought a silver-gray Jaguar and hired a chauffeur to drive her to and from the studio and appointments around town. Some nights, on the way home from the show, if John were away on a flight, she would ask the driver to take her and her secretary, Joyce Lasky, out to Nathan's in Coney Island for a hot dog before returning to the brownstone.

Joyce had been George Wood's secretary at the William Morris Agency. Wood, Jane's agent for twenty years, had died suddenly of a heart attack, and Joyce was awaiting transfer to another department. Abe Lastfogel knew that Jane was looking for a private secretary. He phoned Joyce.

"Miss Froman is appearing in Cleveland at the Mounds. Fly out to see her. She's ready to hire a secretary."

"Oh, I couldn't do that," the mature twenty-year-old Joyce replied. Leaving like that on the spur of the moment for a job possibility that had no guarantees was not Joyce's style. She lived at home; her mother would be horrified. Joyce waited until Jane returned to the city from her engagement at the Chez Paree in Chicago, and made an appointment to see her.

"We hit it off right away," Joyce said.

Jane liked the pretty, well-spoken young woman and her eagerness to learn. Joyce was sweet, but she could be firm, and she had a practical side that impressed Jane. Before long, Joyce became Jane's right hand, not only taking dic-

Jane with Joyce Lasky

tation and answering fan mail, but running errands, helping her make costume changes, taking Jane's calls and speaking for her.

When John was away and Jane and Joyce worked late, Joyce stayed over, sleeping in the third floor room that served as her office. On those nights they would order take-out from a nearby Chinese restaurant, storing the leftovers in a small refrigerator that Jane kept in the office. The next day, they ate the cold leftovers for lunch.

When John was home between flights, the couple entertained their friends—from opera singers to John's flying buddies. Aileen Brenon had introduced the Burns to Mrs. Roosevelt, a close friend of hers, who took a particular liking to John. "She welcomed young people who were interested in politics," he explained in an interview, "and I asked a lot of brash questions, that today I shudder thinking about, about the behavior of her kids and their relationship with their father, and so on. She loved to say that she was not a sentimental person, and I'll tell you this story and let you judge." His admiration for her was clear as he told this story:

> It was a terrible night, thunder and lightning, pouring rain . . . and somewhere around 9:30 or 10 o'clock the doorbell rang. . . . I couldn't imagine who it was at this time of night. I went to the door, and there stands Mrs. R with a large bundle in her arms of wet newspapers. She said, "Johnny, be a dear and take care of the taxi for me will you? I'm going down into your kitchen." I said "Sure." So I went down to the kitchen and she was opening this thing out there—it was full of mint plants and she said, "I thought it might be something you'd like. I know you and Jane have been working on the garden in the back—"
>
> I looked at this a little bit puzzled, and she explained that she was one of the directors who maintained Jefferson's home, Monticello . . . and she had been down there that day.

She said, "I know your admiration for Jefferson, and," she said, "I know you're fond of me, and I thought you might like to have some mint for your garden—from a mint bed that was planted by Thomas Jefferson and was picked by me."

John shook his head. "I became unglued," he admitted. "And I said, 'You have the nerve to try to tell me you're not sentimental!'"

Jane tried to draw John into her career, but he chose to maintain the position of observer. As her husband, admirer, and amateur photographer, he left career management to the professionals, content to take pictures from a front row seat as Jane rehearsed. On one subject, however, he had a strong opinion. With her figure, Jane ought to wear gowns with a different line, contoured to hug the body. Jane considered the idea but continued to wear the bouffant style that the public had come to identify with her image.

Television shows were performed live in the 1950s, and the strain under which performers worked was huge. Jane had Dr. Kanev come before each show to relax her with a massage or sometimes to give her an adjustment, but there were times when even Dr. Kanev couldn't help her. When Jane had laryngitis or bursitis and couldn't perform, other singers would be brought in to do the show for her. One of these entertainers was a personable young man with a good voice by the name of Merv Griffin. CBS liked what he did subbing for Jane and hired him to co-star with singer Betty Ann Grove as the summer replacements for *The Jane Froman Show*.

Jane took a real vacation in the summer. She was tired after a season of her television show, and she just wanted to play a little golf and get in some relaxing time with John when he wasn't flying. At Fred Waring's resort in the Pocono

**Overseeing work at the E.
93rd Street brownstone**

Mountains, Shawnee-on-the-Delaware, she got off the putting green and hit her first golf ball since the crash.

At last, Jane had a home of her own, and a husband she truly loved with whom she could share it. This was also a good time to put into some serious decorating. Although her funds were not exactly unlimited, she had enough and planned to enjoy it. Life seemed pretty complete, except for the family she and John wanted. It was harder than she thought to have a baby. She saw doctor after doctor who found her perfectly capable of bearing a child, but she did not get pregnant. Hopeful, they kept trying. She wanted very much to have a baby.

Jane put her energy into making a beautiful home. The job came easily to her, with her natural sense of beauty and taste. Jane firmly believed a family's surroundings ought to reflect that family—its personality and its life. Mama sent Jane her grandmother's painted china, linen, silver, and a cutting from the rose bush that her grandmother had brought in a covered wagon to plant at her home in Clinton—a bit of Old Missouri, which became part of her decor. Their home was shaping up into a gracious, friendly one.

The first-floor living room and smaller parlor at the back of the house were almost complete. Downstairs, on the kitchen level, the dining room was yet to be done. The upstairs bedrooms, too, were still unfinished. There was no hurry. She had a fondness for antiques and searched until she found the right piece, or she would recognize it in the first five seconds spent in a shop. She was a regular at auctions. "Fifty-seventh Street knows me well!" she quipped. "They can smell me coming, I think!"

Jane bought John a small antique side table for his birthday. Her prize was a Queen Anne desk-secretary, but she was just as excited over a $9 cruet set she discovered. Her eyes lit up when she mentioned her six dining room chairs. It had taken quite a while to find six matching ones in the Queen Anne style she loved, but she was patient and finally acquired them. She recovered the seats with her own needlepoint. The rose-colored drapes that hung in the living room were from the end of the bolt used in the Rose Room at the White House. "Sloane's got it for me," she said with delight.

The house still needed pictures, although there was one—an oil portrait of Jane in cool pastel shades, predominantly blue, painted by artist Luis Corbellini. It was impressionistic in style, sad, slightly distorted. Draped over Jane's arm is a fold of sheer fabric, vaguely covering a dark mark. John said that Jane hated the portrait, but to friends she confessed feeling a peculiar attachment to it and took great pleasure in showing it off. The portrait always had a featured place in her home.

Corbellini had lived and painted in Paris, but visited this country—the West Coast—from time to time to exhibit his work. He was represented by Victor Hammer, a close friend of Jane, so it is possible the painter met Jane through that

The portrait of Jane by Corbellini

connection. It isn't clear exactly when Jane sat for the portrait, but it was after 1943, as she bears the scars of the crash,
and it had to be before 1952, when the portrait first appears
in photos of Jane in her home. Jane was not in Paris in that
period so she could have sat for it in New York, on one of
Corbellini's visits to the Hammer Galleries, or during one
of her stays on the West Coast, perhaps while the movie was
being made. The longer hair is also a clue; her hair was longer
before she cut it for her TV show.

John Burn said Corbellini, a flamboyant person who flaunted his colorful personality, had been quite a challenge to Jane, playing on her feminine charms. Jane let the painter know in her forthright manner that she was married, happily, and had no interest in his advances, but this must have been an enormous, if cockeyed, ego boost to a woman who saw the physical damage to her body every day.

Jane looked forward to the work that lay ahead. Right now her life was active, and full. When John was gone on flights, about a third of the month, she was busy with her show, or making gifts for birthdays and Christmas. She gave away dozens of rugs she hooked herself and hand-knitted baby sweaters, socks, mittens, stoles, scarves, and afghans. She even knit a dress for her mother.

Jane got John involved in her shows. He remembered:

> . . . she got me involved in everything. I was always on the lookout for new songs, because I knew her voice and the sort of thing that she did best, and I found it very interesting and was very pleased that she wanted my advice. But at one point she started talking to me about clothes! I doubted that she'd listen to me on that score, but I didn't buy her notion that because of her injury she could only wear bouffant dresses —you don't need armor plate to conceal the fact that you're wearing a brace—nobody can look under a long dress and see what you're wearing. I told her, "With your figure, I think you ought to wear more classic lines, what I would describe as Grecian." She tried it, and was very pleased with it. And here, she looked like she was in a hoop skirt all the time!

Jane did not have a whole lot of close friends because of her shyness, but among those who were close to her were

Victor and Ireene Hammer, actress Helen Menken, and Paul Draper, the dancer. Getting people together who had similar interesting tastes and styles was one of Jane's gifts. Deems Taylor was a favorite guest at her parties. Taylor told Jane he was a stutterer in his youth, and was taught to inhale before consonants. The word "hello" helped. He spoke beautifully. Interestingly, Paul Draper was also a stutterer.

On a daily basis, without the glow of celebrity and the sparkle of witty conversation, the brownstone had a down-to-earth quality. The smell of hops from the Rupert brewery on Third Avenue would come wafting into Joyce's third floor office. Jane kept all her awards in another room on that floor.

Upstairs, on the top floor of the brownstone, in a room furnished with two built-in racks, Jane kept her gowns. Some were from the early days of her career, including an early Valentino in flapper style.

More and more, Jane enjoyed just staying at home with John. They amused themselves playing poker and watching football on TV. They shared a good sense of humor and could laugh at themselves, remembering times like their first meeting in the Tagus River, that now sounded like a second-rate soap opera. John said that every time Jane hit a high note, another piece of the plane seemed to pop out of her skin.

John noticed that Jane enjoyed her isolation from the rest of the world. She found real contentment in being alone, just the two of them; out of the whirl that a life in show business forced on her so much of the time. He, on the other hand, loved meeting people, traveling. Jane was excellent company and he wanted to share his favorite places with her—Paris, for example, which he knew well and loved. Each seemed to bask in exactly what the other didn't want or need.

Still, life was swimming along, with Jane and John playing their parts as the lovers of destiny in their storybook romance. Jane continued to take drugs to alleviate the wracking pain she still often felt from her injuries, but they had not affected her voice, and it was easy enough to ignore a potential problem when things were looking and feeling so good.

The only blot on the horizon now was having to go through the accident all over again, because the lawsuit that Jane had brought against Pan American was about to go to trial.

16

THE TRIAL
1953

TEN YEARS AFTER the Clipper crash, Jane's suit against Pan American Airways came to trial on March 10, 1953, in New York County Supreme Court. She had had twenty-seven operations to save her leg, fighting every doctor's advice to let the leg go. She had had a breakdown over her constant battle against infection, and only her strong will and motivation to be of some help to others had gotten her through this far. Pushing forward with her life meant no looking back. Now, because she had to, she lived the experience over again.

Accompanied by John, Jane walked into the crowded court room on the first day wearing a gray checked suit and a black hat with red flowers. Judge Aron Steuer presided over a jury consisting of eight men and four women. The 200 seats in the courtroom were filled, and spectators were being turned away at the doors.

Jane had hired attorney Harry Gair, who was known for his astute handling of negligence cases, and who was particularly successful in cases against domestic airlines. Gair had not lost a jury verdict in ten years. He hired a young attorney to assist, Stuart M. Speiser, who was a pilot himself and familiar with aviation law.

The suit was not going to be an easy one to win. Pan Am had grown into the world's leading international airline, flying to sixty-two countries on five continents, and the Warsaw Convention—a treaty signed in 1929 when air travel was new—protected the airline from claims like Jane's.

Jane had first brought suit in 1944, a year after the crash, asking damages of $1,000,000, but in a series of legal moves and countermoves, Pan Am succeeded in getting the suit dismissed on the grounds that the Warsaw Convention limited damages for death or injury in an international flight to about $8,300. The $8,300 limit did not apply, however, if the airline failed to deliver a ticket without notice of the Warsaw Convention printed on it, if the transportation was provided by the U. S. Government, or if it could be proved that the accident was caused by "willful misconduct" by airline personnel. The plaintiffs had spent years gathering evidence to support this last exception, their only hope. By the time the suit finally came to trial, Jane had spent months of her life in hospitals, suffered through dozens of operations, and medical bills were still accruing. She had increased her demand to $2,500,000, for medical expenses and loss of earnings while hospitalized. Gypsy Markoff joined in the suit with a demand for another million.

Don Ross, as usual clinging to Jane's success for his own gain, was also suing Pan American Airways. He had not even a sprained pinky from the accident, but felt it had cost him his marriage, which inevitably meant his meal ticket, to the tune of a million dollars.

Jane could not talk about her experience without emotion. She agonized at having to relive the Lisbon crash and the medical ordeals that followed it. It was one thing to put on a pleasant face in public, and to let fan magazines talk about her struggle to overcome her physical limitations.

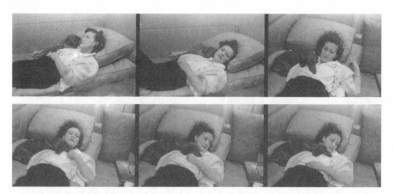

Jane, at home, resting her leg on a particularly trying day

In reality, when there was no stage or microphone nearby nor strangers waiting to be entertained, Jane was still a shy woman who did not like to dwell on the painful past. She still had nightmares when she was overtired. If she sensed the topic was coming up during a conversation, she would offer tea or coffee to her company, or dash out of the room for something she'd forgotten, anything to lead the talk in another direction. If John were around, he would generally take over the story for her.

For the period of the trial, John was on a temporary leave of absence. When reporters asked Jane if John's job with Pan American made her suit against them embarrassing, she answered, wisely, "I don't think so. This is an entirely separate matter. If John was injured in the CBS building where I work I wouldn't be embarrassed."

When Jane took the stand on the third day of the trial, the courthouse was again packed. She was nervous, stammering as she spoke. "I have a speech impediment," she informed the court as she testified, halting when the memories became too painful. When she removed the jacket to her suit, her short-sleeved black silk blouse revealed long scars on her right arm.

Jane testified to the landing of the *Yankee Clipper* as the others had. It was dusk as the plane approached Lisbon and she could see the outline of the hills back of the town. There was a storm over the hills, and she saw flashes of lightning.

"What happened then?" asked her counsel, Harry Gair, slowly guiding her through her testimony, allowing for pauses when she hit an emotional moment, as in the moment of impact, when she fell silent for a moment, or as Harry Gair read the dire reports of her physical condition, taking her through years of surgery, during which she stuttered badly. Gair asked, at one point, if her stuttering interfered with her singing. Jane smiled and answered, "No, it doesn't."

Her testimony became more difficult as she was asked to identify photos as they were held up for exhibit, showing what the accident did to her legs through repeated operations. The jury saw a left leg that was slender and shapely—and a withered right one that looked like nearly fleshless bone. This leg was the one that was supported with a metal and leather brace from knee to ankle.

When Jane left the stand, in tears, doctors, including an orthopedic specialist, took over, describing her injuries in detail. Her wasted right leg, they reported, was heavily scarred and measured a full inch shorter than the left. She could no longer place her foot flat on the ground. Without the support of the sturdy brace and specially made shoe, she could not stand on that leg or she would re-fracture it.

Gair read various hospital reports revealing Jane's emotional state following the air disaster: "Patient very depressed—patient feels life has nothing to offer." "Pain very severe in right leg—patient asks 'give me a strong hypo—maybe I will be able to sleep and forget.'" "Patient very depressed. Wants to die."

Defense counsel William J. Junkerman contended that the accident had been a boon to the singer, citing her earnings while on crutches and braces were higher than those prior to the crash and at present she was earning $4,000 a week for two fifteen-minute television shows a week, plus record royalties.

On the eighth day of the trial, both sides had presented their cases and while it had looked good for Jane, the mood changed swiftly when Justice Steuer charged the jury, advising them on the law that was applicable to the claims charged. Steuer began a long-winded discourse leading the jury to observations and conclusions that leaned heavily on the side of the airline.

First, he lectured them for nearly ten minutes about letting sympathy get in the way of their decision. If he had seemed cool to the plaintiffs before, he was totally devoid of compassion now. He described the Warsaw Convention as a wonderful bit of insurance that made certain passengers were reimbursed for their losses, without mentioning the limitations of that compensation. Finally, he bent the phrase "willful misconduct" to mean that the pilot not only had to have intended to crash but also meant for the results of that crash to happen—a preposterous notion. Appeals by the defense were rejected. Requests for further illumination were denied.

Jane must have felt the chill in the courtroom when the jury returned with its verdict after two hours of deliberation.

They had absolved the airline of blame for the crash in an eleven to one vote against the plaintiffs. Jane and Gypsy broke down in tears. They had not proved "willful disregard on the part of the pilot" and therefore Judge Steuer was bound by the rules of the antiquated Warsaw Convention. He awarded to Jane and to Gypsy limited damages of $8,300 plus $750 for lost luggage—$9,050 each.

As in other difficult times in her life, Jane's back was straight and her head was high as she left the courtroom. On the way home from the court house she sat in the car quietly, John on one side, Joyce on the other, her thoughts to herself.

At home she couldn't sit still and paced the floor, venting her anger at the outcome of the trial, filling the profound silence. That small print on the back of every airline ticket, based on an agreement drawn when international air travel had barely begun, was the final winner in the suit. This was a bitter blow.

The only justice that seemed to come out of the trial was the outcome for Don Ross, who received nothing but a tongue-lashing when Judge Steuer chastised him for his claim that the accident cost him an idyllic home life. Don had revealed the private details of his marital situation before the public to gain support for his claim that the accident had broken up his marriage, his contention being that disagreements over Jane's medical treatments and her nature under the influence of pain medications had resulted in "lack of services." Few people in the courtroom, including the jurors, could listen to his testimony without squirming.

Stuart Speiser, one of Jane's lawyers, wrote in his book, *Lawyers and the American Dream:*

Don Ross reached a new low in morality, even for him, by attempting to collect a chunk of the $9,050 that Jane Froman finally received from Pan Am for her injuries. The fact that all her lawyers had waived their fees and expenses so that Jane could get the benefit of that miniscule compensation did not deter Ross from claiming most of it for himself.

It would hardly enhance the court's opinion of this so-called "perfect partnership," Steuer told Ross, to learn that he sought to be recompensed out of Miss Froman's funds.

The case was later appealed, citing that Jane's passage was bought by the United States government under an arrangement with the USO, but she lost again.

Jane would continue to work for many more years to pay her medical bills, and would never walk again without the metal and leather brace on her right leg. Her heated anger at the mean-spiritedness of Justice Aron Steuer's behavior and at the injustice of the decision died down over time but was never quite extinguished. Over the years one could still see it smoldering when Jane talked about the unfairness of the small print on the back of every plane ticket—the Warsaw Convention—and advised everyone she knew to take additional insurance before boarding a flight.

Although the amount of compensation under the Convention was increased by amendment to $75,000 in 1966, the pact remains an outmoded relic in this day of commonplace jet air travel.

PART III

17

THE STOOP SITTERS' SOCIETY
1953

AFTER the release of *With a Song in My Heart*, teenage fans seemed to appear out of nowhere. Adolescents, whose parents might have seen Jane at the Roxy or heard her in the heyday of radio, were an unexpected delight for Jane. Bright, eager, and bursting with youthful energy, they were at the stage door following every TV show and sent cards and letters pouring out their hearts.

Jane had known ardent fans before. There was Stella Kingsbury, of course, the fan from Syracuse, who had given her the little gold cross that she now kept always by her bedside, draped by its chain around her alarm clock. Others wrote to her over the years, bought her records, listened to her faithfully on the radio, and even petitioned Congress in her behalf. Long after the war, Jane still received mail from ex-servicemen who were devoted to her.

Now, a decade later, there were fan clubs popping up for her everywhere—not of servicemen, but of high school kids. The first one had surfaced in Chicago, shortly after the release of *With a Song in My Heart*. The movie fan magazines spread the word about the clubs, and soon there were several. There was even one for Jane and John together.

Jane knew the importance of fan clubs to a star's career—these young people were buying up her records and watching her shows—but that wasn't all. These kids saw in her a role model. Her personal struggle had moved them, and she felt a responsibility to make herself accessible to them.

Mostly girls, with a few males spread among them, the fans represented thousands of teenagers across the country and beyond who adored Jane. A devoted group in the New York area called themselves "The Fromanettes," came to the live telecasts, and began to meet on Saturdays on the stoop of her brownstone. They compared their latest photos, magazine articles and records, chatted about the shows, DJs who played Jane's records, and anything else even vaguely about Jane. Often Jane looked out from her third floor bedroom window and chatted with them. It was great fun having them around. When she left the house to go shopping, she stopped to talk to them, getting to know them by name.

Windy, Deena, Babs, and Joan (half hidden) on the stoop

"Where's the gal with the big brown eyes?" she asked one day.

"Babs? She couldn't come. She had to take care of her little sister," Windy explained.

"Look, Jane," said Joan, twisting around. On the back of her red jeans was stitched *Jane* on one pocket and *John* on the other.

Jane's laughter was her immediate response. "Joan, you're wonderful!" she cried.

Deena showed Jane a scar she had between her thumb and index finger in the shape of a J. The most horrified look came across Jane's face.

"Deena! Y-y-y-you didn't . . ."

"Oh no," Deena assured her. "I didn't do it on purpose. It's from an old cut. I just thought it was funny that it was in the shape of a J."

Jane's relief was genuine. "I hope you'll never do anything so foolish," she said, concerned as she stared into Deena's worshiping eyes.

In these brief encounters a connection was made. Jane found herself looking forward to seeing the girls, listening to their stories about school and boys and parents, worrying about them. They amused her with their youthful exuberance and creative imaginations, referring to themselves as "The Stoop Sitters Society." Eventually, the girls began calling her "Aunt Jane," and she loved it.

Even Mama, when she came to visit, loved talking to the girls. She brought them candy, sat on the stoop with them, and chatted. She got into the spirit, too, and soon found herself writing postcards to the girls on a regular basis.

The Fromanettes had sweaters made up with the club

Jane's curtsy at the end of every TV show became a tradition.

name across the back. They met whenever they weren't in school, usually at one of the girls' houses. Parents seemed slightly overwhelmed by the lively group, but most welcomed them and made their homes available for meetings, record-playing, and endless chatter.

Jane saw to it that Joyce placed reserved tickets at CBS's Studio 50 stage door each week for the Fromanettes, and arranged for them to attend rehearsals. To Jane, who had been such a lonely child, with her mother her closest and often her only friend, it was a thrill to watch these gregarious youngsters with their thirst for life.

Sometimes Jane's mood was dark or troubled and it touched the girls, but they were too young and idealistic to see the larger issues that might be facing their idol. They rallied after these occasional cool moments from Jane, and Jane did not harbor any anger or discomfort from one meeting to the next. She continued to show great affection for them and was constantly amused by their antics, so far removed from her own strictly supervised girlhood.

At a concert in Central Park in which Jane was scheduled to sing, the girls arrived, unaware that they needed tickets to get in. Jane could not help this time—tickets were not in her control. She was tickled afterward to hear that they had devised a clever plan to get in—by helping band members carry in their instruments.

Another time, she was ill and had to miss a show, and the girls chipped in to buy her flowers. At the last moment, as the flowers were placed in the delivery truck, the girls persuaded the driver to let them be "delivered" with the flowers. Sick as she was, Jane laughed at the sheer fun of it.

John was adored along with Jane, and met the challenge. When Ellen G. asked him to write a piece for the next fan club journal, he agreed to it, but when it did not arrive immediately, Ellen got on his case. He responded with quick wit and charm.

A Studio 50 ticket for The Jane Froman Show

Dear Ellen,

I want to thank you for reminding me that I have not sent you an explanation as to why I have not yet written the article for which you asked.

This has been thoughtless of me and I hope you'll forgive me this time.

I did explain why I was unable to do the article before Christmas. (I was unexpectedly called for a trip to London.)

As for my failure to do it since then, I'd like to explain that my work has allowed me to spend very little time at home in the past year. I'm sure you'll understand that Jane is the most important and wonderful thing in my life—as well as my favorite singer. So perhaps you won't blame me if I have used all available time just enjoying the nearness of the one I love.

The article you shall have as soon as possible. One point in this regard; where did you get the idea that it would require no thought on my part?! Ask for discourse on Napoleon or Frederick the Great—no thought. About my wife—come, come, what can you be thinking of?!!

Why don't you suggest what you would like for me to write about Jane?

Yours,
John Burn

The girls tried to be like Jane in every way they could, sometimes to the point of ludicrous mimicry. They walked like Jane, talked like Jane, added "Jane" to their own names and signed themselves "Fromanly yours." Some used makeup far too advanced for their young faces, and they all bought the brands that Jane used—from Coca-Cola to Revlon's *Moon Drops* and Guerlain's *Shalimar.*

Since Jane smoked, the girls did that, too. Smoking in the 1950s was promoted as attractive, with movies and advertisements showing beautiful people, in sophisticated poses, holding cigarettes to their lips. The girls watched their idol take a dramatic puff of her cigarette and nonchalantly blow smoke into their midst, and soon after, chipped in and bought Jane's brand of cigarettes, Parliaments, then in their vogue in a unique gold and white box. They passed it around when they met on the stoop on Saturdays. A box could last for several weeks.

Their enthusiasm sometimes got them into trouble. One Saturday, as Jane practiced a number with her accompanist in the living room, the girls sat on the stoop, sharing magazines, listening. The song was bouncy. They moved up the steps to hear better. At the very top, they moved onto the door sill and Ellen S. pressed her ear against the big oak door, while Deena climbed on the small railing to lean over and take a peek inside. Jane happened to look up at that moment. Seconds later, the door opened and Ellen fell in at Jane's feet.

The look on Jane's face said it all. The girls gathered their belongings, said they were sorry, and left. They knew they had crossed a line.

Jane not only loved hearing their stories; she answered their letters, sent them postcards when she went on vacation, and supported their efforts to run a good club. When some of them seemed to be undisciplined, lonely or troubled, she never gave advice but listened, something she did so well. A rare few had run away from home, appearing on her doorstep. Jane saw to it that their distraught parents were contacted and they were sent safely home to work out their problems, sometimes with references for professional help to guide them. She was thrilled and proud of each new fan club journal and told them so. Her initial surprise at the teen fans gave way to a deeper understanding.

"I couldn't figure it out at first," she said. "Then I realized that every young girl dreams of overcoming some big obstacle and finding the right guy. I guess I sort of became the symbol of that dream."

On Jane's birthday, the girls arrived at Studio 50 during

rehearsal with a cake. Joan, president of the fan club, asked Jane if she had a favorite cause that they could adopt as their pet charity. An idea of a similar nature had been working in Jane's mind from the time the girls first started showing up regularly at her shows and on her stoop with all sorts of small gifts—all affectionately bestowed. And she remembered the children at Southard School, who had so moved her. This could be a way of redirecting their well-meant generosity to- ward a more important cause. She said she would let them know, and soon after, she sent out invitations to a party at her house on February 13, 1954, to discuss it.

"Hi, darlings!" she greeted them at the door as they ar- rived, her bright eyes glowing. "Put your coats upstairs and then come and meet everybody." Eva Davis, Jane's devoted housekeeper, showed them to Jane's bedroom, where they left their coats on the bed. They memorized everything about the room and went downstairs to join the party.

Jane's grand piano, the one they knew so well from pictures in fan magazines and which had been played by famous guests like Deems Taylor, as well as by Jane and her accompanists, sat at one end of the spacious living room. They recognized the elegant rose colored draperies that hung at the front windows; they had been featured in magazines, too. The girls had read every article about Jane and had seen all the pictures.

In the less formal parlor at the back of the house, people milled about, chatting, looking out over the terrace and gar- den. There were about a dozen youngsters and a few older people. John was among them, his camera in hand.

Over the sofa hung a portrait of Jane, in predominant shades of blue. Bobbie stared at it.

"Do you like it?" Jane asked, coming up behind her.

First party at Jane's house. Everyone sat on the floor, even Jane.

"I—don't know. It doesn't look like you."

Jane giggled. "Yes, but it does show the *suffering*." Anyone close to Jane knew she was no tragic figure; the irony seemed to amuse her.

The girls gathered in the cozy parlor, most of them sitting on the floor. It was hard to believe that Jane sat there with them, cross-legged, in spite of the brace she wore. Her eyes sparkled as flashbulbs went *pop—pop—pop* constantly. She didn't complain, listening intently to what each girl had to say.

When lunch was served, Jane led them downstairs to the dining room. The table, neatly arranged buffet style with assorted sandwiches, overlooked the patio and garden, now in repose for the winter. Cokes flowed freely as Jane and the girls talked and laughed.

Nobody noticed as Eva brought out a cake and began to light the sixteen candles on it. The noise died down and everyone gasped, especially Babs, surprised that anyone had remembered, in the shadow of the party at Jane's, that today was her "sweet sixteen" birthday. Having a round of "Happy Birthday" sung to her, led by Jane, made up for it a dozen times over.

After everyone had finished eating and chatting, Jane began to unfold her plan. She introduced noted psychiatrist, Dr. William C. Menninger, her old friend from the Menninger Foundation. She referred to him as "Dr. Will."

"You asked about a pet charity for the club," Jane said. She told them she had attempted to start a charity for mentally disturbed children once before, and had asked the help of well-known people. Their reaction had been one of discomfort and avoidance; disturbing topics like mental illness just weren't talked about in polite society.

Jane told them that she knew firsthand how important it was to recognize and deal with mental problems. She remembered being a patient herself at the Menninger Foundation in Topeka, Kansas, when she had been at the breaking point. She never forgot the young people she met at Southard School, the children's division of Menningers, when she herself had been a patient. She thought this would be a wonderful pet charity if the girls liked the idea.

She had talked it over with Dr. Will, the man who had helped Jane overcome her own breakdown a few years before. She told him of her idea to engage the Fromanettes with their energy and ebullience, demonstrated in so many loving acts directed toward her, in a cause to help the children of Southard School. He thought it was a fine idea and said he would do his part in getting the wheels turning.

Jane put it to the girls. Were they willing to adopt the

plan? The clubs could raise money for a scholarship for a child at the Clinic.

The girls eagerly accepted the challenge, thrilled that Jane would consider asking them to play an important part in her dream. There were many steps ahead to legalizing the proposal, to register it and have it approved as a bona fide charitable organization according to the laws of the State of New York, but Jane was willing to take it through whatever channels were necessary.

The Fromanettes were the first on board, but all of Jane's fan clubs—The Golden Tones, The Burning Brights, the Fromaneers—ultimately responded enthusiastically and came up with their own creative ideas. Diane L. raised a champion show dog, "Fromaneer," and turned over the money from the sale of the dog's puppies to the charity. Luanne, president of the California fan club, started "Operation Jokebook," inviting members to send in jokes, each with a two-cent entry fee that would go to the charity; the resulting book of all the jokes would be sent to a hospital for disabled vets. Babs organized a penny fair at her church in Weehawken, New Jersey, where children and adults could play various games of skill and chance for a penny and win prizes. The pennies added up. Windy carried around a roll of adhesive tape, asking people to stick their spare change onto the tape for Southard School. Soon all the girls were carrying rolls of tape.

Jane's instincts about the girls had been good, and belief in them had paid off. Their youthful enthusiasm and open-mindedness was just what she needed to throw herself into the project. They took on raising funds for Southard School with a passion not unlike her own.

They produced a fan club journal, *The Velvet Chords*,

Bibs, Joan and Babs printing the club journal

containing articles, poems and news about their pet charity, Jane's recordings and appearances—written by the fans or people they admired like Mrs. Hetzler, John, or Sid Feller. Jane delighted at the enterprise as well as the artistic talent showing through the journal's contents. She purchased a mimeograph machine for them to make the job easier and more cost-efficient. Bibs's mom let them keep it in her Brooklyn basement, which is where they printed each issue while Windy used a makeshift bathroom darkroom in the Bronx to print out photos to glue onto its pages.

Along with the fans came the fan magazines. Articles on Jane appeared regularly. Stories of her courage and determination to walk again were now common knowledge, but there was an ever increasing interest in the public mind about what it was that had sustained her through so much. Jane had once described how music had helped her; doctors could report on her recovery from a purely medical standpoint. What about her faith? It had been tested time and again. How had she held on to it through all she had been through? What did she herself have to say about her own beliefs?

In typical midwestern fashion, Jane had been brought up with Christian values, going to Calvary Episcopal Church on Sunday, singing in the choir, attending church social events and helping the less fortunate. Her roots were strong, but her beliefs had always been a private, personal affair. They were not something you talked about; they were something you lived, every day.

Stirred by the mail she received in response to articles in the magazines and her recording of "I Believe," Jane became less uneasy talking about her more private self. It was in her nature—and in her upbringing—to share any experience if it could help others. An excellent writer, she even wrote some personal experience stories herself, and talked about her faith in God.

Never one to take herself too seriously, she also reminded people, with a gleam in her eye, that she was from Missouri, the "Show me!" state. Stubbornness was in every Missourian's DNA, and it had served her well.

18

ILLUSION
1954

THE JANE FROMAN Show was renewed again for the 1954-55 season. Jane was at a good place in her career. Talking to reporters who clamored for interviews, she told them she loved television. "It doesn't really feel like hard work when you like it as much as I do."

In spite of her enormous success, or perhaps in part because of it, Jane and John were having difficulties keeping their storybook marriage intact. There were problems that might have been anticipated from the beginning, but perhaps they had always looked at each other through the particular scene in the Tagus River, when they clung to each other for everything. The strain of all those years of hospitals and operations, the constant pressure to pay off the bills, the stress of trying unsuccessfully for a family, and now a career that demanded her full time attention, plus John's shattered nerves from his second plane crash—all of it was catching up to them.

Probably more than anything else, Jane's dependency was putting a strain on their relationship. It's true that she leaned on alcohol, but as time went on, it was her dependency on John that wore down their marriage. She wanted more from him than he could provide.

Understandably, Jane was fearful about John flying, but

trying to talk him into giving it up, and suggesting that he become her manager, was a mistake. John was horrified at the idea of a rank amateur like himself assuming responsibility for a career like hers. That had been a fatal element in her marriage to Don. He wouldn't consider it.

Even more difficult was Jane's desire to shut themselves off from the world and live like hermits. They would go for months, and outside of professional contacts, not see anyone at all.

Jane had the most extraordinary charm, and could cover up her shyness to entertain. Then she would seem like the most gregarious person and be a marvelous hostess, but at great cost. Afterward, she would be exhausted and irritable because the tension had been so great. Quarrels would erupt over nothing at all, simply from the emotional strain.

They were pulling in two different directions. It got to the point where John seriously considered leaving and discussed it with Dr. Kubie. The doctor agreed, for Jane's benefit, but he wanted to time it. Jane had to learn to stand on her own, but he thought he'd be the one to decide when she was ready.

When Jane became aware of Kubie's role in John's decision, she was furious. She blamed him for destroying their marriage. John didn't think Kubie deserved the blame; he believed the psychiatrist had tried to help them. In the end they separated. It was a combination of things—the irrational quarrels that came while Jane was drinking, and the demands on John that he couldn't fulfill—and didn't want to, for fear they would destroy them both.

In February, John finally got Jane to travel with him to Paris, her first visit there since performing with her USO troupe in 1945—and her first time on a plane since John's crash in Puerto Rico. She thought after that she would never fly again, but the only way they could swing ten days together in Paris was to fly—and even then she had to miss one show.

Aware of the exhaustive training pilots went through, plus the statistics about flight safety, Jane knew intellectually flying was the safest means of travel, yet she couldn't help being nervous. With a handful of Bonamines from her doctor, she got on the plane.

In Paris, they avoided big hotels and fancy restaurants. Like honeymooners, they found a charming little French hotel with a courtyard, where tea and little cakes were served in the afternoon. John, an experienced traveler, knew many intimate restaurants off the tourist trail, and they would order cocktails, linger over a delicious dinner with a bottle of wine, and talk, something they didn't have much time for at home, with the hustle of TV rehearsals and John's flights. Nobody recognized Jane, so there was no fawning over her or special treatment; people were kind to her for no other reason than they wanted to be.

She came back from Paris with her spirits high, humming "I Love Paris" as she swept through the studio to her dressing room after a show.

The restorative effects of the trip to Paris began to wear off almost immediately back in New York, where she was once again dealing with the pressures of two weekly television shows and the preparation of a new night club act. Jane Froman was returning to the Copacabana.

Jane's appearance at the Copa eight years earlier was under markedly different circumstances. She had been propped up on the motorized platform with a mechanical device to move her around the floor with her pianist because she couldn't stand on her own.

The day before Jane's opening, she ran around, talking to electricians about getting the spotlight just right; running through a song with her conductor, Hank Sylvern; tapping her foot to the beat; stopping to say hello to someone who had just walked in; discussing an arrangement with Sid Feller. There was no outward clue that this was the same person who had been on the same floor, on a moveable platform, eight years earlier. The irony was not lost on the critics on opening night, as they all fell under her spell.

> "Jane Froman, opening brilliantly at the Copa, mentioned Ike throwing out the first ball 'when he'd rather have thrown out a couple of Senators.'"
> —Earl Wilson—*New York Post*

> "A real pro of show-business in my book . . . Jane Froman is singing as only Jane Froman can. Never mind the titles because she makes all songs sound better. Singing is her business and she certainly knows her business. . . .
> —Gene Knight—*New York Journal-American*

> "Miss Jane Froman . . . hypnotizes the audience with her music-magic. She has a way with a tune that makes you think each note was custom-tailored for her exclusive use. . . ."
> —Hy Gardner—*New York Herald-Tribune*

> "JANE IS SUPREME in the vocal department. Her deep, rich voice, with organ-like qualities, stirs listeners as no one currently around."
> —Lee Mortimer—*New York Mirror*

". . . Jane Froman received an unprecedented ovation—
the only word to use—as she came on to sing—and even a
greater one when she finished her act."

—Louis Sobel—*New York Journal-American*

". . . she is dynamic. . . . it was a personal triumph of the
sort that makes show business the business there is none
like."   *—Variety*

It was clear that the show was put together by a pro.
After an entertaining warmup by the Kirby Stone Quartet
and comic George DeWitt, the lights dimmed and soft
music played under the host's offstage voice announcing
". . . Jane Froman!"

The light had never gone out of her sparkling blue eyes,
nor had her spirit been dampened by the years of struggle it
had taken to reach this point. Her brunette hair pulled back
regally, she appeared in a platinum peau de soie coat lined
with orange velvet, which she slipped off to reveal a matching gown trimmed in exquisite embroidery and tiny antique
pearls. The audience applauded before she had sung a single
note.

When they settled down, Jane crooned the Peggy Lee–
Victor Young ballad, "Where Can I Go Without You?"
followed by a cheerful pick-me-upper, "It's a Great Life"
from Cole Porter's *Red, Hot and Blue!*, a song that appeared
regularly in her shows. Two ballads came next, "Here" and
the popular "Young at Heart," to which she added special
lyrics to name a few people who were especially young at
heart—Sophie Tucker, Marlene Dietrich, President Eisenhower—and maybe a touch too young at heart—Porfirio
Rubirosa, the international playboy then making headlines

for his jet set lifestyle and legendary dalliances with well-known women.

Jane then asked the stage crew to bring out the expensive prop the Copa had arranged for her next number. A single waiter brought a stool over to Jane, for which she thanked him, bringing a laugh from the audience. Perched on it, with Hank Sylvern accompanying her at the piano, she sang a medley of tunes from her movie biography: "Tea for Two," "I'll Walk Alone," "Embraceable You," "Get Happy," and "With a Song in My Heart." The show ended with Jane taking two bows.

The image of grace and beauty that Jane had created for her public was in her control but not so her tolerance for alcohol.

John Burn recalled, "It wasn't so much the amount that she drank but the changes in her personality that it caused. I think the best description of her personality I ever heard came from Larry Kubie, who said Jane was the most winning person you would ever know . . . here is this lady with all of her celebrity—she was such a wonderful human being—and that made it all the more painful to see the changes when she drank. It didn't take very much. . . . I was never concerned about her becoming an alcoholic but I didn't like the changes it caused in her. . . ." John believed she was just one of those people whose systems cannot take alcohol, and at those times she was difficult—she could cut and demean.

Joyce, working with her on a daily basis, had seen Jane at moments like these, and had learned to stay out of her way. Once, when she was new at the job, and Jane struggled to get a word out, Joyce mistakenly offered her the word to make it easier. In return she received a ferocious glare from Jane that she remembered with a chill many years later. She learned quickly, however, and the two got along famously.

John found it remarkable that when others were around Jane could cleverly keep her secret. Even Jane's good friend Ruth Barnard, a frequent house guest, had never observed a problem with Jane's drinking and Ruth had been Jane's therapist.

Agreeing to try to work out their problems, Jane and John kept up a brave and loving public front. It is no wonder their marriage was under a strain. The effort that must have gone into protecting their public image on all counts was probably, in the end, loosening the bolts that had held it together.

Among the first to know about Jane and John's problem were the girls, although they didn't know why and were only able to guess. One Saturday at the stoop, no one seemed to be home; there was no sign of Jane or Eva; there wasn't even a sound from Til Eulenspiegel. Deena and Ellen G. arrived early to find Joan already waiting on the top step. Windy arrived a little later, then Babs, who had to come into Port Authority by bus from New Jersey. Last were Bobbie and Bibs.

In the small tiled front yard of the brownstone, the trash cans were neatly lined up, ready for pickup by the Sanitation Department. Later on, nobody could remember how it had happened, but someone—perhaps looking for a memento from their beloved Jane—found a scrap of paper with the names "Jane" and "John"—a score of some kind, maybe from a card game. Excitement grew over their find and they continued to search. There was a torn page from an account book showing household expenses, a thank you note from a guest at a recent party, and a discarded sheet of the familiar pale blue Saks Fifth Avenue stationery with Jane's personal imprint across the left hand corner embossed in red. Something was written on it—in Jane's handwriting. They ran off, away from the house, to read their prize in the doorway of a shop on Madison Avenue. Some words had been stricken out as Jane composed a note. . . .

> Dear John,
> You are probably right in your decision that we be apart.
> Dr. Kubie says if this separation is to continue . . . (stricken)
> Please let me know what to do with your clothes—
> My love darling,
> Jane

Slowly, the girls absorbed the shock of what they had discovered, and the seriousness of their intrusion. Safely away from the brownstone, they read the letter again, choking on the words.

What could they do? They could not say anything to Jane; in public, they were the same old Jane and John the girls had always known—John came down to the studio and they were just as loving toward each other as always. They had gone on a romantic trip to Paris together. No one would ever guess anything was wrong between them.

The girls—Joan, Deena, Windy, Babs, Bobbie, Bibs, and Ellen G.—decided emphatically to say nothing to anybody, lest newspapers and magazines get hold of it. They vowed to keep the secret among themselves. With all in agreement, Deena copied the letter carefully on a page of her school notebook, imitating Jane's backward slanted script, then Joan folded the letter and tore the original into eight even pieces, with each of the girls getting a segment and tossing away the odd segment with no writing on it. As they tucked their sacred scraps into their wallets, their hearts ached—Jane and John, the perfect couple in the love match of the century—were breaking up.

A worried neighbor, concerned about seeing kids rummaging through the trash, phoned Jane, and she called the girls together for a short visit.

"I think you'd better not come around for a while," she said, pausing. "There have been complaints from the neighbors. And they're right, you know?" she added, without mentioning specific transgressions. The girls took the advice and stopped coming to the stoop, while Jane, a conscientious neighbor, hired a private collection agency to pick up her trash. Perhaps she surmised the extent of the girls' snooping, but she never mentioned it that day, nor did she bring it up again.

John might have been better able to cope if he weren't having problems of his own. Ever since his plane went down off Puerto Rico in 1952, he had been under a terrific strain, with the enormous loss of lives weighing heavily on him. In the Lisbon crash lives were lost, too, but he had not been at the controls of the plane. The tragedy caused him great mental anguish, in spite of the rescue efforts he had made and the lives he did save.

Following the disaster, when Pan Am tried to claim pilot error rather than mechanical failure for the disaster, John had to fight with everything he had to clear his name and fly again as a pilot for the airline. The strain cost him dearly. Jane had encouraged him to talk to Dr. Kubie, her own psychiatrist. Kubie was a most extraordinary man, in that he dismissed the traditions of classical analysis to know what was going on with the stresses and strains of a patient's life.

It was with this attitude that a friendship formed between him and John. And it was Dr. Kubie's suggestion that Jane and John try living apart.

John moved to a nearby apartment to try to work out his problems. He and Jane agreed to continue with the public illusion of their happy marriage.

Work on her television show consumed Jane's long days and lonely nights. She made public relations trips for her sponsor, General Electric. She pored through hundreds of pages of music to select the ballads that had been her standards over the years and worked on arrangements to help build her shows around the works of songwriters she admired. She kept up with her young fans, who had turned into the most constant of friends through this stressful time in her life. Their love and support lightened her days and gave her comfort when her marriage to John ruptured.

The girls were invited over to Jane's house for another party. A few—Alice, Carol S. and Joann among them—came in from out of town. John was not around; it was just Jane and Til. They talked for hours. They ran through what the various fan clubs had done to raise money for the charity and caught up on everyone's latest news.

Win had joined the Navy in January and was home on leave. When she had arrived that afternoon, Jane had hushed them all and made them salute as Win walked into the room. It cracked Win up and they all had a good laugh. They made Win tell them all about the Navy. The only sea duty she had seen so far had been on an officer's yacht, where there was a party, and she had passed her swimming test swimming from one end of the thirty-foot pool to another holding her breath because she didn't know how to swim and breathe at the same time.

They stopped for lunch, then all gathered around the Steinway to sing while Ellen S. played song after song by ear. Jane curled up in the arm chair and lit a cigarette, while some of the girls stood by the piano and others sat on the floor. Carol S. was on the floor near Jane. As they sang, Jane leaned over her.

"I want to hear you sing something by yourself," Jane said.

Nervously, Carol told her she was not prepared, but Jane coaxed her into it, and Ellen said she'd try to help. Carol knelt on the floor near Jane and sang "You'll Never Walk Alone." Luckily, Ellen was able to play it in the original key of C, with no music. Jane sat back and listened.

"Have you ever taken lessons?" she asked.

"No," the sixteen-year-old answered, shakily.

"You should study," Jane told her. "Your voice has a unique and lovely quality to it."

Carol, who had been timid in pursuing a vocal career, began voice lessons not long after.

Jane's show was running for its third year. Jane and John had problems, but they also loved each other and were good friends, bound by extraordinary circumstances. Time alone would show them how this would play out.

The TV show of June 17 closed out the television season. Jane had not had a long vacation in twenty years; she planned not to sing a note for three whole months. On July 4, she and John attended the wedding of Joyce Lasky to businessman Elliot Liskin. Jane was the matron of honor, wearing all pink, topped with a big picture hat.

On the day after Joyce's wedding, Jane left by train for Los Angeles, where she was to meet her mother. From there they would sail to Honolulu. She planned to check into the

Jane dances with the groom and John dances with the bride at Joyce and Elliot's wedding

Royal Hawaiian Hotel and loaf. Her bags were packed with the latest bestsellers and a lot of suntan lotion.

Tropical sun and warm breezes from the sea worked their usual magic on Jane. For weeks she bathed in the sun, enjoyed the profusion of exotic flowers growing wild, and relaxed among the friendly people of the islands. She and Mama traveled thousands of miles touring the islands and could not believe the orchids growing wildly everywhere or the beautiful sunsets. Hawaiian music, with its twangy sounds, was not appealing to these two women trained in classical music, but the charm of the islands made up for it.

On the way home Jane and Mama stopped in Denver to visit John's mother, then both mothers were sent ahead to

New York while Jane visited Dr. Will and Cay Menninger in Topeka. It may have been a professional visit, to help with the stress of having her marriage break up, but there is no record of it, to be certain.

There is evidence, however, that Jane had a personally guided tour of the whole Foundation by Dr. Will himself, who had a rigorous schedule arranged for her so she had something to do every hour on the hour. She went through all the buildings, and visited Southard School, where she saw the patients for whom the fan clubs were working so hard.

She was walking across the grounds with one of Dr. Will's assistants. Her new camera was slung over her shoulder. Suddenly, she spied a young boy in the midst of a small cornfield. She asked the assistant if she could talk to him and maybe take a picture.

"Well, Miss Froman," he said, "you can try. But, please don't be insulted if he calls you by a dirty name. You see it's kind of a habit with him. He's never learned to be civil. Just can't get along with other people."

She said she understood and walked over to the boy.

"Hello," she said. No answer. "That's nice corn you have there."

The boy eyed her apprehensively.

"Thank you," he said. "You may take a picture of it if you like."

The assistant was astounded. Jane took the picture.

"Would you like me to show you around our school?" the boy asked.

"I would love it," she replied.

The boy, Johnny, showed her around, then they sat down and talked for about an hour, just the two of them. When

Jane got back to New York, she had Johnny's picture blown up to send to him. Before she could send it, she received a letter from the boy.

> Dear Jane,
> I hope you enjoyed your trip. I hope my picture turned out fine. It was so nice while you were here.
> Good-bye.
> Johnny

Jane cried when she read Johnny's letter. She had heard similar stories, but this one had happened to her. Johnny had sent that letter on his own. No one made him write it. She knew he was going to be all right.

It was one of Jane's proudest moments when, shortly after this visit, she was asked to be a member of the Board of Governors of the Menninger Foundation, a post she retained for the rest of her life.

When she got back to New York, she needed to play some golf. She and John and both mothers drove to Pennsylvania to Shawnee-on-the-Delaware, where they had played golf before with Fred Waring and his brother, Tom.

Jane had been hanging out on the putting green, watching all the other gals drive off the first tee, and she began to get the itch. Jerry Stulgaitis, the football coach at Stroudsburg, coaxed her to come and hit a few. She borrowed some clubs and hobbled around. She blew her first drive but wound up with a 7, which she didn't think was so bad. Then she got a 5 on the next hole and a ladies' par 4 on the third. She was so excited she walked into the golf shop and bought a whole outfit: clubs, bag, two sweaters, two skirts, gloves, the works. After that, she got in a few holes any time she could manage it.

Playing golf again at Shawnee-on-the-Delaware

John had been told not to play golf, because of his injuries, he couldn't swing well. Frustrated, he would pick up a club, but Jane got right on him. "You put that down or I'll walk off the course and I'll never play again as long as I live."

So John watched as Jane and Tom, Fred's younger brother, played and he followed them around. John found Tom an irreverent character, hilariously funny. He referred to his brother Fred as "himself." One day Tom made a hole in one. The first thing Tom said was "For God's sake, don't tell himself. I didn't have his permission."

At times, the effort Jane and John made to maintain the image of a happy couple dissolved. There was little laughter;

the country club air was filled with tension. With no cameras or reporters around, Jane and John did little to check their frustrations. Tempers flared, heated words were exchanged, a car door was slammed. Perhaps it was just a tiff. Or perhaps things were deteriorating far beyond their attempts to hold together a marriage that no longer worked. It was hard to tell, with the illusion so carefully managed. In November, John threw a surprise birthday party for Jane. He wrote the article he had promised the fan club for their journal:

> Have just finished reading your latest issue of the journal and wish to express my admiration for the work you and all the members of the club are doing. Please convey my congratulations to all for the high quality and excellent organization of the journal.
>
> Please know that I am very proud that Jane has the admiration and affection of such a wonderful group of girls.
>
> I think you may be interested in the details of a birthday party I gave for Jane on the night of the ninth. In order to surprise her, I had told her that we were going out to dinner and implied that I had great plans for the evening, such as going to the theatre and a club—just a lot of things.
>
> Meanwhile, Mrs. Gardner, our cook, and Eva were secretly preparing turkey, hams, and all the trimmings. Joseph, our chauffeur, was alerted to be on hand to bring guests in by the kitchen door—so that no one would ring the doorbell—and to keep them hidden in the dining room.
>
> Meanwhile, Dr. and Mrs. Menninger, who were in New York, were brought in on the plans and came over for a visit late in the afternoon, very adroitly holding Jane's attention until all the guests arrived.
>
> Even Til cooperated to the extent of not barking when

guests arrived at the lower entrance. However, he would trot to the head of the kitchen stairs at each arrival so I could count the guests as they came in.

When all our friends assembled, Joseph came up (as previously planned) and announced that he was standing by with the car and that the cook wanted Jane to see a special Swedish delicacy being prepared for Jane's birthday (the next day). Naturally, Dr. and Mrs. Menninger wanted to see too, and came along.

When we arrived in the kitchen all of our friends crowded in from the dining room, singing "Happy Birthday."

By Jane's expression, I knew she was completely surprised. Do you know how difficult this is?

It was a very happy evening and much fun. For example, I very much enjoyed Jane teasing Deems Taylor into playing the "Missouri Waltz" for her birthday. I don't believe that it is one of Mr. Taylor's favorite waltzes. However, in his hands, it became a symphony.

I am just too full of birthday cake to write more.

> With all the best,
> Yours,
> John Burn

Had the girls not had those little scraps of blue paper in their wallets to prove it, they would not have believed their beloved Jane and John were having difficulties in their marriage.

On November 11, 1954, when the girls threw another party for Jane on the set of Studio 50, she showed off one of the two beautiful rings she had received from John, an enormous heart-shaped amethyst surrounded by diamonds. Things could not have seemed more perfect.

Birthday party backstage at TV show;
note the "Fromanettes" album on table

When everyone on the set had their fill of birthday cake, and the girls presented Jane with a scrapbook containing photographs of themselves and "The Fromanettes" carved in wood on the cover, Jane was visibly moved. Little did anyone know at the time how much this gift from the girls meant to her.

19

THE BREAK-UP
1955

Wᴵᴛʜ ᴄᴀʀᴇꜰᴜʟ ᴘʟᴀɴɴɪɴɢ so that it took up no more than a day or two in the newspapers, Jane and John announced their separation. They agreed that they wanted only the best for each other and would remain friends. Skipping one week of her live TV show, she went to Florida—to recover from bursitis, she said. John, meanwhile, was in Acapulco. On March 1, 1955, headlines appeared in papers across the country:

JANE FROMAN AND MATE PART

JANE HOPING LOVE SONG IS NOT ENDED

JANE FROMAN QUITS HUSBAND WHO
SAVED HER IN AIR CRASH

Jane talked with reporters briefly, saying she and John agreed to a temporary separation but declined to say what caused the breakup. "I'm afraid I can't tell you that," she said. "It's pretty personal."

When Jane returned from Florida, John had moved to a hotel. He would come back for his clothes and personal belongings later. When the dust settled, they would resume their lives, separately, as friends. Jane had to get used to the idea that she was alone again and face the fact that the chapter of her life with John was over. She threw herself into activity.

General Electric had not renewed Jane's contract at the end of the TV season. Immediately, invitations for guest appearances on all the major variety shows arrived, along with offers from the night clubs, one after the other. Jane Froman was hot, and there was no cool-down in sight. At forty-seven she remained a startlingly beautiful woman, with her voice in excellent shape, and she gave a darned good show. The Desert Inn knew this and paid her a whopping quarter of a million dollars to play three four-week performances in the next eighteen months.

The canceling of *The Jane Froman Show* was a great disappointment, but Jane looked forward and put everything she had into the final months of the show, offering her own interests and areas of expertise as thematic material for the writers. She invited Deems Taylor to guest star on one, and strolled down the avenue to shop for antiques on another. Other shows paid tribute to song writers like Frank Loesser and Vincent Youmans. Even the fan club got into the act when a commercial for GE flash bulbs featured the Fromanettes, in their club sweaters, with one of them taking a picture of Jane with her flash camera.

Jane hired a new secretary, Gertrude Palmer, a mature no-nonsense woman who kept Jane's affairs in order more like an army sergeant than a private secretary, in sharp contrast to the gentle, soft-spoken Joyce, who was now starting to raise a family.

A new act had to be prepared; Jane had signed contracts for multiple night club appearances across the country. She changed her hair style, bought chic new gowns, then posed

Publicity photo in her new look

for updated publicity photos. She worked on arrangements and hired song writers Robert Wright and George Forrest to write special material for her. Jane had been using their delightful "Millionaires Don't Whistle" in her act for years, and Wright and Forrest had written material for her before: "A Bag of Popcorn and a Dream" was a regular part of her repertoire. Now, about to play Ciro's in Hollywood, she needed another piece of special material. Jane was a master at balancing her act so that it never seemed either too brooding or disappointingly lightweight. Wright and Forrest gave her "The Southern California Blues."

> They wine and dine in dungarees
> And go to church in shorts in California
> They make their cemeteries sound
> like underground resorts in California. . . .

Jane loved it. It was just the kind of witty interlude she needed in an act that featured the romantic ballads she sang so well.

Underestimated was Southern California's emotional reaction to the lyrics. Not usually one to receive negative press, Jane garnered some ire when Hollywood stars came down hard on what they perceived as an insult to their fair town. Jane added an aside in her routine, "If Darryl Zanuck is listening, I'm kidding."

It had been her intention to remain good friends with John, but while they started out according to plan, Jane could not avoid harping on old issues each time they met. Although Dr. Kubie himself had suggested the separation, Jane could not let go without a fight. John avoided seeing her; it was just too difficult.

It is likely that alcohol was at the root of these flareups. When Jane's temper was unleashed, as could happen when she drank, look out! During one of these times, she found John's Leica among the belongings he had planned to pick up and she smashed it, cutting up his expensive leather camera case as well.

Jane put her energy into her work and her various charitable affiliations. She proposed an idea to Dr. Will for a fund-raising campaign for Southard School. With the help of the girls and her fan clubs everywhere, she would write a letter to everyone in her address book asking for a donation of a dollar and a promise to get another person to contribute a dollar and a promise, and so on. Dr. Will thought it was a clever idea, and at a board meeting of the Menninger Foundation asked Jane, as a newly appointed governor on the Board, to speak about this. Among the many famous people she was to address was Bernard Baruch. As she told it:

> Bernard Baruch got up and gave a terrific speech. Some of the others did the same. Everything was very formal with the gavels and such. Well, as these fabulous people got up to speak I slid lower and lower in my chair. Finally everyone was finished—or so I thought. Then Dr. Will got up to speak, and said: "Janey—how about telling these folks your plan?"
>
> Now I love Dr. Will dearly, but right then I could have shot him. Well, I got up and told them that each member in my fan club would go out and get another member for $1.00. The new member would, in turn have to get another member—in sort of a chain fashion. Well before I could go any farther, Bernard Baruch came up—took out a dollar bill and said, "Jane, I'd love to become a member of the Jane Froman

Fan Club." No sooner did he come up when the others followed suit.

Jane always finished that story with a great laugh. She loved playing to a good audience.

In the spring, she called a meeting about the charity. The girls arrived, as always, eager and loaded with ideas. They counted the money that had come in for Southard School, to which Jane added the ten dollars she had collected at the board meeting. They sat on the floor, as usual, and as Jane opened envelopes and read off amounts, Deena wrote them down. Jane doubled the total by matching it with a check of her own, establishing a tradition on the spot.

Dr. Will, delighted with the devotion of Jane's fans to help Southard School, wrote to them.

Dear Jane Froman Fans:

It is grand of you to have taken such an interest in the job we are trying to do here at the Menninger Foundation to make life happier and brighter for lonely, unhappy children. Jane and I have talked many times about the big job of stopping mental illness where it starts—in children—and about ways she might help. I am absolutely delighted that you have joined with her in this great interest of hers. . . .

This was the beginning of a long and remarkable correspondence that lasted for the next several years between the famous psychiatrist and the girls in the fan club. Dr. Will showed genuine interest in their activities and guided them when they shared confidences with him, from parental problems to worries about Jane being upset with them for some youthful indiscretion.

THE MENNINGER FOUNDATION

A NON-PROFIT CENTER FOR TREATMENT AND PREVENTION, RESEARCH AND PROFESSIONAL EDUCATION IN PSYCHIATRY

Topeka, Kansas
September 12, 1955

Miss Deena Hirshman
2020 Arthur Avenue
New York 57, N.Y.

Dear Deena:

Yours is kind of a sad letter of September 6. I wish
I could help you but I don't know anything really I can say
that would make much difference.

These thoughts do come to me. Jane is just another human
being after all. In your days gone by I know you have put her on a
very high pedestal and, of course, with good reason. I think all of
us go through a stage in life when we have our idols and it is
terrible if they ever have to fall. I hope Jane really doesn't fall
from being your idol either. I can tell you that in a very different
kind of a way, I seem to have a good many admirers. I get lots and
lots of "fan mail" about articles I write. One was in THIS WEEK
magazine just a week ago Sunday with my picture and I have had many,
many letters about that. I get annoyed with some of the letters. I
dont' want to see some of the people who try to see me. A lot depends
on my mood. Some times I am up to it and at other times I just don't
want to be bothered. I am sure that Jane must have the same kind
of difficulty. She is always in the show-case--on parade in a sense.
I am sure she just hopes that your understanding will be such that if
she doesn't give you as much time or house or attention--or apparently
some times even appears rude, I know she fundamentally isn't. I
can assure you that you can bank on that too. She is a very sweet
affable person.

You perhaps know too that I never hear from Jane or almost
never. I write her many times. She is on my Board of Governors but
I know she is busy. I think if I was in a jam and it really had to
be, that Jane would be right on the job. In the meantime, however,
I don't take offense that I don't hear from her every time when I
wish I could. I hope you will take this attitude and I am sure these
two years since I met you have given you a chance to grow up enough to
know that this is true with everybody--especially people in important
and prominent public view.

Just stay steady.

Cordially,

Dr. Will

William C. Menninger, M.D.

WCM/lf

At the end of June, 1955, Jane closed her television show for the last time singing "With a Song in My Heart." The cast and crew came out to sing with her. In an elegant champagne-colored beaded gown designed for her by Christian Dior, she bid goodbye to the audience, the cast and crew, and a cluster of the girls. As always, she seemed to be the one to cheer everyone through this sad time.

There wasn't a moment to dwell on the past. She had to work on her night club act. She vocalized daily, worked on arrangements, went to rehearsals and planned her clothes. In between, she attended openings and parties, generally on

**Jane and members of the cast and crew
at the last show**

the arm of handsome young BBD&O advertising executive Dudley Field Malone, Jr., whom she had met through her TV show—General Electric was one of his accounts.

Malone was dashing, witty, good company and, as far as Jane's vulnerability went, "safe." His interest in Jane was not romantic. Columnists like Dorothy Kilgallen penned poisonous innuendoes in their gossip columns about Malone, as divergent lifestyles were not open in those repressed times, but in spite of the occasional barbs he remained a steadfast friend throughout Jane's life.

When Gisele MacKenzie, singing star on TV's popular *Your Hit Parade,* invited her to a masquerade party, Jane went at it wholeheartedly. She had to find a disguise for not only her leg brace but the deep lilting sound of her voice—as well as

the terrible stutter—if she were to keep people from guessing her identity before the unmasking at midnight. She called on Eva, who knew where everything was, to collaborate with her on coming up with a perfect solution: she would go as Emmett Kelley, the famous sad-faced circus clown in tramp clothing who never spoke. Eva had to find old clothes and an old broom, Kelley's

Jane, right, as Emmett Kelley

signature prop that he used in his act as he tried to sweep away the spotlight. Jane, skillful with makeup, added the clown's unique face. Jane and Eva had some good laughs as the results of their handwork grew.

Guests at the party were mystified as she moved among them, never speaking a word. All evening long people tried in vain to guess her identity. Singer Snooky Lanson, another singer with *Your Hit Parade,* asked her to dance. "I don't even know if you're a man or a woman!" he said, but as he put his arms around her and hugged her to him, he announced, "It's a woman!"

At the unmasking, folks gasped as Jane's identity was revealed. Everyone had expected her to show up as Madame DuBarry or Marie Antoinette, in an elaborate ball gown. Jane, in her baggy pants, won the prize for best costume hands down.

Booked into the biggest clubs in Miami, Chicago, Reno, Las Vegas and New York, Jane threw herself into work with a vengeance. She packed the room every night. Critics, in awe, felt her energy and remarked on her great artistry. The heavy club schedule did not keep Jane from taping a Jimmy Durante show on the coast, looking bright and youthful, or from cutting a new record for Capitol.

When the tour was over and she returned to New York, the large empty brownstone reminded her too painfully of what was missing. The life she had hoped for there, with John, was over. In August she sold it and took an apartment on East 67th Street.

Jane saw the year out in high spirits. She was going to have fun, focus on the future, not the past. With "Deadly Dudley" Malone and another couple, she booked passage on a boat to

Aboard the banana boat:
(top row) unnamed accordionist, Jane, Bibs, and Babs;
(bottom row) Bobbie, Joan M., Ellen G., Deena, Louise

Costa Rica for late November. It was not a luxury cruise, but one of United Fruit Lines' freighters—a banana boat. "Before we left," Jane wrote later, "there was a sort of 'farewell party' on the boat. Some of the gals came to see me off and it was so much fun." An accordionist appeared out of nowhere and provided the music. A photographer snapped pictures.

Jane looked forward to the trip, expecting—needing— a whale of a good time. Unfortunately, it turned out to be a dreadfully dull voyage. Halfway through the trip, with Dudley as co-conspirator, she convinced the captain that she had a medical emergency—not a card she pulled out easily. There, on the high seas, she and Dudley disembarked, were transported by small boat to Panama, and got on a plane for New York.

The rebellious streak that had first shown itself during the long boring days at the Holy Rosary Convent had surfaced again.

20

IT'S A GREAT LIFE
1956

JANE STOOD AT the steps to the Empire Room, pulling on her long evening gloves. Friends said hello as they passed but left her alone with her jitters.

She heard Nat Brandwynne's orchestra start up with the opening strains of the song that had become indelibly associated with her, "With a Song in My Heart." At the crescendo, she entered the room and the spotlight beamed on her as applause rose to greet her.

A vision in the stunning Dior gown with its matching stole, she began with the melancholy "Everybody's Got a Home But Me" from the new Rodgers and Hammerstein musical, *Pipe Dream,* following it with one of her regulars, "It's a Great Life," an observation that no matter what life tosses your way, it's pretty wonderful anyway. Coming from anyone else, the song might have seemed a mere change of pace, but to anyone who knew Jane's story, it spoke her heart.

With accompanist Ronnie Selby at the keyboard, she sang several more songs, mesmerizing the audience with a seductive arrangement of Cole Porter's "It's All Right With Me," coming to the last line with her shoulders thrown back, singing her powerful final note with her head held high, tossing the mike cord to the side. Her rich mezzo voice was that of Jane at her peak, with magnificent color and phrasing.

The second part of her act was a witty medley of Irving Berlin songs that spanned four decades, with Jane donning a different hat to fit each period.

The audience wouldn't let her go without a double encore. Mama, in the audience that night, must have been in awe, to see how that little child who sat, enthralled, under the piano when she gave a lesson with a student, had grown into this lovely singer!

Card advertising Jane's appearance at the Empire Room

A few nights later, on January 15, 1956, the Theater Wing held its First Night ball, "Command Performance," honoring Helen Hayes for her fifty years in the theater. People swarmed to the Waldorf-Astoria to pay tribute to the actress. Among the performers lined up to entertain was Jane, portraying Elsie Janis, the stage actress who was the first popular American artist to travel abroad in wartime to entertain the troops, during World War I. Wearing a World War I uniform, Jane belted out, without the help of a microphone, "How're You Going to Keep Them Down on the Farm?" and George M. Cohan's rousing "Over There," stopping the show. A couple of hours later, she was back in her gown at the Empire Room, doing her second show.

The hectic pace only energized her. Once again, she went on tour, first in February to Birmingham, Alabama, for a concert with the Birmingham Symphony; then in March to the

Eden Roc in Miami; and off again to a smashing reception at
the Cocoanut Grove in L.A. in April; to the Painted Desert
Room of the Desert Inn in Las Vegas in May and the Riverside in Reno in June. The same wonder held each audience as
Jane appeared. When the welcoming applause subsided, they
were dazzled by the woman, the gown, and always the voice.
She was a sensation.

The rigorous work of her night club act was what she
needed, but off hours were a problem in Las Vegas. There was
nothing to do but gamble, and women did not enter the casi-
nos alone. She phoned Ruth Barnard, who now lived in L.A.
Maybe her fun-loving friend would join her for a weekend.
Ruth had barely hung up the phone when she was on her
way. The two gals had a ball.

Ruth had a down-to-earth sense of humor that matched
Jane's and made her a terrific companion. Like Jane, she had
a huge capacity for fun. At Christmas, knowing Ruth's weak-
ness for furs, Jane presented her with a mink-lined toilet
seat. Ruth gave her an album of songs poking fun at psy-
chotherapy called *Songs for Couch and Consultation,* including
numbers such as "Stay As Sick As You Are" and "Schizo-
phrenic Moon."

Ruth helped Jane dress for her performances, joined her
for cocktails, listened to her sing, and made the rounds of
the hotel casino with her, going from blackjack to roulette
to poker. They didn't do too badly. One night it seemed they
could do no wrong. When they were done for the night, Jane
bought a pack of cigarettes and got three silver dollars in
change. She shrugged, holding up the coins.

"Put them on number three," said Ruth. Jane placed the
coins on the roulette table and the wheel was spun, landing

on number three. Taking their winnings, they laughed all the way back to their rooms.

During her stay at the Desert Inn Jane filed for divorce from John on grounds of desertion. Even with their amicable agreement that this was the least damaging route for both, it was painful. The tabloids had noted that John was dating Charlene Hargrove, a young showgirl in Broadway's *Pajama Game*. The decree came through in June, with Jane waiving alimony. A property settlement left each party in control of personal possessions.

The marvel of Jane's resilience was that the more she suffered personally, the stronger she became as a performer, and the illusion of well-being and optimism dominated her public persona.

On the West Coast, she had managed, between night club engagements, to appear on one TV show after another, do a radio interview, and sign a new contract with Capitol.

It was one thing to deal with immediate concerns, but doubts about her future were creeping into her thoughts. Would she ever pay off her heaping medical bills, which grew with each new malady that struck? Would she be able to continue with her work to keep earning? When she had had nagging worries before, she had faced them with John, and had learned to depend on his moral support. She continued to hold herself together in public, as she had been taught to do by her stiff-backed mother and grandmother, but at home, she resorted to more alcohol to get her through. Miraculously, the incessant smoking, and now drinking, had not affected her voice.

Jane called the girls. Their sweet outpouring of love and constant devotion had often bolstered her sagging spirits.

They never let her down. A good dose of them was just what she needed now.

"Just have to tell you about Til," she said cheerily as they got comfortable on chairs and floor. "You know whenever I go on tour I usually bring home some little toy—and he gets so mad when I play with it. I go over to it and say 'nice baby' and jealous little Til tears it to pieces." The girls reached out to pet the long brown dachshund, who somehow knew he was the center of discussion. "Well," continued Jane, "on the way back from Vegas I saw the most adorable stuffed toy tiger—one of those big life-size ones—I brought it home to Til expecting him to tear it to shreds when I played with it. He toddled over, sniffed and went zooming under the couch! The tiger is still in one piece—Til's scared to death of it!"

They laughed, told Jane their latest stories, and the hours passed as they sat and talked. At last, it was time to tell them about the break-up. They had waited patiently and had a right to know the truth, and to hear it from her.

The problems she and John had came out of so many issues, she explained; it had been John's first marriage, and he took on a woman more experienced and to complicate things, one in show business. Of course there was the crash in Lisbon and the injuries they had both sustained that had drawn them together, but John's crash in 1952, off the coast of Puerto Rico, had been more personally devastating. This tragedy, where he was the pilot, and where so many people had been killed, had affected his confidence. He had sought counsel from a psychiatrist.

Her own work schedule, first with the daily pressures of a TV show and then with the night club circuit, rehearsing and traveling, increased the strain on their marriage. They wanted it to work. They had taken it slowly, not rushing into anything; they cared too much for each other for that. For a year they had talked about it, discussing it at length with Dr. Kubie and taking his advice. When they planned a separation, they did it intelligently, to attract as little attention as possible.

"We both have great respect for each other, and there are no hard feelings," she told them. "We've been pondering it for a long, long time, and came to the decision that this was the best thing to do. Everything was clean, and nobody got hurt."

Looking at the girls' sad faces, she added: "There was none of this." She made a fist, as if to say, there was no meanness.

"I wouldn't hurt John for anything in the world," she continued. "If he ever got in a jam and needed me, I'd be the first one at his side, and if ever I got in a jam and needed him, he'd be the first one at my side. We're still very good friends, and there's been no quarrel or anything. We just figured, between us, after many long discussions, that this would be the best thing for both of us."

The girls accepted this; the bond that had developed over the Lisbon accident could not sustain Jane and John as their differences grew. The girls had questions; Jane answered them, adding, "All the love in the world can't help a person sometimes. At one time, even John couldn't help me, and I went out to Menninger's. Now he's having his chance. All the love I could give him still wouldn't help right now."

Before their visit was over, they talked about Jane's new album, *Faith*, a copy of which was on the coffee table. "It's the first time I wrote the liner notes myself," Jane said, proudly. "I always thought that these really beautiful songs such as 'You'll Never Walk Alone,' 'One Little Candle,' and such, should be done without a lot of bongo drums in the background so I did it with a wonderful chorus. I do hope you enjoy listening to it. . . ."

Babs picked up the album and read Jane's liner notes aloud.

> FAITH—It moves mountains, raises the human spirit, brings joy and confidence to the hungry heart.
>
> It is faith that has made men great. It is faith that has made great men meek. It is faith that has given strength to the lowly and tenderness to the strong. It is faith that has kept aloft the torches of freedom and liberty, and it is that same faith which has brought contentment and peace to the simplest hearth side.
>
> I like to hope, in recording these songs of faith now part of our glorious heritage, that these songs from my heart will bring joy where there may be sadness, hope where there may be despair, courage to faltering footsteps, and a song to many a heart which will sing with me—"I believe."
>
> Jane Froman

Everyone's spirits were lifted. The talk about Jane and John parting had left them in a solemn mood; it was good to leave on a reassuring note that things could be good again.

For Jane's birthday the girls planned an elegant luncheon at the Waldorf Astoria, hiring the Carpenter Suite—complete with piano—for the event and inviting several club members from out of town. Jane deserved something special; she had had a lot on her shoulders with the divorce, sinus problems that had worsened in the L.A. smog, and her hard work preparing her new night club act. They couldn't let her be alone on her birthday.

Dudley was commandeered to steer Jane to the Waldorf

that afternoon, and to get her to wear the new blue hat she had showed them during one of their visits. Jane arrived on Dudley's arm, wearing a smart black sheath dress and the hat, a pancake-shaped affair trimmed with a border of puffy blue netting that sat atop her head at a slight angle. The blue color brought out the incredible luminescence of her eyes. She walked ahead of Dudley into the Carpenter Suite to find a gaggle of friends shouting "Happy birthday!" The surprise nearly knocked Jane off her feet as she spun toward Dudley and said, "Dudley, you louse!" then turned back toward the well-wishers.

"No wonder Deadly Dudley insisted that I wear this hat today! He called and said he wanted to take me AND the blue hat out for lunch for my birthday, and I thought to myself, 'Now where in the world can he be taking me that I MUST wear this hat?'"

Jane greeted each guest: Sam Salzman, a longtime friend who had worked with her in *Artists and Models* and at Bill Miller's Riviera night club; Aileen Brenon Harrity, Jane's good friend and publicist; John Grant, a good friend; Joyce and Elliot Liskin and a handful of the girls.

Jane listened to a toast from Babs, then was handed a beautifully wrapped box in silver paper and blue ribbon. She opened it and found inside a pile of cards from her fans, which she read aloud. As she opened one, a butterfly flew out and Jane jumped back, scared to death. Everyone turned to Bibs, even Jane; it was just the sort of thing she would do.

In the final envelope was a check for the children at Southard School. Jane stared at it pensively. Finally, she looked up and said, "You couldn't have done *anything* that would have pleased me more than this."

Soon everyone moved into the dining room, where a long banquet table had been set for lunch. Joan took out a beautiful white orchid corsage and pinned it on Jane's dress.

Talk and laughter went on throughout lunch. At the mention of the girls' most recent pajama party, Jane reminisced about some that she had gone to when she was in college. "I learned more things at those parties!" she giggled. "I haven't had one in such a long time . . . we were supposed to have one once, weren't we?"

They had talked about one, but Jane's health problems had prevented it from materializing.

When the last plate was cleared, everyone moved into the other room. Deena handed Jane a hat box from the famous Fifth Avenue milliner Mr. John. A bewildered look crossed

Jane at the Waldorf party with the Elvis hat

Talking to Mama from the Waldorf

Jane's face as she opened it. Under layers of tissue paper was a hat, but not a Mr. John creation; it was an Elvis Presley souvenir hat. Jane howled as she held it up for all to see.

"I'd love to put it on," she chuckled, "but if I took this off," she said, pointing to the blue hat, "I'd never be able to get it on again!"

Bibs, her hair pulled into a fashionable chignon, sat down at the piano to play while several of the girls gathered around to sing the song that they had rehearsed, "Our Best to You," a birthday greeting to Jane. The serenading continued as Babs sang a solo to Jane, adapting the words from the charming "Getting to Know You."

A telephone call for Jane interrupted the conversation after the singing, and Joan led Jane to the telephone. It was Mama. Delighted, Jane told her mother about the incredible party that the girls had given her and how Dudley had played a sneaky role in it.

The party continued over coffee and birthday cake, rolling on into the late afternoon until, finally, Jane had to excuse herself. A young fan from Illinois was in town and was stopping by her house and she had to be home to meet her at five o'clock. Jane left as she had arrived, on Dudley's arm, and in high spirits.

Just before Christmas, Jane was back in the hospital for emergency surgery. Her sinus problems had reached a point where nose sprays no longer relieved her and she couldn't breathe. She postponed a meeting that was scheduled for the election of officers of the Jane Froman Foundation.

Mama came to New York to be with her. Cards and letters from fans cheered her during her recovery, but it still hadn't been much of a Christmas, with just Mama, Eva, her new secretary, Helen Ryan, and Miss Loken, a private nurse, so Jane agreed to a visit with the girls. Even feeling low, she knew the girls could bring some cheer into the holiday.

Six of the girls arrived around three o'clock, as planned, bearing several bulky packages. Eva took their coats. A fire crackled pleasantly in the fireplace. Music—opera—played softly on the radio, but Jane was nowhere in sight.

Sprawling all over the living room, they got to work, chattering as they did. Windy was on her knees setting up a small Christmas tree that they had brought for Jane, when out came

Mama, shushing them. "Jane is still sleeping," she whispered. "Girls—listen," she continued. "This will do you good!"

Ben Gross was speaking to Deems Taylor during the Metropolitan Opera broadcast intermission. The music resumed and a lovely aria drifted through the room. Mama seemed lost in thought as she listened. "That could have been Jane," she mused. Indeed, it could have. Those who knew music, as Anna Froman Hetzler did, knew a good operatic voice when they heard one. Opera star Rise Stevens, now a friend of Jane's, confessed that she had practiced emulating the Froman sound to such a degree that the NBC radio network once asked her to appear in her place when Jane couldn't make it for her nightly coast-to-coast broadcast. The audience never knew the real Jane Froman wasn't there.

Jane came out around five o'clock, the sleep still in her eyes, but happy to see them. Smiling, she introduced the girls to Miss Loken, who appeared a bit timid amidst the sudden burst of life around her. A lively conversation ensued. Jane told them how she had lost her steam after this last surgery and couldn't wait to get it back again.

"I have no P-P-PUSH," she exclaimed. "And y-y-you know that's not l-l-like me at all."

The stuttering she was so proud to have had under control was back at its most profound. The girls had learned early on, as Joyce had, never to help her when she got stuck on a word, no matter how long it took for her to get the word out. At times, the seconds seemed like minutes. She told them about the ordeal of the sinus operation.

"It was ghastly," she told them. She had to be awake throughout, according to the doctors, and heard the scraping of bone and saw everything that was going on.

Pointing to her leg, she said, "I'd m-m-much rather go through a bone graft a-a-any day than to have to go through that ag-g-g-g-g-ain!" Her voice rose and fell in a singsong way, as she tried one of her rhythm exercises to avoid the worst stumbling blocks to her speech.

She admired their tree and asked them about themselves. Christmas had been good to all of them, and they talked of family, clothes, music, college. Bobbie disappeared for a few minutes and came back dressed as Santa Claus, carrying a bulging pillowcase. She pulled out one lighthearted gift after another, handing them to Jane, who giggled as she opened each one: a football pump, a small glass dachshund, bird food, earrings in the shape of musical notes, a tiny hot water bottle, a miniature Mexican sombrero, which Jane put on immediately. The last package was oddly wrapped, with a plastic palm tree sticking out of the top. Inside were two tiny turtles.

"Their names are Deadly and Dudley," cried Deena.

Jane howled and slapped her knee with delight.

No longer limp as a rag doll, Jane got up and left the room, coming back a minute later with her camera. She had everyone pose for a picture, making sure she had one of herself sitting on "Santa's" lap. Windy snapped the picture.

Jane thought of one thing after another to show or tell them. Weren't the Academy Awards wonderful this year? . . . she loved Ingrid Bergman and Yul Brynner. It had been hard being without Til. She had developed an allergic reaction to him, suffering swollen eyelids and difficulty in breathing when she was near him. He had been sent to live with Eva, who gave her regular reports on him. She had had genuine diamond earrings made from stones she had accumulated over the years. . . .

Much to Miss Loken's dismay, the short visit had turned into hours as Jane kept thinking of more things to share with the girls. Finally, even Miss Loken listened, entranced. Jane could spin a good story:

A little while ago I went down to see a favorite designer. He told me that he had something he thought I'd like to see. So we went up in this little tiny elevator—it's open—you know?

Well, we went up in this elevator and finally came to the fur department. We got out and he took me over to this chinchilla coat. He asked me if I liked it. GAD—of course I like it! I've always dreamed of having a chinchilla coat—ever since I was a little girl.* Well, I admired the coat and he told me that he was making it for a certain opera singer. I can't tell her name—you'll understand why when I tell you the rest of the story. He asked me if I'd like a coat like that. I just didn't know what to say! Of course I wanted one! He told me that there were a lot of furs left over that were all paid for—enough to make a jacket from. He said that if I'd pay the tax and the labor, he'd make one for ME! I was so stunned—but I've got the jacket!"

"What's it look like?" Deena asked.

"It's a sort of gray and white—and so soft—wait—"

With that, Jane flew out of the room and came strutting back wearing the gorgeous jacket. The Mexican sombrero was still on her head. The room erupted in giggles as one girl

---

* In the 1950s, the public consciousness had not yet been raised regarding animal rights, in particular the use of furs in fashionable clothing. Most women in the 1950s still accepted furs as a sign of success and glamor, representing the most luxurious of possessions next only to diamonds.

after another felt the silky fur and tried the jacket on. Jane stared at Janet, the last one to try it on. "It looks better on her than on me," Jane said. "Because of her coloring—you know?" That's all Janet needed. Tossing her blonde hair back, she almost had to be peeled out of the jacket.

After the chinchilla excitement was over, Jane remembered one more thing—a beautiful pale blue chiffon stole with royal blue flowers on it; Dudley had given it to her for Christmas. She modeled it for the girls, draping it over her head and shoulders.

At last, the party was over. As they were leaving, Jane was a lot more energetic than when they had arrived. She felt better, too. What was it—their vitality? their buoyant spirit?

Clearly, her "girls" had grown up. They were young women now, planning birthday parties at the Waldorf, dating and planning weddings, engaged in careers, some showing enormous talent. The joy she felt in seeing them grow into intelligent, thoughtful and responsible women warmed her heart. Their friendship meant so much to her; they had gotten her through her lowest moments just by being there—did they have any idea? Some day she would have to let them know.

21

THE FINAL ROUND
1957–1960

A T LAST, AFTER a long journey through the courts, the charter for The Jane Froman Foundation arrived, incorporated by the State of New York on March 26, 1957.

"I've never been a whole foundation before!" Jane exclaimed when she told the girls.

This was what they were waiting for. Now they could move forward in earnest, as a legitimate charity. Always ready to serve on boards or volunteer her talents for others, Jane realized with great joy that she would now be able to lure the finest professional people to help her with her cause.

Serving on the board of the Jane Froman Foundation, Inc. were Jane, of course, as President; Abe Lastfogel and Dr. Lawrence Kubie were elected Vice Presidents; Michael Halperin, Jane's attorney, was Secretary and Dr. Sydney Kanev was Treasurer. Dr. Will was elected Chairman by a unanimous vote. Also serving on the Board were Marion E. Kenworthy, M. D., of New York; Victor J. Hammer of the Hammer Galleries in New York; Mrs. Alfred E. Hess of New York and Dr. Ruth Barnard of Los Angeles. A junior or auxiliary group was formed, using the same officers of the fan club as officers of the foundation. It was decided that one representative from the auxiliary group should be present at each Senior

Board meeting. Barbara (Babs) Buoncristiano was elected as first rotating representative to the board meetings.

All funds would go directly to Southard School, at least for the time being. A new Research Division for Children was planned that would absorb Southard School, and that was probably where funds would go in the future.

Jane called a meeting at her house for April 19, 1957, to get the ball rolling. Dr. Will greeted the girls with a cheerful hello and an affectionate hug. "You're so grown up!" he remarked. He hadn't seen them since that first meeting at Jane's house on East 93rd Street in February of 1954. "Last time I saw you you were a bunch of brats who didn't know anything!" Jane laughed her hearty laugh and looked on with a twinkle in her eye.

Spirits were high and voices eager as they discussed plans for raising funds for the foundation. They would have pins, buttons or cards for anyone who contributed to the foundation. Jane would write a letter kicking off the "dollar and a promise" campaign and the girls would help her send them out.

Dr. Will, who traveled around the country trying to raise funds on behalf of the Menninger Foundation, explained that publicity was not what actually brought in the money; that 98

Discussing the charity

percent of gifts to Menningers were through personal contact. "If you want to get money," he told them, "you must meet people and ask!" While the girls didn't know that many people, the big wheels on the board did.

The meeting couldn't end without a lot of lively chatter among friends, and Dr. Will joined in for the fun. Jane showed off the new Easter bonnet Mr. John had created for her.

A week later, the *New York World Telegram and Sun* published an article about the meeting at Jane's house, and on May 17, 1957, staff writer George Montgomery followed up with another piece, going into detail on the history and purposes of the Jane Froman Foundation. It began:

> Jane Froman, the gal who kicked fate in the teeth, presides over America's most unusual chain of teen-aged fan clubs. . . .

Jane and the girls were thrilled. On the heels of the good publicity, Jane's "dollar and a promise" campaign went into effect immediately. The girls helped Jane type up letters on her personal stationery, stuff them into envelopes, and send them out to all the people in her file, asking for a dollar and a promise.

> 39 East 67th St.
> New York 21, N. Y.

Dear ----------- ,

I am writing to you about something that is very close to my heart.

The Jane Froman Foundation has recently been legalized,

according to the laws of the State of New York. Our purpose is to help disturbed children who are patients in the Children's Division of the internationally famous Menninger Foundation in Topeka, Kansas. These children are housed in two old weather-beaten frame buildings. Not a single bed, desk, laboratory or treatment room is endowed. The recreation room is a made-over cubbyhole in the basement. Toys and equipment are sadly needed.

These children, bewildered and unhappy, need our help. Will you give a dollar and a promise? The dollar, to be of immediate assistance. The promise, to get a friend to give a dollar and a promise! This friend, in turn, gives a dollar, and a promise to get a friend, and so on. In this way not too great a demand is made on your pocketbook and still you can be a part of a wonderful undertaking, to help a frightened child on the pathway toward a fuller, richer life.

In return for your dollar and your promise, a membership card in the Jane Froman Foundation will be sent to you. The Jane Froman Fan Clubs throughout the country are helping me in this most worthy undertaking. Won't you be a part of it, too? I would be so proud if you would join us.

Here's hoping!

                                        Sincerely,
                                        Jane Froman

Dr. Will appeared frequently on radio and TV talking about the need for more research on mental health, hopefully breaking down the myths and fears surrounding the subject. A new era was dawning, with psychoanalysis becoming more common among the well-to-do, but there were still some who regarded it on a plane with voodoo and magic. The New York *Daily News* published an editorial on Dr. Will that clearly came from this kind of thinking, stating that a mentally ill person "never has a stab of worry."

Babs wrote an indignant letter to the *News,* refuting the ignorant claim and telling them about the work of William Menninger and people like him who were trying to gain more understanding and support for the mentally ill. "The use of the terms 'head shrinkers' and 'nut houses' in your editorial is enough to set your newspaper back years, sir, not psychiatry," she wrote.

A portion of the letter was printed, and Jane, proud as can be, dispatched a telegram:

> DEAR BABS:
> YOUR LETTER TO DAILY SIMPLY
> SUPERB. AM SO PROUD TO SEE EVEN
> SMALL PART PRINTED IN TODAYS NEWS.
> AM VERY PROUD OF YOU. BEST LOVE.
>   JANE

Windy's solemn poem accompanied several published articles on the foundation, Dr. Will, and mental health.

> A jigsaw puzzle
> Its pieces
> Twisted and bent,
> Broken and missing.
> The beautiful picture
> That once it depicted
> Distorted and ugly, —
> Dark blotches and cracks.
>
> Hold gently the fragments,
> But firmly in grasp;

Touch not at the weak spot—
It may crumble and fall.
Work patiently, thoughtfully,
Determinedly on it, —
Press out the scarring defects;
Rebuild the lost pieces;
Return to its beauty
The mind of a man!
                    —W. Glasgow

Windy's poem was an eerie portent of things to come. Jane's life itself had become a maddening set of broken and bent pieces that desperately needed rebuilding.

In June, Jane appeared in a two-week engagement at the Beverly Hills Country Club in Newport, Kentucky, just across the Ohio River from Cincinnati. Three fans from the Chicago area met at Chicago's Union Station after work on Friday. Although they had been fans of Jane's since they were young teenagers, they had never met their idol, or each other. They were well acquainted by the time they arrived in Cincinnati, making it to the club in time for Jane's first show.

The show was especially thrilling for the three young people. Jack had made attempts to meet Jane, but all had been thwarted by bad timing. Carol K. had come close, but appearances had been canceled or postponed just as she was about to leave for them. Carol P. had been to New York and attended the telecast of Jane's show, but had never seen her in a night club.

When Jane heard they were in the audience she asked them to come backstage and welcomed them warmly, with a hearty handshake. Carol K., whose hands were icy cold from nervous excitement, remembers Jane telling her how good her hands felt, as she was so warm after doing a show. They talked about themselves, as Jane had turned the conversation to them. Jane asked Helen, her secretary, to tell anyone who came to the door that she was busy having an "interview and pictures," and they went on chatting, uninterrupted.

When Jane learned that the three were returning the next day for both shows, she reserved a ringside table for them, and Helen joined them. Cameras were not allowed in the club, so Jane had them bring their cameras to her hotel before they left for the club. After the first show on Saturday, Helen led them backstage, where she pulled their cameras

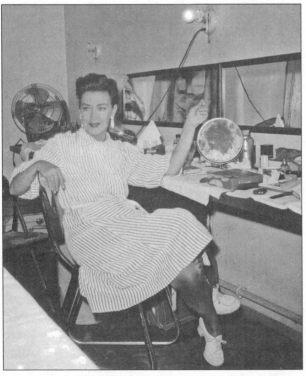

**Relaxing with her visitors in the dressing room
of the Beverly Hills (KY) Country Club**

out of her handbag and they snapped all the pictures they wanted to. Jane, wearing a robe, even changed into her gown for them. Following the second show of the evening, Jane came back on stage, saying, "A few years ago on my television show I introduced a song which is now on its way to becoming a standard. I would like to sing it tonight especially for three friends of mine who came all the way from Illinois." She sang "I Believe" directly to them.

After that engagement, Jane virtually disappeared from the world of entertainment. Back pain that had nagged her for months had become intolerable, and attempts to relieve it were unsuccessful. She found it increasingly difficult to perform. A spinal fusion—a grueling and risky procedure that could leave her worse off than she was—might be the only solution.

Old anxieties returned along with the new; going out on stage was stressful, and the longer she stayed out of work, the more frightening it became to perform. Dr. Kubie felt she needed a break—a real break—from her responsibilities as a performer, and wrote a letter on her behalf to Abe Lastfogel at the William Morris Agency. The cumulative effect of Jane's personal disappointments and her physical suffering plus her mother's recent failing health, he explained, had left Jane emotionally depleted. She had become depressed. He recommended a leave of absence so she could relax and regain her health.

When it appeared that she no longer had any choice in the matter, Jane agreed to have the spinal fusion, knowing that she would have to go through months of tests on her back before surgery was finally performed, and dreading the long and difficult recovery that she knew so well from earlier bone grafts.

She told friends she was going to find a nice quiet place to rest and swim and take care of her back. She enjoyed swimming; it was one activity in which she could engage without a brace. She didn't tell anyone about the upcoming surgery; they must be tired of hearing about her operations by now.

The surgery—her thirty-fifth since the crash—took place early in 1959. Afterward, encased in a steel brace while the bones in her spine fused, she lay in the hospital, seriously depressed, wishing to see no one. Even Mama wasn't allowed to visit.

When it was time to leave the hospital, the gnawing pain had ceased, but only if she remained stooped over, with her arms dangling. Physical therapy was recommended, but she thought she could get well without it. Month after month, there was no improvement. She dared not move for fear of that terrible pain coming back. Finally, she listened to her doctors and entered a rehabilitation center, the Burke Foundation in White Plains, New York, for an intensive program of physical therapy and psychiatric help.

At Burke, recovery was effected through rigorous workouts. She was up at 8 A.M. and into the gymnasium in spite of her tears and complaints. Every hour on the hour she was forced to exercise: to walk, pull pulleys, stretch or bend. They didn't care whether she complained about pain. The arduous routine left her exhausted. On Fridays she was rewarded with free time to relax with a chosen activity. She painted, as she had done at Menningers, and enjoyed it tremendously. Slowly, she started to feel better, and could walk upright without pain.

The wisdom of the intense training at the Burke Foundation paid off as Jane regained her mobility and stood and

walked erect again. Full recovery was slow. She walked a bit
every day and was amazed that she felt no pain.

It was the first time since the plane crash that she was
totally free of pain, and Jane tested it every way she could.
She played golf again when she wasn't working, hoping to
regain her low 80s game, starting with two holes, then four,
and five. She had no pain. She went to parties and danced—
and didn't have to pretend that she was fine. It wasn't long
before she found herself thinking about going back to work.
The feeling was not unlike the time in 1945 when she left
hospitals and doctors behind to go to Europe and finish the
job she had started two years before. This time, she headed
for Chicago.

She and Helen arrived with eleven pieces of luggage
which barely fit in the compartment of the Twentieth Century Limited or the dressing room at the Chez Paree. In her
bags were couture gowns from the finest designers—Dior
of Paris, Simonetta of Rome, Hattie Carnegie of New York.
She had paid $22,000 for them. They were as much a part of
her act as her singing voice.

She opened on Friday the 13th. Could she defy the fates
any more than that? Superstitious, she brought a few lucky
charms with her. She needn't have worried. When the lights
went out and orchestra leader George Cook announced, "And
now the Chez Paree management is very proud and privileged
to present Miss Jane Froman," she appeared, a vision in a white
satin gown with a red velvet bodice, to thunderous applause.

She opened with "All of You," the hit song from Cole
Porter's *Silk Stockings*, recently released as an MGM musical
starring Fred Astaire and Cyd Charisse, sung as a personal
welcome to her audience. After she thanked them for coming "to see Susan Hayward sing," she sang more beautiful

ballads, putting her audience in a warm and mellow mood. Then came a few oldies by two of her favorite composers, Richard Rodgers and George Gershwin, whose music she loved and sang so well. She added the special material by Bob Wright and Chet Forrest now in her repertory: "A Bag of Popcorn and a Dream" and "Southern California Blues," which Charlie Dawn in *Chicago's American* called "a comic valentine, dipped in acid, to Los Angeles."

On November 14, 1959, reviewer Sam Lesner of the *Chicago Daily News* wrote that Jane Froman,

> with the grace of a bird, took the Chez Paree by storm Friday night . . . a living testimony that we once knew beautiful singing when we heard it. . . . Beautiful singing is an art, whether in a night club or a concert hall. . . . You never forget Froman once you've heard her.

The rest of Chicago agreed with Lesner.

Here she was, at last, in front of an audience, totally free of pain for the first time in all the years since the accident. She felt like a new woman. Her worst fears over, she could now go on with her plans to perform at other clubs around the country. It was good to be singing again. She didn't want to stop.

Back in good form, Jane opened at the Persian Room of the Plaza just before New Year's, working with Sid Feller on brilliant new arrangements. Once again, she dazzled her audience. After the opening night performance, composer Richard Rodgers, who was there with his wife, Dorothy, rose from his table and kissed her, saying "That's the way to sing my songs." He wrote her a note afterward:

> The whole presentation at The Persian Room is exciting, completely musical and emotional. I should think that you

**With Richard and Dorothy Rodgers backstage at the
Persian Room**

would be extraordinarily successful wherever you go. . . . Just
go on giving yourself to the vast number of people who will
find joy and inspiration in what you have to say and sing.

Dick

A string of night club appearances filled her calendar for
the new year, from the Casino Royal in Washington D.C. to
the Venetian Room at the Fairmont in San Francisco. The
San Mateo Times said of her performance there:

> Miss Froman . . . is of that rare (nowadays) genre—a
> singer who can sing. There is nothing meretricious about her
> songs, her style or her act. She sings today with the same
> verve and style that has made and kept her a star of the first
> magnitude since her debut with Paul Whiteman.

It was hard to see, in the light of Jane's busy engagement calendar and ensuing accolades, that the dawn of a new age was approaching.

By the late 1950s, rock and roll was sweeping the world. Jane's songs were still played on the radio, but were being eased out by the new sounds and rhythms. New York disc jockey and fellow Missourian Jim Lowe met Jane around that time, when he was new in town. She was kind to him, introducing him to people and encouraging him, even using one of the songs he wrote, a beautiful ballad called "I Still Have a Lifetime Before Me" in her night club act. Jane and Jim became good friends—and they both loved a good martini.

One night, the two were having dinner, and after each had a couple of drinks, Jane grew introspective. Jim asked her, "On TV, you never stutter. How is that possible?"

She answered, using a noise in her throat combined with the words "I mean" that told friends she was getting in gear: "I mean—I could stop stuttering right now and not stutter again all evening if I wanted to."

"Why, then, don't you do it?" he asked.

"I mean—I w-w-wouldn't enjoy it!"

Jim was introduced to Jane's mother early in their friendship. Mama was a forceful lady, he found, probably much like her forebears, but Jim found her interesting. When she was in town she and Jim had lunch. As they talked about this and that, Anna Froman Hetzler made a confession that Jim found rather startling.

"Nobody knows this," she said. "Jane's father, my husband, stuttered so badly that, walking down the street in St. Louis, if he saw a neighbor, he had to rev himself up to speak." This was the only known reference ever made to Jane's father having had a stuttering problem.

The major clubs were beginning to disappear. Soft music and sentimental ballads—the kind of music that made the clubs the romantic rendezvous of polite society—were becoming passé. Those that remained, clustered in Las Vegas, became more glitzy. Tastefully orchestrated ballads were replaced with off-color humor and lots of flesh. The flashing strobe lights and sounds of disco were only a few years down the road.

Jane saw a change in the offers that came her way. She was still a popular guest star on television, singing Gershwin on the *Bell Telephone Hour* or dancing the cha-cha and the waltz with choreographer James Starbuck on the *Arthur Murray Party,* but soon after her latest sweep of the night clubs, jobs were fewer and farther between despite everything the Morris Agency did to find things for her to do. Recent medical bills were again nagging at her; she hated the loathsome feeling of being in debt. In one of her rare admissions of despair, Jane wrote to her old friend, Abe Lastfogel, who had seen her through the roughest spots in her career, admitting that she felt it was time to retire. The only thing stopping her, however, was the money she owed the Agency. She would work to pay off the last of her debts and call it quits.

Lastfogel wrote back immediately with the encouraging words he hoped would change Jane's mind:

> . . . it is most vital and important you not become discouraged and decide to quit. You have already made an investment in your arrangements and clothes and you can handle your expenses so if there is a stretch of time when you are not booked you can enjoy the many good things you can do in the lay-off period. You certainly have proven your

courage and fortitude in handling much greater problems than the temporary disappointment in your career. I urge you to again call upon your inherent strength and understanding to overcome this immediate hurdle.

Lastfogel's heart was, as always, huge and generous, but nobody knew Jane the way she knew herself. Some people called it stubbornness, and perhaps it was, but that stubbornness had saved her life, saved her leg, and given her a career the envy of the show business world. She trusted those strong instincts. It was a matter of paying the bills. She would work toward that end, and then consider the future.

In May, she appeared on the *Ed Sullivan Show* looking lovelier than ever. In a stylish black sheath gown that clung to her figure, long white gloves, and a new shorter hairdo, she extended her arms and smiled her welcoming smile and the audience was in her hands. Few noticed that in the familiar old ballads Jane sang, her voice showed signs of wear.

To those who knew the amazing Froman voice, there was first a shaky note in the upper register, then another note not quite on target, and a thin quality that was unusual in a voice always so rich and strong. Fortunately her regal bearing and remarkably effective stage movements and gestures highlighted the joy in the music, and even Sullivan himself unabashedly bent to her beauty and style—but it was to be her final television appearance.

The long years of pain medication and drinking to ease the relentless pain, the physical strain from one operation after another, plus major personal disappointments had caught up to her and were now affecting her voice. She was tired. Was she up to facing a life without singing? Could she?

There must be more to living than this, and perhaps it was time to find out.

Her left knee had begun hurting, probably from favoring it over the years, and she needed another operation. She decided to have it in Columbia. There was still one more commitment to fulfill and she prepared for it—a concert under the stars with the Connecticut Pops, on July 15, 1960, in Fairfield, Connecticut, with guest conductor Paul Lavalle.

Friends, her beloved "stoop sitters society," drove up to hear her sing, and that lifted her spirits. They knew her heart was no longer in it; she had told them so, but she had contracts to fulfill and she would give them the best show she knew how. Worried about her voice and the reception she would get, the group placed themselves strategically in the audience to spread the applause.

They needn't have worried. The crowd cheered as Jane swept onto the stage in a cloud of yellow organdy. She did her favorite kind of show, songs that paid tribute to America's great songwriters: Jerome Kern, George Gershwin, Cole Porter, Rodgers and Hammerstein.

At the first intermission, a fellow in an American Legion uniform dashed up onto the stage with a bouquet of roses, "to the sweetheart of the Armed Forces," he said, with deep affection and appreciation. Although he fumbled for the appropriate words, Jane was obviously moved, and kissed him on the cheek, leaving him in a glorious daze as he found his way back to his buddies. The scene had probably been played out a thousand times before, and still it was deeply moving.

The mood was high and Jane's voice did not betray her. It was not the voice of ten years ago, but allowances could be made for time and age. An electric charge was in the

Connecticut air that summer night as Joyce Liskin and her husband, Elliot, met Jane in her dressing room along with Windy, Bobbie, Deena and Babs. Only Jane, among them, knew that it was to be her farewell performance.

At last, her medical bills and other debts were paid. It was time to go home.

22

MRS. SMITH
1961–1980

AFTER THIRTY-FOUR YEARS in show business, Jane Froman went home to the town where she had grown up, Columbia, Missouri. It was still a staunchly collegiate town set in the heart of middle America. Its values had not changed much since Jane had left.

Although she had had several recording and television offers in the past year, Jane could no longer maintain her own standards of excellence. An honest artist, she said, knew when the time had come to cease performing professionally, and she retired officially.

Mama had purchased a small home for herself after her husband's estate was settled, and Jane moved in with her, much like the old days when they shared a small apartment on the Christian College campus.

With a small income from record royalties and a few prudent investments to sustain her, Jane enjoyed her new role as a citizen of Columbia. She savored the privacy of her life, but remained active and involved, working with civic and church groups and her beloved alma mater, now known as Columbia College. She did needlework and knitted gifts for friends.

Earning her way back into the community after being away for three decades was not easy. Jane understood this.

After all, she had grown up among these diehard "show me" people. Columbia was going to be a tough audience.

Health problems still dogged her, and in June she was in the hospital again. Her left leg was troubling her now. Adhesions had formed in her spine after her disc and fusion operations in 1957 and 1958, and were pinching nerves going down her leg. She had four peridural blocks in her spine to relieve the pain and hydrocortosone was used to break up the adhesions.

Back on her feet again and out of pain, Jane enrolled at the University of Missouri to study art history and appreciation, hoping to earn credits toward a degree. She had always been interested in the arts. Learning to paint at Menningers, then renewing her interest in painting at the Burke Foundation, had opened a window for her. With leisure time now, she pursued it with eager anticipation.

The other students were friendly and often shared conversations over coffee. They took an interest in her work as she did in theirs. The faculty, however, was not at all convinced Jane hadn't returned on some sort of a publicity scheme. Her instructor,

Jane in art class

using the university's system of "excellent," "superior," "inferior" and "failure" instead of the more traditional A, B, C, D, F grades, graded her "inferior."

Swallowing her pride, Jane dug in her heels and took on the challenge. She took courses in composition and introduction to art and drawing; three afternoons a week she was in class from 12:40 to 5:30. The other two days she had a shorter schedule.

Although she had to cut her studies short late in 1961 when she was hospitalized for pneumonia, she returned to school when she was well again, taking a course in drawing with the same teacher who had found her work inferior. Her drawing revealed obvious talent. This time, she earned a "superior" grade, qualifying her for the dean's list. Mama, still conscious of anything that might tarnish their reputation, was so proud that her daughter was now an honor student, she called everyone in town.

Occasionally, local reporters would seek Jane out for an interview, and she always obliged, remembering her own beginnings as a journalist. Was it tough? they asked her, referring to her return to school after so long.

"Don't think it doesn't take some doing to go back to school after more than thirty years," she said. "These students today are smarter than we ever were. They are as keen as can be. The wars, the bomb and TV have made an impact which definitely shows. They are darling. I just love them. . . . If I'm drawing and do something wrong, they come over to help me. I'm having a ball."

Social life began to fall in place, too. Jane and Lita Spencer, a fellow alumna of Christian College, had become reacquainted, and Lita and her husband, George, saw to it that Jane got out to meet people. They invited her to a New Year's Eve party, where Jane was introduced to Rowland Haw Smith, Assistant Managing Editor of the Columbia *Tribune*. Smith had been a newspaperman since he arrived in Columbia from Charleston, Missouri, in 1926, at the age of seventeen. Smith's first wife had died a year earlier after a long illness.

Jane and Rowland had actually met before, when they were both young students at the University of Missouri. He had never dated Jane then, he said, "because she was booked up three or four months in advance!" Rowland had seen Jane perform in Bad Hamburg, Germany, but stayed in the background, letting the fellows in the military get all the attention. A mild man, Rowland was tough at his newspaper job. Known by everyone in Columbia as "Smitty," he was honest, intelligent, and witty. Jane was attracted to Rowland, and they began going out together.

Jane and Rowland found they enjoyed each other's company and both loved to dance. When Rowland showed greater interest in her than that of a companion for the country club dances, Jane found herself enjoying the attention. Rowland knew everyone in town and helped ease her into Columbia social life. They enjoyed much in common, especially watching the Tigers play.

One night when Jane came home in the wee hours of the morning after a date with Rowland, Mama scolded her for staying out too late. This time her mother's strict rules amused her; at last she was not being treated as a star, and she and Rowland laughed about it long afterward.

When Rowland called at the end of the semester to ask Jane if he could help her clean out her locker, she knew the relationship had become serious. They became engaged

Jane always relished a chance to meet with "her girls."

shortly after and planned to marry in June.

As the date of their wedding neared Jane had an anxiety attack. What was she getting herself into? Mama's health had been deteriorating. Was she so terrified of being alone? Rowland was a respected member of the Columbia community, with a forty year history at the *Tribune*—everyone knew and loved him. The world she imagined with him was safe and secure. He was willing to take her on with no money and a lot of health problems. What did she fear?

What did Rowland expect of her in return? The long years of medical problems had left her physically exhausted and emotionally drained. Would he understand her needs? Was this too much of a burden to place on him? He had been through a difficult time with the long illness of his first wife. Was it fair to him? Was it too much of a commitment for her?

In a panic, she asked Rowland to be released from her promise to marry him. Smitty, showing remarkable insight, stood firm on their agreement, insisting that he loved her and wanted to marry her, and that she had to uphold her end of the bargain. Jane, perhaps needing that reassurance, and someone who could stand up to her, unafraid, went ahead with the wedding. If she had any doubts after that, no one ever knew about them.

On June 22, 1962, Jane and Rowland were married in the chapel of the First Presbyterian Church student center. Among the guests were Mama, the Spencers, who had introduced them, Ruth Barnard, her friend and former psychotherapist from Menningers, and a few other friends, including Carol Kennedy and Carol Peck.

The Smiths honeymooned at the Lake of the Ozarks, a beautiful resort area in the heart of Missouri, after which they moved into Rowland's house while they had a house of their own built in the quiet southwest part of Columbia, not far from the *Tribune* offices and the University.

Jane and Rowland after their wedding, June 22, 1962

Browsing the antique shops around Columbia, Jane spotted a couch in a shop window that she liked and showed it to friends. It represented what she had missed all those years in show business: a real home, and roots. Friends thought it looked more suited to a bordello than Jane's and Rowland's home, in its bright red upholstery, but they humored her. When Abe Lastfogel heard about it, he told Jane to buy it and have it upholstered the way she wanted it. He would give it to her for a wedding present. The couch disappeared from the shop window and didn't reappear until the Smiths moved into their new house on Cowan Drive, reupholstered in a blue floral fabric chosen by Jane, looking elegant.

Jane made their house a fine home. In the dining room. she put her grandmother's hand-painted china punch bowl, strewn with pink and white roses and rimmed with gold. She gave another place of honor to the hot chocolate pitcher her grandmother had painted, sprinkled with violets copied from her garden.

The only painting on the walls was the Corbellini, over the blue sofa in the living room. Victor Hammer offered to give her a Dali to hang and she refused it. "Can you imagine the worry of having something like that hanging in your house?" she asked. No, thank you. Jane and Rowland were happy living simply.

She did enjoy an original Ludwig Bemelmans drawing of a doctor that hung over her bed, however. She loved that picture; thought it so apt, portraying all the doctors in her life—"always in a hurry and looking like they know so much!"

Jane learned to prepare several dishes. "I never learned to cook," she explained. "I never had a home life as a child, for

I was raised in girls' schools. Now, after a thirty-four-year career, I'm beginning to learn how to prepare a few things."

One of her favorite dishes was spaghetti. The sauce, she said in triumph, was from opera legend Enrico Caruso's own recipe, and she loved making it for friends when they visited. When asked in an interview what it was like to go from stardom to housewife, Jane said she loved it. "When you enjoy cooking spaghetti more than singing then you know you are really retired."

Having her own home, a husband who was known and loved by everyone, and a rich full life of homemaking like every other woman in town was what Jane had dreamed of for so long. As Mrs. Rowland Smith she had the glorious feeling of being home now that her work was done.

In October, 1962, John F. Kennedy signed a congressional bill awarding Jane $20,000 as "full and final payment" for damages in the 1943 plane crash. Her expenses at that point had reached $500,000. It's easy to imagine her chuckling over the irony of it with Rowland, but hard to believe that there was not a touch of bitterness as she swallowed this last pill regarding the crash.

Mama fell ill that fall. At eighty-eight, she was still teaching, and gave her last music lesson on the day she went into the hospital for the last time. Once the talented and promising pianist Anna Tillman Barcafer, and later first lady of Columbia, Anna Froman Hetzler died on November 20, 1962. The one stalwart person in Jane's life, always supportive in spite of her doubts about her daughter's musical choices, was gone. Whatever the tension between Jane and her mother had been over the years, there is no doubt that their love for each other ran deep. Jane buried her mother in the pearls she had bought early in her career, when she could first afford them.

The trauma of Mama's illness and death was difficult enough, but pain in Jane's back and leg was once again impairing her ability to walk. Doctors had informed her that the only solution was to have another spinal fusion. If she went ahead with it, she faced the odds that she might not survive another surgery and, if she did, she could possibly end up a helpless invalid. It was a terrifying proposition. She chose instead to do intensive therapy and lay in traction many hours a day.

A bird feeder that was in the backyard was difficult to see from her bedroom window, as their little trees had grown up to obscure it, but Rowland put another feeder closer to the window and Jane would watch the activity around it from her bed.

To help her tolerate this latest challenge, Jane saw a psychiatrist regularly. Pain was not new to her; nor was time spent alone, in bed, thinking. This was one more hurdle in a life too generously packed with challenges. If she needed a couple of drinks or pills to help relieve her pain, she did not hesitate to use them.

A substantial drinker himself, Rowland did not judge Jane, but did tell the story, after her death, of how, during a fierce argument, Jane had deliberately picked up a stack of his former wife's dinner plates and dropped them one by one to shatter on the floor. "Living with her was not easy," he said with a grin.

Contented in her role as Mrs. Rowland Smith, Jane continued to help raise funds for mental health, the physically disabled, muscular dystrophy, and many other causes. It was sometimes impossible to keep a low profile, however, as people remembered her for who she was and what she had done before. She still got letters from GIs she sang for, twenty years later.

In 1963, Jane was awarded the Distinguished Alumna Award from the Alumni Association at Christian College, citing her for her "artistry as a singer in the realm of fine art and her inspiration which she has given to millions and which have transformed her into a living legend." Rowland bought her a pink evening gown for the occasion, the first gown any man had ever bought for her. And in 1965, Jane was instrumental in bringing old friend and renowned actress Helen Hayes to Columbia for the college's Distinguished Women of America Award.

When Abe Lastfogel was honored in 1968 for his contributions to the founding of the USO, Jane was eager to

With old friend Helen Hayes

attend. The award was made in Dallas. For years, Lastfogel had repeatedly declined invitations to accept public recognition for his work, but finally gave in, with the understanding that in accepting the award he would do so on behalf of the American entertainment industry, honoring them for their patriotic contributions and for building the morale of America's military forces.

Jane was to receive an award, too, a specially designed gold medallion, struck for the occasion, for her "exceptional example of courage and devotion to duty despite great personal sacrifice." Asked to deliver a speech about Abe, she said, "That will be no problem at all. I could talk for hours about that dear, sweet man."

Jane bought a new pink gown to wear to the USO dinner, and she and Rowland even bought a bright red '65 Dodge, with air conditioning, power steering and power brakes, for the occasion, deciding to drive rather than take the train.

Another honor that gave Jane great joy came in 1971 when she was elected into the Academy of Missouri Squires, founded by former governor, James T. Blair, to honor Missourians for their accomplishments in community, state, or nation. "It's easy to get awards all over the world, but damned hard to get one in your home town," Jane remarked with a chuckle. It was one of her proudest achievements.

Jane's health began to deteriorate. Her incessant smoking had surely contributed to the eventual failure of her voice, and it had also left her with emphysema. Pulmonary specialist Dr. Hugh Stephenson, looking at an X-ray of Jane's lungs, didn't like what he saw. With Jane's history of heavy smoking and of her emphysema, he suspected that the spot he saw on the film was bad news and he proposed lung surgery. On December 14, 1965, he performed a thoracotomy and pulmonary resection, removing the part of the lung in question. It was a surprise to find out that, even with emphysema, Jane's lungs were still good.

Dr. Stephenson, who was Head of General Surgery at the University of Missouri Medical Center, was in awe of Jane. The surgery didn't phase her a bit; it was just another step in her unusual journey through life, one that included dozens of anesthesias, operations and procedures. "She was one of the best patients I ever had," he said. "She had the ability to breathe with one lung or the other and control her breathing because of her singing. It was a talent that I have never seen other people have as far as patients are concerned."

After her surgery, which involved an incision from her spine to her sternum, Jane's right arm, once again, did not work very well. Scar tissue had formed, making it difficult for her to use that arm, especially when it was cold or when it rained. Knitting and crocheting, her constant companions, kept her fingers moving as much as possible, but the right arm had little strength and the fingers little control. Even writing a check became difficult for her; it might take seven or eight tries before she got it right. She was forced to stop writing the long chatty letters she had been writing all her life, and she couldn't speak on the phone, but friends understood and continued to write to her. Some, who had been out of touch for a while during her retirement years, were jolted into action when they heard of Jane's fragile condition.

Many of the fans who had known Jane since they were teenagers were in frequent contact with her. Others had fallen out of touch. Former Fromanettes Bobbie and Win had been working at General Electric's *Progressland* exhibit at the 1964 World's Fair when Bobbie noticed a familiar name on the register of VIP visitors expected at the pavilion: Dr. William C.

Menninger. Eager to see him again, she and Win met him as he arrived. It was a happy reunion—it had been said of Dr. Will that he spent his life radiating warmth everywhere he went and it was certainly true that day—but he also lost no time in putting the young women back in touch with Jane.

"When did you last write to Jane?" he asked, after a warm hug.

It had been a long time.

"Write a note to her right now and I will deliver it to her personally when I see her in a few days," he said. You didn't say no to Dr. Will. On the spot, they penned notes to Jane, breaking the long spell of silence, and watched him slip them into his jacket pocket. They were never out of touch with her after that.

Within and around the Columbia community, Jane kept busy in endless charitable causes and alumni activities. Rowland, following his retirement from the Columbia *Tribune*, had joined the University of Missouri as Associate Director of the Office of Public Information, bringing to him a whole new set of responsibilities as well as social events, which Jane attended with him. Perhaps most dear to Jane's heart among all her activities, however, was the establishment of a music center in the town of Arrowrock, a few miles from Columbia.

Not even deteriorating health could keep her from taking part in that. The idea of the center intrigued her, because she remembered how wonderful it was to live and breathe music twenty-four hours a day at the Oscar Seagle music camp at Schroon Lake when she was a girl.

Arrow Rock, as it came to be called, was the vision of Jay Turley, a playwright who had, like Jane, come home to small

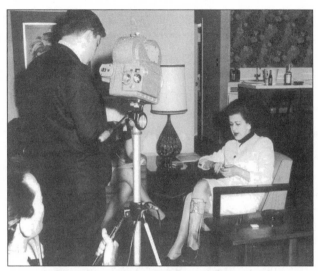

Being interviewed about Arrow Rock

town Missouri after a career in the entertainment world. He had helped found the Jane Froman Music Center at Columbia College in 1969. Turley's idea of having a place where young musical talent could be encouraged to grow was just the thing to appeal to Jane's talents as well as her abundant energy and need to contribute.

She enjoyed being around talented young musicians. She threw herself into brainstorming ideas with Turley and pitching in to help raise money for the center.

"The spirit of the whole thing is the most contagious, beguiling thing you ever saw. If you could do this all over the world, you'd never have a war."

The popular music scene had changed, Jane admitted. "Some of my best work was done on my TV show in the '50s," she said. "I thought I was pretty hip then. But I've never been as hip as the kids are today."

She appreciated the Beatles, who had captured her imagination. "The Beatles are inventive and I think they are trying to get onto a new sound," she said, prophetically. "Their song, 'Yesterday,' is one of the most beautiful I have ever heard. And what impresses me is that they did not stop there; they seem to be looking for new things."

In 1969, for two days, Jane briefly interrupted her retirement for a benefit Christmas concert to raise money for the music camp, scheduled to open in June. Singing in public for the first time in many years—and after lung surgery!—she was the featured performer in "A Party for Jane," a production of the Arrow Rock Opera House. She had a time getting her diaphragm back in such a short time, but the audience loved her, and she got standing ovations, singing "Good King Wenceslas," "The Christmas Song," and "White Christmas."

For one of the Christmas concerts, Sue Gerard, the swimming instructor who had debunked the myth about Jane diving headfirst into the Christian College pool, was in the audience. Gerard recalled being there with her husband, Chub and a small group of Christian College girls:

> It was a wonderfully informal evening of song. . . . Jane "slid" forward as if she were on skates. . . . Jane sang with us, not to us! It was true friends singing together. . . . It was breath taking for those college girls—and for Chub (a fine bass) and me (a husky alto). It was a relaxed. . . . family of singers and the greatest voice in the world, in its waning years. I shall never forget it.

The music camp produced a few musicals, and Jane worked hard to do her part. It appealed to her professional honor that, as she had been helped by show business professionals in her youth, she might pass on what she knew about stagemanship, movement, and voice to the young people in the productions. However, Arrow Rock never achieved the success everyone had hoped for, and in 1972, the last concerts were performed there. It must have been a terrible disappointment.

The early part of 1976 saw a decline in Jane's health, when she was hospitalized with cardiac and pulmonary problems. She came home from the hospital on March 20th. Rowland hired a woman to help out at home, as Jane was up against a long recuperation period. Her weight was down to ninety-three pounds. Daily phone calls from "the kids"—the fans who had grown as close to her as her own children—kept them in touch with Jane, who chirped in the background when Rowland talked on the phone. When they heard that Jane wasn't doing well, Bobbie, Deena, and the two Carols paid a visit.

The women were entertained by Rowland as they waited for Jane to come out; Bobbie and Deena had not seen her for several years. Rowland could throw no light on the state of Jane's health, except to say that she always seemed much better after one of the visits from her kids.

At last, Jane joined them, wearing a red and white hostess gown. Her face with its electric blue eyes and perfectly shaped lips was the same, with makeup carefully applied, but her hair was now its natural gray, rolled back from her face. Her head tilted leeward. She was thin, extremely thin. As always, she walked on her own, no cane in sight.

In no time they were all sitting around, talking, laughing. The women had brought gifts—her favorite Fanny May chocolates, with the cream centers; coffee from the renowned delicatessen, Zabar's, in New York.

The mood mellowed as the conversation turned backward in time. The women recalled how Jane had helped them with their adolescent troubles with parents, school, boyfriends, careers, heartbreak and loss.

"Why did you do it, Jane?" asked Bobbie. Jane looked at her thoughtfully.

"Because I love you," she answered, without hesitation. "You'll never know what you did for me. You got me through some very tough times. You were there, darlings, loving me, when it seemed like nobody else did."

Jane spoke about how they had done as much for her in difficult times as she had ever done for them. "You'll never know how much," she said. The Fromanettes album they had presented to her many years ago, she told them, was one of the finest gifts she had ever received, and how she treasured it.

Hours passed as they remembered those times, when the girls were too young to appreciate the depth of Jane's grown-up concerns, but turned up, nevertheless, pouring out their enthusiasm and their love. They talked about those times when she lived in the brownstone and they gathered there to meet, complete with lunches, Coca-Colas and school papers. She recalled when they first called her "Aunt Jane," and how she loved it. Jane sat back and chuckled. "We had fun, didn't we?" she said with a twinkle, after hours of stories and memories.

Visits like these became more frequent, as more of "her children" learned of Jane's fragile condition and stopped by to see her. Diane L. came in from Washington and brought her dog, Cabaret, to Jane's delight. Carol S. and Joann, traveling around the country, stopped in Columbia, bringing more chocolates that Jane devoured, and having the good fortune to taste Jane's famous spaghetti sauce that she swore was opera star Caruso's own recipe. Bobbie and Win made a stopover on a trip to Santa Fe and brought coffee from Manhattan's renowned Zabar's as well as Bobbie's latest picture book for her to autograph and a stoneware casserole that Win had made. They talked about politics—how people on the West Coast felt about Ronald Reagan, and the possibility of Bobby Kennedy running for president; about literature and poets and the disappointment of best sellers; about movies and gardens and recipes and painting and music, always music. It was during one of their conversations that Carol S. got Jane to tell her, once and for all, that she was a mezzo, not a contralto, as some had described her. Jane loved each visit and grew more excited as they went on.

Carol P. and Carol K. had remained fast friends since their weekend at the Chez Paree in 1957 and met every year in Columbia to visit Jane. If if was a good day for Jane, and they had shopped, they had show and tell.

"Show me what you bought," Jane would say. "I want to see." And they'd go to it. They might also go through the women's magazines and catalogues, ordering something here or there.

If Jane needed to lie in bed to elevate her leg, they sat quietly and watched TV together with her. They might spend hours without saying a word. At dinnertime, Rowland would go out for a pizza.

In a thank you note after one of these visits, Rowland wrote:

> Wish I could report a remarkable recovery for her, but I can't. She's just about the same, having good days and bad days, and the best days when some of her "kids" are on hand. Carol K and mother were here last week, and we're expecting

Deena, hubby and two children Aug. 20. Maybe that'll get Jane off to a good Fall start. . . .

Deena made the trip with her husband and two young boys, to introduce them to this woman who had had such an impact on her life. They had a wonderful visit but shortly after, in September, 1977, Jane was in the hospital again with cardiac problems, pneumonia, pulmonary edema, a broken toe, and emphysema. She was there for nearly three weeks.

In late November, Jane could hardly get out of bed, much less celebrate Thanksgiving. Bobbie and Win phoned Rowland and said they were coming out and they were bringing the holiday with them. Rowland passed the message to Jane, and in no time, she rallied and asked the two Carols to come and join them. By Thursday morning, all had arrived and were in the kitchen, cutting, chopping, preparing the turkey. Bobbie and Win had carried a blender with them, along with fresh oysters packed on ice for Jane's favorite dressing.

Limp as a rag doll when they arrived, Jane rallied as the preparations went on. She flitted in and out of the kitchen all morning, eager to join in the conversation as the women prepared the Thanksgiving dinner. Suddenly, she seemed to have her doubts about the safety of the turkey. She had read about botulism, and no amount of persuasive talk satisfied her. At last she did what she did whenever she had an insurmountable problem: she called her friend, Rosa Guitar. Rosa knew just about everything from how to grow an eggplant to racing horses to redecorating a room. At ease, finally, Jane continued setting the table for their dinner.

She took out her Bavarian china and suggested using the floral arrangement on her coffee table in the living room for the centerpiece on the dining table. More than once, she checked the menu and made changes. She insisted on putting the cranberry sauce in little cups made from scooped out oranges—something she had seen in a women's magazine that had caught her fancy. At the last moment, she brought out her pinking shears to cut a decorative rim on each of the orange cups.

Dinner was served buffet style. Carol P. said grace, and all bowed their heads as she gave thanks for being together, and for Jane's improving health. After many good helpings of food, the old friends sat around the living room, Jane on the blue couch that was her wedding present from Abe Lastfogel, her knitting needles clicking, talking on through the evening. Rowland enjoyed the chatter as much as anyone did,

"The happiest Thanksgiving ever," Carol K., Rowland, Jane, and Carol P.

Win, Bobbie, and the turkey

throwing in the occasional story about the Tigers or his days at the *Tribune*.

By the next evening, Jane was in good enough spirits to make a pot of chili for everyone.

"What's that ingredient that's so important in chili? I just can't remember it."

"Cumin?" Bobbie suggested.

"Of course! Cumin!" Jane happily returned to the chili pot. Whether it was puttering in the kitchen or talking politics, Jane did it with gusto.

As they had the night before, they picked up on the conversation again, and talked until it seemed right to end it. Jane could have gone on and on. The goodbyes were long and warm, and it seemed a shame to leave, when the company had revived her so.

Several days later, Rowland reported that Jane was doing better, and was gaining weight. "She says it was her happiest Thanksgiving ever," he said.

Jane continued to get physically stronger, but after a while, there were longer and longer periods of depression between short spurts of higher spirits.

In October, 1979, Jane insisted on a trip to New York where the doctors could surely figure out what was wrong with her and make her well. Rowland felt she had enough good doctors in Columbia, but he could not talk her out of it. What's more, Jane wanted to do this alone. Old pal Dudley Malone arranged for Jane to stay at his mother's apartment while she was away for a few days, and Jane boarded the train for New York.

At first it looked like things would work out well. Dudley took her to a couple of favorite restaurants on the East side, but the walk to one of them was too much for her.

In the tiny New York apartment, Jane took over the only bedroom, her clothes hanging all over, her medicines and pill bottles covering the night table and bathroom sink. The small living room was hardly a place for a party, but she called on Joyce to host the reunion. A dozen people crowded together— and arranged themselves on the few chairs and floor as they had once done in Jane's large apartment and the brownstone.

Unfortunately, the good fun did not last. The next day Jane became really ill and ended up in the hospital. Rowland had to be fetched when she felt better, to take her back home. This last desperate attempt to set things right physically took its toll. At home again, she retired to her bed and rarely got up.

On Christmas night, 1979, Jane felt well enough to have dinner with friends Rosa and Len Guitar, who lived just a little north of town. Rowland drove. It was dark, and as he turned to go into the driveway, he went beyond the intended turn, heading for a ditch instead. A car was coming toward them on the passenger side where Jane was sitting, so he accelerated and went for the ditch. The oncoming car hit them anyway, but Rowland's move saved them from serious injury. Jane spent several days in the hospital, suffering only bruises but under watch. Rowland was unharmed, as were the people in the other car. Although Rowland's quick thinking had probably avoided a real tragedy, those who knew Jane said she never completely recovered from this accident. She told friends that, as they were hit, she thought, "God, you finally got me."

On the morning of April 22, 1980, Rowland had seen to Jane's breakfast and had left the house for his morning ritual of taking a walk and getting the paper. When he returned, he found Jane in her bed; she had died in her sleep. The cause of death was noted as cardiac arrest.

Dudley and Joyce were at the funeral. Bobbie, Deena, and the two Carols were there, too, as were friends of the Smiths and some of Rowland's cronies from his *Tribune* days. It was Dudley's proposition on arrival to tell only funny stories about Jane for their two days in Columbia, because she would not have wanted them to be gloomy. Everyone agreed. He offered up the first one.

He told once of being on a train with Jane, when she excused herself, got up and went to the next car for something. In her short journey from one car to another, she spied a movie star with a reputation for sleeping around. She couldn't wait to tell Dudley. When she came back, she was all excited.

"Y-Y-Y-Y-You n-n-n-n-know who's on the t-t-t-t-t-train with u-u-us?"

In her rush to speak, her tongue failed her.

"No, who?" Dudley, the biggest tease in the world, with a sense of humor to match, grinned, waiting for the information to come. They had made jokes about her stutter throughout their relationship, and she loved it. He even told stories like this one in Jane's presence, without removing the stutter from the telling.

"J-J-J-J-J-J . . ." She tried again. "J-J-J-J-J . . ." She got madder and madder, and the madder she got the more she stayed stuck. "D-D-Dudley . . ." she pleaded, "y-y-y-y-y-y-you know who I mean . . . J-J-J-J-J-J-J-J-J-J-J . . ." She was exasperated by now. She forced out one final word. "c-c-c-c-*crabs*!" They broke up.

Rowland managed to keep himself together for the service at the First Presbyterian Church in Columbia, but he, along with the other mourners, broke down a little when the organist played "I Believe."

She was laid to rest in a white casket in the Columbia Cemetery, as Jane Froman Smith, next to the space reserved for Rowland, not far from her mother's grave. Mama had been buried next to *her* husband. The little gold cross, which had been with her through every operation and every journey since the crash, was buried with her.

Back at the Smiths' house, Rowland accepted condolences from friends and read the cards and notes that had come in. He showed one to the group gathered in the living room. It was from John Burn, expressing his sympathy at Rowland's loss, with a few words more about what a remarkable woman she was. At this, Rowland could no longer hold back his tears, and Dudley comforted him.

He said, simply, "We both know it was time."

For those who were close to Jane, no truer words could have been spoken. She had done her work, borne her burdens without bitterness, sung her songs well, and kept her faith.

A voice like Jane's could not be denied, and so in life she sang, from the moment she could open her mouth to the last good breath she was able to draw. When asked why she continued to sing, no matter what befell her, Jane Froman had answered easily.

"Singing has always been my way of life," she explained. "Coming back to it again is partly a labor of love, partly my *raison d'etre*. People are happiest when they are paying their way, giving something for being alive, making themselves useful in society. Some may think it's easier to give up—sit under a tree, like Ferdinand, and watch the world go by. To me, that's the difficult way. It's easier to fight."

We are so lucky she did.

EPILOGUE

J ANE THOUGHT OF "her children" often. In her papers, found
after her death, was the following, in her own handwriting,
probably written before lung surgery left her hand too weak
to write. Up to then, she had written all her personal letters
by hand, partially as therapy for her weak right arm. Probably
intended for publication, names are not actual, and there is
an occasional generalization, but for the most part, she told
it as it was.

I miss my children—all one hundred and seventeen of
them! They have grown up, some are married and having
babies, others are holding responsible positions in large business firms, still others are finishing their educations. But I
hear from them regularly and am delighted with their progress. It all began this way.

In 1952 the Columbia Broadcasting System, at the in-
stigation of Producer Irving Mansfield, gave me my own
television program, a half hour on Saturday night. It presented original musical numbers, usually featuring a guest
star and a "story one" or theme. It was called USA Canteen
and members of the armed forces were welcomed. Fortunately it caught on immediately and was such a success that
it was divided into two fifteen minute sessions and sold to
General Electric Lamps and Revlon Cosmetics.

I had been appearing on radio for years but television was a new medium for me. The script conferences, musical rehearsals, dress fittings, interviews with the press, meetings with the producer and director, the final dress rehearsals and then the show itself (live, not on tape!)—all of it was hard work but gratifying. I loved it.

Imagine my surprise when groups of teenagers began to appear at the stage door. Their ages varied from twelve to seventeen and they were typical—blue jeans, pony tails, too much make up and an overabundance of enthusiasm. Our rehearsals began at twelve noon and rather than have these children standing out in the cold I got permission from our producer for them to come in and sit in the empty theatre while we did our run through provided they were quiet and did not interfere with our work. I got to know them by name—Mary Ann with the beautiful brown eyes; Janey, ill at ease and longing for friendship; Barbara, who was studying singing and eager for a career; Patty, whose main problem was reducing; Carol, who wanted to be a writer; John, whose dream was to be an industrial designer; Sue, who was just starting in High School; Joany who was already drawing dress designs; Marilyn, who wanted to teach school—all these and many more. They, in turn, began to call me Aunt Jane.

At the time I was living in a lovely old brownstone house on 93rd Street. These teenagers formed what they called the SSS, the "Stoop Sitters Society." It was not unusual to find my stoop crowded with children, complete with lunch boxes, coca-colas and school papers. They compared Jane Froman scrapbooks and pictures taken at the studio. Letters began to arrive filled with confidences regarding boy friends, school problems, clothes and complexion problems, and anything that was troubling them at the moment. I did my best to answer every letter, giving what advice I could but most of all, I'm afraid, acting as a sounding board.

One evening while I was rehearsing alone at home the front door bell rang. When I answered there stood a forlorn girl, tears in her eyes and eager, as I could see, to tell me her troubles. She had run away from home, after a quarrel with her mother, and was determined never to go back. I was aghast when I learned she had walked, alone, through Central Park at ten o'clock at night. After a long talk, in which I tried to point out that her mother was probably just as sorry about the quarrel as she was and was worried about her, she agreed to call her home and tell her mother she was all right. I gave her taxi fare and exacted a promise that she would go directly home. This she did and called me to tell me she was safe and that her quarrel with her mother had been resolved.

Not all such contacts with my children were so serious. The SSS went to the corner drug store to bring back for me what they called a Froman Surprise. It consisted of a scoop of every kind of ice cream available and every kind of syrup too—you can imagine what kind of conglomeration resulted when it was all mixed together in a cardboard container. Once they spent an hour and a half buying me a bouquet of flowers. Each SSS member wanted a different kind of flower and the result was astounding when they were all thrown together. The florist must have been completely confounded. He certainly took a dim view of their accompanying the bouquet. They wanted to be "delivered" too but he made them unscramble themselves and get out of the truck. On all holidays, they would make clever posters with cut outs, cartoons and drawings. St. Valentine's Day brought a heart as large as I was, signed by all the members. Easter produced a poster covered by rabbits made out of cotton and painted by hand. Their imagination knew no bounds and to realize that all their stunts were motivated by love and admiration gave me a warm glow.

I began to notice they were copying my handwriting, my clothes, my way of walking. I gave them parties at my home and it was interesting to see them arrive in pretty party dresses—very feminine—with the latest hair styles, no more blue jeans! They decided to form a fan club called the Froma-nettes and publish a Journal called "The Velvet Chords." In the Journal were articles to interest everyone. Reviews of the current best selling books, recordings, both popular and classical, that were selling best, reviews of operatic performances, puzzles, word games and articles based on experiences of their own.

They would give me parties on my birthday—some at the studio, one at the Sulgrave and another at the Waldorf Astoria. They were planned beautifully, to the last detail. My children were growing up! They would bring me gifts—flowers, jewelry, dainty underwear, books, replicas of my dog, Til. It was at a party in my home that an idea occurred to me. I was, and am, a governor on the Board of Directors of the Menningers Clinic in Topeka, Kansas. Why couldn't the money these children were spending on me be put into a fund for the benefit of the children's division of the Men-ningers Institute and why couldn't we incorporate into the Jane Froman Foundation? In this way, all the energy and drive of the teenagers could be channeled into a worthwhile cause, thus giving them a goal, a purpose.

Dr. William Menninger was in town at the time and

agreed wholeheartedly with our idea. It took us some time to get our charter but it was indeed a gala day when it was legalized. In the meantime, a California branch of the fan club called the Fromaneers was organized and they, in time, merged with the Fromanettes and have since called themselves the International Fromaneers.

Ideas for fund-raising sprang forth from eager young minds. A dance at Columbia University with door prizes donated from interested firms; beach parties; a Christmas tree trimmed with dimes; interviews with disc jockeys regarding the Foundation; raffles with substantial prizes; cake bakes; the "dollar and a promise" idea (whereby each member gives a dollar and a promise to get someone else to give a dollar and a promise); sororities donating half their dues—all these ideas and many others slowly filled our coffers. As a result, last year we sent a check for a thousand dollars to the children's division of the Menninger Institute. We are hoping to send more soon.

The members were so proud to be a part of such a wonderful organization. The teenage drives and enthusiasm were channeled into productive and positive outlets. As the girls grew older their thoughts turned toward marriage and homes of their own. Every so often now I get an announcement that a new International Fromaneer has arrived. Every Christmas and birthday I get cards from the members of the club. We have become great friends throughout the years.

Last week the virus bug attacked me and I was forced to be quiet for a day or two. Along with many lovely cards, a box of beautiful red roses arrived and on the card was the message "International Fromaneers." The members aren't the only proud ones. I am proud, too—of my children—and grateful!

The Fromanettes and the other fan clubs continued to work for the Foundation, and over a period of ten years, from its start in 1955 to 1965, without any major campaign or publicity, and mainly from contributions of members in small increments, was able to send more than $25,000 to the children's wing of the Menninger Clinic.

Many of these fans—now senior citizens—have remained in touch for more than fifty years. In 2003, they celebrated the 50th anniversary of the Fromanettes with a reunion at Tavern on the Green in New York City. Here is a glance at them over time:

Alice Armstrong, from Fall River, Massachusetts, visited New York frequently to see Jane's shows and attend her parties. She became a registered nurse and married a young man in the Coast Guard, Paul Cummings. She and Paul raised five children, giving them eight grandchildren. Still a New Englander, she now visits New York again because her son lives in Manhattan.

The Fromanettes on their 50th anniversary

Barbara "Babs" Buoncristiano received her degree from Barnard College, where she first became involved in the women's movement and was instrumental in winning a class action suit for maintenance workers at Columbia University. She was nominated for various fellowships while working on her doctorate and is Director of Compliance for the New York State Division of Human Rights.

Barbara "Bibs" DeFlories (Manzo) worked as a secretary in the Wall Street area until she married. When husband Tony died and she had two young boys to raise, she returned to work at Kingsborough Community College in Brooklyn as an assistant to the Director of a Human Services program advising students preparing for careers in social work. Now retired and a grandmother, she lives in Florida.

Ellen Galtrof (Friedman) was married and has one daughter. She received her Ph.D. in History from the City University of New York Graduate Center in 1975. She became a professor of history and women's studies at Boston College and is the author of one book and numerous scholarly articles. She is involved in the music business as well.

Winnette "Windy" Glasgow served four years in the Navy, then became an elementary school teacher. She was handpicked by renowned educator Deborah Meier to teach at Central Park East, an alternative school in Manhattan. Several of her students have gone on to pursue their doctorates. Retired, Win designed and maintains the Jane Froman Centennial Web Site (www.janefroman.com).

Joann Grandi attended Penn State University and the University of Delaware, where she received a Master of

Science Degree in chemistry. She worked for a large chemical company, taught college chemistry, and later switched careers to become the Director of Media Services at a liberal arts college in Pennsylvania.

Joan Hecht attended many rehearsals for Jane's television show at CBS Studio 52. After she moved to Palm Springs, Florida, she became social secretary to Victor and Ireene Hammer, friends of Jane. Victor owned an art gallery on 57th Street in Manhattan, but when the Hammers were in Palm Beach, Joan was called on to work for them.

Deena Hirschman (Meiner) and husband Bernie raised two sons. After her boys were grown, Deena returned to school to earn her degree in Spanish Languages and Latin American Culture. She became involved in HIV/AIDS work to give bilingual HIV prevention and parenting workshops. She and Bernie have two grandchildren.

Diane Leschner (Dagley) became a veterinarian who raised prize-winning show dogs. She married and had a son. Although she did not get to see Jane during the television years, living far off in Washington state, she was always in touch with Jane and the other fans. She finally met Jane in Columbia.

Joan McCarroll (DeFontes) and husband Angelo raised two sons and a daughter who have given them four grandchildren and a great grandchild. Joan worked for Cablevision on Long Island for eighteen years before she and Angelo retired to Florida. Joan was always attracted to people with great voices—Angelo sings, too.

Carol Peck and Carol Kennedy, sometimes referred to jointly as "The two Carols," met when they lived in Illinois and became best friends. When Carol P. moved to Hilton Head Island, South Carolina, they continued to get together and visited Jane and Rowland in Columbia regularly. Carol K. had worked for the Amoco Oil Company for many years but is now retired.

Diane Pollock grew up in the same town as Babs, so the two made frequent trips in from New Jersey together to see Jane's television shows. Diane worked in journalism and public relations while raising her son, who is now married.

Janet Schmidt (Leeb) and husband Chuck raised a daughter and two sons, who gave them ten grandchildren. Janet, the oldest of the Fromanettes by a slight margin, was affectionately dubbed "Mom" by the others and was the first of the Stoop Sitters' Society to have a baby. Her daughter was the first Fromanette baby held by Jane. Sadly, Janet passed away just four months before this book was published.

Barbara "Bobbie" Seuling attended Columbia University before becoming a children's book editor as well as a writer and illustrator of her own books. She continues to write, speak and teach, running writing workshops in Vermont every summer. Bobbie wrote this book to honor and repay Jane for her constant support and encouragement when she was lost in adolescence and to tell the story that Jane wanted told. (www.barbaraseuling.com)

Ellen Stein (Greenwald) attended the H.S. of Music and Art in New York and made theatre her lifelong career, although she tried social work for a while. She has worked as actor, producer, director and teacher and continues to write plays and work with playwrights. She has been married to Peter Greenwald for 49 years and has three children and six grandchildren.

Carol Stess attended The University of the Arts in Philadelphia and also studied voice with teachers and coaches from Temple U. and The Curtis Institute of Music. She sang with local opera companies until ear problems forced her, reluctantly, to pursue other interests. She then became a professional portrait photographer and decor designer.

Some fans never joined a fan club or saw Jane in person. Others were too far away to see her on television and some were not even born in her lifetime. All fans seem to belong to an unofficial network of admirers whose common interest contributes to keeping Jane's memory alive in the annals of popular American song.

Ilene Stone has written two books about Jane. Richard Harcourt of Australia began a biography of Jane several years ago and when he had to abandon the project, generously shared his research with the author of this biography. Shirley Gilroy is working on a book that pays tribute to Jane's music and also shared information.

Robert Beck has collected Jane's recordings throughout his life and donated his collection to the Chicago Public Library, so that more people would have access to it. He, Sheldon Duchin, Miriam Charlow and others have been instrumental in acquiring additional materials for the various archives in Columbia, Missouri, that preserve them for musicians and historians to study.

At the time of Jane's death in 1980, there was still no Internet or World Wide Web hurling through cyberspace. Today you can search for the name of Jane Froman and come up with hundreds of pages relating to her. Ginger Haydon, Ellie Fagan and Winnette Glasgow have put up web sites in

Jane's fans meet every year in Columbia

Jane's honor, the last of which has become a detailed database for students, researchers and admirers.

Singer Valerie Lemon has taken her cabaret show on the road to keep Jane Froman's memory alive with *The Jane Froman Songbook,* a loving tribute. (www.valerielemon.com)

Thanks to these fans, much of Jane's music has been reissued in digitized CDs, and the DVD of *With a Song in My Heart* has finally, after fifty-five years, been released.

With technological advances continuing to astound us daily, there will, no doubt, be new and even better ways to capture, preserve and celebrate the music that has contributed to our enjoyment and our cultural heritage. With this in mind, and in this spirit, we must dare to hope that Jane Froman's voice, one of the finest voices of the twentieth century, will live on.

APPENDIX

RESOURCES

I devoured everything I could find to illuminate the life of a singer of Jane's stature emerging during the resurgence of American popular music and performing for nearly four decades. As a friend, I knew her in certain modes and situations, and had had many conversations that gave me crucial insights into her life, but I still had to learn much of the background that went into making her the person she was. There are far too many sources to include, but listed here are those materials that gave me the greatest sense of the people, the events and the mood of the times as well as the development of what is popularly known as the great American songbook.

Museums and Collections

Boone County Historical Society/Walters–Boone County Historical Museum, at 3801 Ponderosa Avenue, Columbia, MO 65201, holds a permanent exhibit devoted to Jane Froman, as well as recordings, video tapes of Jane on television programs, an oil portrait of Jane and various memorabilia.

Columbia College (formerly Christian College), Columbia, MO, holds Jane's unfinished memoir, "Time to Go Home," various awards and citations, an oil portrait, photographs and gowns in the Jane Froman Collection.

The Henry County Museum, 203 West Franklin, Clinton, MO 64735. A collection of historical interest about the origins and growth of Henry County, including a genealogy library containing original wills that were filed in Henry County from 1836 to 1989.

The Library of Film and TV at the University of Southern California houses comprehensive archives of movie history. The Twentieth Century–Fox Special Collection has production notes from outline and treatment to first draft, continuity, comments, shooting script, etc. pertaining to *With a Song in My Heart*. The Warner Brothers Special Collection has production notes, correspondence and publicity folders for *Stars Over Broadway*.

The New York Public Library for the Performing Arts, Dorothy and Lewis B. Cullman Center, 40 Lincoln Center Plaza, New York, NY 10023, houses the Rodgers and Hammerstein Archives of Recorded Sound and The Billy Rose Theatre Collection, both of which have material on Jane's career.

The Paley Center for Media (formerly The Museum of Broadcasting), 25 West 52 Street, New York, NY 10019 and 465 N. Beverly Drive, Beverly Hills, CA 90210, has a collection of radio and television broadcasts from the past including several of Jane's radio and television performances.

The Western Historical Manuscript Collection, 23 Ellis Library, University of Missouri, Columbia, MO 65201, is a joint collection of the University of Missouri and the State Historical Society of Missouri, housing the Jane Froman Papers (personal correspondence, music arrangements, photographs, scrapbooks, family records and other documents) and the Jane Froman Collection (commercial

recordings and those from radio shows as well as video-
tapes of television appearances).

BOOKS

Bach, Steven. *Dazzler: The Life and Times of Moss Hart.* New York: Alfred A. Knopf, 2001; Cambridge, MA: Da Capo Press, 2002.

Bishop, Jim. *The Golden Ham: A Candid Biography of Jackie Gleason.* New York: Simon and Schuster, 1956.

Brokaw, Tom. *The Greatest Generation.* New York: Random House, 1998.

Chaplin, Charles. *My Autobiography.* New York: Simon and Schuster, 1964.

Cohen, Stan. *V for Victory: America's Home Front During World War II.* Missoula, MT: Pictorial Histories, 1991.

Cox, Jim. *Music Radio: The Great Performers and Programs of the 1920s through Early 1960.* Jefferson, NC: McFarland, 2005.

Follett, Ken. *Night Over Water.* New York: Morrow, 1991. Fiction; setting is a PanAm B-314 Clipper in September 1939.

Furia, Philip. *Ira Gershwin: The Art of the Lyricist.* New York: Oxford University Press, 1996.

Gavin, James. *Intimate Nights: The Golden Age of New York Cabaret.* New York: Limelight Editions, 1992.

Goldman, Herbert G. *Fanny Brice, The Original Funny Girl.* New York: Oxford University Press, 1992.

Goulden, Joseph C. *The Best Years: 1945-1950.* New York, Atheneum, 1976.

Green, Stanley. *Ring Bells! Sing Songs! Broadway Musicals of the 1930s.* New Rochelle, NY:Arlington House, 1971.

Grossman, Barbara W. *Funny Woman: the Life and Times of Fanny Brice.* Bloomington: Indiana University Press, 1991.

Hale, Allean Lemmon. *Petticoat Pioneer: The Story of Christian College.* Columbia, MO: Christian College, 1956, rev. 1968.

Hemming, Roy. *The Melody Lingers On: The Great Songwriters and Their Movie Musicals.* New York: Newmarket, 1986.

Hoopes, Roy. *When the Stars Went to War.* New York: Random House, 1994.

Kimball, Robert, and Alfred Simon. *The Gershwins.* New York: Bonanza Books, 1973.

Miller, William D. *Pretty Bubbles in the Air: America in 1919.* Urbana: University of Illinois Press, 1991.

Nagel, Paul C. *Missouri: A History.* Lawrence: University Press of Kansas, 1977; rev. 1988.

Perry, Dick. *Not Just a Sound: The Story of WLW.* Englewood Cliffs, NJ: Prentice-Hall, 1971.

Rose, Frank. *The Agency: William Norris and the Hidden History of Show Business.* New York: Harper Business, 1995.

Secrest, Meryle. *Somewhere for Me, A Biography of Richard Rodgers.* New York: Alfred P. Knopf, 2002.

Sennett, Ted. *Warner Brothers Presents.* New Rochelle, NY: Arlington House, 1971.

Speiser, Stuart M. *Lawyers and the American Dream.* New York, M. Evans and Company, 1993.

Thomas, Tony, and Jim Terry. *The Busby Berkeley Book,* Greenwich, CT: New York Graphic Society, 1973.

Vallance, Tom. *The American Musical.* New York: Castle Books, 1970.

Wilder, Alec. *American Popular Song, The Great Innovators 1900-1950.* New York: Oxford University Press, 1972.

Winslow, Walker. *The Menninger Story.* New York: Doubleday, 1956.

Zinsser, William. *Easy to Remember: The Great American Songwriters and Their Songs.* Jaffrey, NH: Godine, 2001.

JANE FROMAN PERFORMANCES

BROADWAY STAGE

Ziegfield Follies of 1934. Winter Garden Theatre.
Keep Off the Grass, 1940. Broadhurst Theatre.
Laugh, Town, Laugh, 1942. Alvin Theatre.
Artists and Models, 1943. Broadway Theatre.

MOVIES

Kissing Time. Warner Brothers-Vitaphone, 1933.
Stars Over Broadway. Warner Brothers, 1935.
Radio City Revels. RKO, 1938.
With a Song in My Heart. Twentieth Century–Fox, 1952.

RECORDINGS

Available in Compact Disc (CD):
    Gems From Gershwin: Magic Key Program. RCA Victor.
    Jane Froman On Capitol. Capitol, Collectors' Choice.
    My Heart Speaks. Jasmine (UK).
    With a Song In My Heart/Pal Joey. DRG.
    Jane Froman: Songs at Sunset/Faith. Encore.

No longer commercially available but look for them in auctions and on used book and record outlets online:
    Faith. Capitol.
    Jane Froman Sings. Royale.

Meet The Girls. Halo.
Moonlight and Roses. Royale.
Songs At Sunset. Capitol.
Souvenir Album. Decca.
Yours Alone: Love Songs By Jane Froman. Capitol.
Jane Froman: The Star thru Three Decades. Encore.
The Memorable Radio Years. Star-Tone Records.
Jane Froman on Capitol. Capitol, Collectors' Choice.
But Beautiful. Janey.
My Heart Speaks. Jasmine (UK).

WEBSITE

Trying to list and detail all of Jane Froman's appearances on radio, TV, in films and on stage, in night clubs and on recordings, would be an endless task and would never be complete, as so many dates and events have been lost over time. I am giving here only a brief summary of the accomplishments of this talented singer. However, there is a web site to honor Jane and add to the information known about her. It has the most complete listing of her achievements ever put together. You are encouraged to contact Winnette if you have additional information to be put on the site. Please visit it for the information you seek.

www.janefroman.com
Webmaster: Winnette Glasgow

City of Columbia, Missouri • Office of the Mayor

PROCLAMATION

WHEREAS, Jane Froman was born in St. Louis County, Missouri, on November 10, 1907, of musically talented forebears, including her mother, Anna Froman Hetzer, who taught piano and voice at Christian College for fourteen years, and created the famous Double Sextette; and

WHEREAS, she attended the School of Journalism at the University of Missouri, performing the lead role in the musical revue "Bagdaddies," which led to her start in show business and her ultimately being named as radio's most popular female singer in the 1930's; and

WHEREAS, Jane Froman ws the first to volunteer for the U.S.O. camp shows and, while en route to entertain troops in World War II, was in a plane crash which resulted in lifethreating injuries; and

WHEREAS, still on crutches from leg injuries received in the crash, Jane Froman fulfilled her commitment to the USO and in 1945 spent three months traveling thoughout wartorn Europe to bring entertainment to the troops and hope to the wounded; and

WHEREAS, she was invited repeatedly to the White House to sing for presidents Roosevelt, Truman, and Eisenhower; and

WHEREAS, she achieved a second career as a result of a film about her life in which she was given her own network television show on which she introduced the song "I Believe," written for her, which has become a symbol of faith for all religions; and

WHEREAS, she devoted her time and talent unselfishly to many worthy causesa, including mental health, Easter Seals, and music scholarships at the University of Missouri, earning her Columbia's Woman of the Year award in 1968; and

WHEREAS, she received the Alumni Association of the University of Missouri's Faculty-Alumni Award recognizing her distinguished service as well as the Distiguished Alumnae Award from the National Alumnae Association of Christian College in 1963; and

WHEREAS, Jane Froman served as a member of the board of trustees of Columbia College from 1976 until her death.

NOW, THEREFORE, I, Darwin Hindman, Mayor of the City of Columbia, Missouri, do hereby proclaim Saturday, November 10, 2007, as

JANE FROMAN DAY

in the City of Columbia in honor of her great contributions to popular music, to the brave fighting men of World War II, and to Columbia.

IN WITNESS WHEREOF, I have hereunto set my hand and caused to be affixed hereto the Seal of the City of Columbia, this 11th day of Mar h, 2005.

1

arwin Hindman, Mayor

ATTEST:

Sheela Amin, City Clerk

PHOTO CREDITS

Author's Collection: 243, 258, 260, 265, 268, 287, 295, 298, 301, 308, 309

Willard G. Beddow, Tech Sergeant, 9th Air Force, 45th Air Depot Group: 162

Boone County Historical Society: 43, 227, 244

Columbia College: 11, 13, 21, 28, 30, 33, 55, 63, 69, 97, 98, 112, 151, 180, 326, 333, 341

Bette Froemke: 226

Jane Froman, Papers, 1891-1980, Western Historical Manuscript Collection, Columbia, MO: 7, 37, 83, 109, 114, 120, 131, 143, 145, 157, 159, 160, 167, 170, 178, 180, 183, 185, 186, 195, 204, 208, 211, 213, 219, 222, 229, 230, 233, 235, 237, 239, 250, 284, 296, 345

Winnette Glasgow: 261, 316, 362

Joann Grandi: 367

Carol Kennedy: 321, 337, 351, 352

Joyce Liskin: 281

Deena Meiner: 217

William Morris Agency: 177

Sgt. Robert Paulson: 158

Billy Rose Theatre Division, The New York Public Library for the Performing Arts, Astor, Lenox and Tilden Foundations: cover

The Seagle Colony studio portrait by Bruno of Hollywood; used by permission of Pete Seagle: 32

Warner Brothers Archive, Library of Film and TV, University of Southern California: 97

INDEX

Photographs indicated in ***bold italic***